Evelyn Waugh

ALSO AVAILABLE FROM BLOOMSBURY

Dangerous Edges of Graham Greene, Edited by Dermot Gilvary
and Darren J. N. Middleton

George Orwell the Essayist, Peter Marks

Graham Greene, Michael G. Brennan

The Pen and the Cross, Richard Griffiths

Works of Graham Greene, Jon Hill and Mike Wise

Evelyn Waugh

Fictions, Faith and Family

Michael G. Brennan

BLOOMSBURY

LONDON • NEW DELHI • NEW YORK • SYDNEY

Bloomsbury Academic
An imprint of Bloomsbury Publishing Plc

50 Bedford Square
London
WC1B 3DP
UK

1385 Broadway
New York
NY 10018
USA

www.bloomsbury.com

Bloomsbury is a registered trade mark of Bloomsbury Publishing PLC

First published 2013
Reprinted 2013

© Michael G. Brennan, 2013

British Library Cataloguing-in-Publication Data
A catalogue record for this book is available from the British Library.

ISBN: HB: 978-1-4411-3111-9
PB: 978-1-4411-0034-4
ePub: 978-1-4411-3503-2
ePDF: 978-1-4411-9417-6

Library of Congress Cataloging-in-Publication Data
Brennan, Michael G.
Evelyn Waugh: fictions, faith and family/Michael G. Brennan.
p. cm.
Includes bibliographical references and index.
ISBN 978-1-4411-0034-4 (pbk.) – ISBN 978-1-4411-3111-9 (hardcover) –
ISBN 978-1-4411-9417-6 (ebook) – ISBN 978-1-4411-3503-2 (ebook)
1. Waugh, Evelyn, 1903–1966–Criticism and interpretation.
2. Anglo-Catholicism in literature. 3. Families in literature. I. Title.
PR6045.A97Z617 2013
823'.912–dc23
2012039218

Typeset by Deanta Global Publishing Services, Chennai, India
Printed and bound in Great Britain

For Geraldine, Christina and Alice

CONTENTS

ACKNOWLEDGEMENTS

I am grateful to Alexander Waugh for his invaluable support while writing this book and for generously allowing me to quote from his publications. His *Fathers and Sons: The Autobiography of a Family* (2004: © Alexander Waugh) has proved a key source of biographical information and I have drawn extensively from three richly informative biographies of Evelyn Waugh by Martin Stannard, Selina Hastings and Douglas Lane Patey. I have received helpful advice on Catholic literature and theology from Geraldine Brennan and Bernadette Barnett. Christopher Sheppard (Brotherton Library, University of Leeds) has been especially supportive and I am indebted to Fay and Geoffrey Elliott for their Waugh bequests to the Brotherton Library. I am also grateful to Catherine Batt, Margaret Hannay, Noel Kinnamon and Francis O'Gorman; the staff of the Leeds Library; David Avital (Publisher, Bloomsbury Academic and Professional); and to Luke Ingram (Wylie Agency, UK: Quotations from the works of Evelyn Waugh © Evelyn Waugh © The Estate of Laura Waugh. Used by permission. All rights reserved), Mary Fox (Penguin Group, UK: Quotations from the works of Evelyn Waugh reproduced by permission of Penguin Books Ltd) and Meghan Tillett (Hachette Book Group, New York: Quotations from the works of Evelyn Waugh reproduced by permission of Little, Brown and Company) for assistance with quotation permissions. Finally, I am grateful to Subitha Nair, Project Manager, and the staff of Deanta Global Publishing Services for their support and efficiency during the final stages of this book's production. All page references given in the text are to the editions listed in the Bibliography.

PREFACE

Graham Greene and Evelyn Waugh

If his religion is the key to his character it is also the side least understood, even by other Catholics. He was not merely a fundamentalist. He was, as Belloc once said, possessed; a man for whom the Four Last Things (especially Hell) vividly existed. (Geoffrey Wheatcroft 1980)

    I see Waugh as a brilliant but awkward, isolated, and neurotic man, with many intimate friends and few lovers, almost frightened but with dauntless bravado, a scintillating manic depressive, not 'possessed' as Belloc suggested, but dispossessed, alienated. (Martin Stannard 1986)[1]

This study of Evelyn Waugh's literary explorations of faith, doubt and authorial versatility does not seek to offer a spiritual autobiography of the writer. Rather, it traces how elements of Catholic belief, theology and liturgy consistently provided Waugh with an inspiring source of narrative creativity, intellectual scepticism and spiritual solace. This perspective echoes that of my *Graham Greene: Fictions, Faith and Authorship* (Continuum 2010), since this book on Waugh is intended as a companion volume to my commentary on Greene's sustained dependence upon religious issues to formulate dominant narrative and thematic concerns in his fictions, journalism, plays, correspondence and other writings. For both Greene and Waugh, a religious mode of thought facilitated an insistent tone of questioning and uncertainty in their works. Both were also preoccupied with the interplay of three key dualities – faith and doubt, hope and despair, and loyalty and betrayal – leading to a sustained and shared literary interrogation of the intellectual and spiritual demands of twentieth-century English Catholicism.

    Henry Graham Greene (1904–91) and Evelyn Arthur St John Waugh (1903–66) were born into comfortable (and, to their retrospective eyes, stiflingly conventional) middle-class Edwardian families with dutiful but undemanding Anglican affiliations. Greene's father, Charles, was a housemaster (later headmaster) of Berkhamsted School, Hertfordshire. Living accommodation was provided for his family within the school premises and several other wealthier members of the extended Greene family resided nearby in Berkhamsted. Waugh's father, Arthur, was a prolific writer and managing director of the publishing firm, Chapman and Hall, with family homes first in West Hampstead and then in the village of North End, between Hampstead and Golder's Green. Although their periods of study at Oxford University coincided (Greene at Balliol, September 1922–June 1925 and Waugh at Hertford, January 1922–June 1924), they did not get to know each other as undergraduates since they belonged to very different social sets.[2]

As newly fledged graduates seeking meaningful employment, both young men tried their hands at conventional jobs – Greene as a newspaper sub-editor and Waugh as a schoolmaster – before focusing full time on precarious careers as writers and journalists. Both also renounced their Church of England heritage by converting to Roman Catholicism: Greene on 28 February 1926 and Waugh on 29 September 1930. While Greene had long admired Waugh's early novels and travel writings, they did not become personally associated until 1937 when Waugh agreed to write a weekly book review for a short-lived journal, *Night and Day*, edited by Greene. This journalistic connection was enhanced in 1938 through their shared experiences of travel in Mexico and their resulting publications: Greene's *The Lawless Roads* (1939) and *The Power and the Glory* (1940) and Waugh's *Robbery Under Law* (1939).

Less than three decades later, on the morning of Easter Sunday, 10 April 1966, Waugh attended a Latin Mass celebrated by his (and Greene's) friend, the Jesuit priest Father Caraman, at the Catholic chapel in Wiveliscombe, a village five miles from his home at Combe Florey, Somerset. The congregation included his mother-in-law, Mary Herbert, his wife Laura and four of their children: Margaret, Harriet, James and Septimus. Back home, Waugh seemed excited over a new book by Father Martin D'Arcy which he was to review for the *Sunday Times* but he collapsed just before lunch. Unresponsive to resuscitation, Father Caraman administered the sacrament of Conditional Absolution, '*Si vivis, ego te absolvo*' ('If you are living, I absolve you'), granted to those in whom life may still not be extinct. The local priest, Father Formosa, was then called to administer the anointing oils. On 15 April Father Caraman conducted Waugh's funeral at the Catholic Church of St Teresa of Lisieux, Taunton, followed by his burial by special dispensation just outside the limits of the Anglican churchyard at Combe Florey. A Latin Requiem Mass was celebrated by Father Caraman at Westminster Cathedral on 21 April, with Cardinal Heenan presiding on the Sanctuary throne. Waugh's demise on Easter Sunday at home, after Communion and a Latin Mass, surrounded by family and shriven on the central Christian feast of the Resurrection, was as ideal a death as any devout Catholic could have desired. He would also have been delighted that his Requiem Mass was celebrated at Westminster Cathedral, the mother church of English Catholics, and presided over by their spiritual leader, Cardinal Heenan.

On 15 April 1966, the day of Waugh's funeral, Greene described him in *The Times* as the greatest novelist of his generation, even though they had held contrasting political views and were divided by their conception of the Catholic Church. Despite these differences, Greene had long respected Waugh's judgements on his literary works. In response to his favourable review of *The Heart of the Matter*, Greene remarked that there was no other contemporary writer from whom he would rather receive either praise or criticism.[3] In his personal memoir, *Ways of Escape* (1980), Greene commented in more detail on his lasting friendship with Waugh. He regarded him as a close friend and a writer of 'genius' and 'insight' (255), commending his generosity and loyalty. He memorably concluded that when he came to die he would wish for Waugh's presence since he would grant him 'no easy comfort' (263).

Yet, it is all too tempting to polarize Greene's angst-ridden and casuistic religious scepticism against Waugh's apparently more orthodox and trusting commitment to the central tenets of Roman Catholicism. Certainly, Greene tended to present himself as an author whose mind was haunted by paradoxical and heretical thoughts, the creator of fictional characters whose bodies (like his own) were frequently entangled in the temptations of the flesh. In contrast, Waugh's writings often suggest that the Catholic faith offers to a depressed and lonely believer (as he often was) the solace of an inviolable trust in an omnipotent Higher Power. As a man, Martin Stannard views Waugh as an 'enigma: malicious yet capable of extraordinary kindness' and defines him, in a striking paradox, as a 'selfish Christian'.[4] But, despite his personal failings, Waugh's writings also offer the Augustinian consolation that no form of personal weakness can overwhelm the infinite compassion and mercy of a Divine Father who seeks from his children only the heartfelt words: '*peccavi*' ('I have sinned') and '*credo in Unum Deum*' (I believe in One God'). Much of Waugh's literary career was dedicated to a defence of the discipline and heritage of Christian civilization and Douglas Lane Patey underlines Waugh's 'enduring concern with the nature and theology of love'. Corroborating this view, the poet Stephen Spender concludes that Waugh increasingly utilized his writings as 'disguised spiritual autobiography'.[5] Another of Waugh's major biographers, Selina Hastings, summarizes the self-conscious interaction of literary creativity and spiritual quest in his writings:

> Evelyn was a perfectionist, and his desire for perfection penetrated every aspect of his life, its lack often causing him acute distress. The Catholic Church was the nearest to perfection this earth could offer. And as an artist, he was attracted to its logic, by the way in which, once the basic premise was accepted, every piece fitted. He appreciated the workmanlike attitude of its officers, the priest as craftsman, who with his apprentice 'stumped up to the altar with their tools and set to work without a glance to those behind them'.[6]

Despite his ardent Catholicism, Waugh was no unquestioning conformist. Once again, it is Greene who gets to the heart of the matter in his *Ways of Escape* when he remarks of their respective religious beliefs that they inhabited contrasting 'waste lands' (257). In this nod to T. S. Eliot's potent influence over their shared preoccupation with the literature of disillusionment, Greene reminds us how often they both focused in their fictions upon isolated, bemused and depressive figures trapped within the cruel secular landscapes of contemporary society. Waugh deplored and repeatedly satirized the twentieth century's relentless displacement of long-established social traditions, artistic values and spiritual continuities with brittle, self-indulgent frivolities, mechanistic aesthetics and meaningless but arrogant secularism. Similarly, Greene laments how the modern pursuit of rationalism within an archly materialistic culture ensured that the idea of faith as a tranquil sea was lost forever. Faith was now more like a tempest in which the fortunate were drowned but the unfortunate survived, only to be cast up on shore 'battered and bleeding' (253).

While envisaging himself and Waugh as two of these chance survivors from a shipwrecked and morally bankrupt modern society, Greene concludes with an observation of considerable importance to an understanding of how his own habitual literary modes of moral and spiritual investigation may be contrasted with Waugh's. Referring to the increasingly desolate inner psychological landscapes of *The Heart of the Matter*, *The End of the Affair*, 'A Visit to Morin' and *A Burnt Out Case* (set in a leper colony in the Belgian Congo), Greene notes that while writing his 'blackest' novel he had 'discovered Comedy' (259). It is true that brief moments of dry and ironically dark comedy flicker through Greene's works from the 1920s onwards. But it is only in his last major novel, *Monsignor Quixote* (1982) – fondly echoing the picaresque adventures of Cervantes' Don Quixote – that a touchingly comic mode of narrative becomes the sustained medium for an exploration of his religious and social concerns. In contrast, from the outset of his literary career Waugh's writings depended heavily upon the brilliantly cruel comedy of his satiric spirit, especially when counter-pointed with an insistent nostalgia for mythical golden worlds, located within the idealized family lives of great English houses or public institutions. Greene concludes that Waugh's creativity always harboured a clash between the romantic and the satirist, in that a satirist is often also a romantic but one who tries not to express his romanticism.

Greene highlights an important contrast between two of Waugh's most distinctive comic styles. In the first, pure fun remains the dominant tone, as with the farcical mishaps ladled upon Paul Pennyfeather, the hapless hero of *Decline and Fall* (1928a). In the second, darker undertones gradually predominate despite the despairing satirist's attempts to disguise his own personal angsts in drollery. Greene shrewdly notes that this bifurcation of comic tone is first evident in *Vile Bodies* (1930). This acclaimed satiric novel opens with scenes of riotous fun and upper-class hedonism amidst the charmed lives of the 'bright young things'. But then it turns at the opening of its seventh chapter (exactly when Waugh learnt in early July 1929 of the infidelity of his first wife) from 'high comedy' to 'a bleak and chilling picture both of human nature and of the period'.[7] By the time of *A Handful of Dust* (1934), his most 'painful' novel, Greene notes, there is 'no fun at all' (260) in Waugh's satires.

The refreshing spirit of anarchic fun spasmodically resurfaces in some of Waugh's later works but for the next three decades his writings tended to focus more upon the tragi-comedy of modern life, in which traditional moral and spiritual values are casually discarded in favour of the false gods of superficial materialism and sensual self-gratification. Waugh's delight in creating comically absurd characters and scenarios provide his fictions with an alluring framework for a sharp-eyed and savage dissection of twentieth-century manners and innate human frailties. But his more sombre and polemical side as a social moralist tends to prevail as he grows older. However urbane, witty or sophisticated Waugh's characters may appear on the surface, from the mid-1930s onwards many of them unknowingly run the risk of tumbling into an impassively brutal world of moral darkness and chaos. For Waugh, satiric comedy becomes a means of holding up a literary mirror to the essentially fallen and irredeemable nature of faithless humanity.

Greene also admired Waugh as a consummate literary stylist whose precision and elegance offer constantly shifting delights since, like authors, readers change and can find new aspects to admire when re-reading his works. In *Ways of Escape*, Greene explains how, at its best, Waugh's style is subtly suffused with implicit touchstones of personal moral values (such as loyalty, generosity of spirit and kindness), hierarchical social norms (such as the efficacy of long-established religious communities and family dynasties) and a searing honesty in analysing individual frailties, including his own. The interaction of these stylistic qualities prompts a sense that elements of self-reflective psycho-analysis became an intrinsic facet of his fictional creativity. In this respect, it is interesting to note that Greene, when listing Waugh's works which he most admired, chose to link *Brideshead Revisited* (1945) as his best and most romantic novel, with his excoriating self-portrait, *The Ordeal of Gilbert Pinfold* (1957), which, despite its focus on mental derangement, showed him 'technically almost at his most perfect' (262).

Following the breakdown of his first marriage, Waugh led an often lonely and rootless existence. Poignantly, the ideal of a secure and reassuring family environment seems to echo constantly through his writings from the 1930s onwards. This longing for personal and spiritual security finds powerful expression in his preoccupation as a writer (and in his own social life) with country houses and their occupants. The grandiose renown of Brideshead, through its novel, television and film identities, now tends to dominate the popular imagination but to this listing may also be added King's Thursday in *Decline and Fall* (1928a). This once grand edifice had been for three centuries the seat of the Earls of Pastmaster but it is swiftly desecrated by the modernist tastes of Margo Beste-Chetwynde (later Lady Metroland) and

her dehumanizing Bauhaus-influenced architect, 'Professor' Otto Friedrich
Silenus. There is also the mysterious country estate of Thatch in 'The Balance'
(1926); and his description in *Rossetti* (1928b) of the architecturally ideal
Kelmscott which for its owner, William Morris, 'sacramentally embodied'
(183) his ultimate aesthetic of beauty, harmony and dignity. Waugh wrote
lyrically in *Rossetti* of Morris's delight in the substantial walls of this
house:

> They alone remained unchanged in Utopia, born of the earth and the
> native rightness of man, as it had watched through a dark age for the
> Renaissance of beauty ... Here, in small compass, lay everything for which
> his art and his work was striving – peace, fellowship, love, childhood,
> beauty, simplicity, abundance. (184)

During the 1930s there is Doubting Hall, Colonel Blount's residence in
Vile Bodies (1930); Hetton, Tony Last's much loved Victorian gothic
mansion in *A Handful of Dust* (1934); and Boot Magna Hall in *Scoop*
(1938), based upon Pixton Hall, the seat of the Herberts (his second wife's
family). In his later works, there is the disintegrating paradise of Malfrey
in *Put Out More Flags* (1942), Finally, there is Broome, the mournfully
vacated great house in *Men at Arms* (1952a), in which Guy Crouchback's
recusant family has resided since the reign of King Henry I; and Mountjoy
Castle, the former home of a maimed World War II V.C., in *Love Among
the Ruins* (1953).

These great houses, with their semi-mythic and Eden-like scenarios, stand
as secular temples to the efficacy of close familial bonds and as a counterpoint
to the less immediately tangible securities provided by institutional churches.
Their stately architectural fabrics and lavish furnishings offer a reassuring
framework for Waugh's pursuit of continuity, security and support. Indeed,
in his fictions he seems far less interested in ecclesiastical buildings – although
throughout his life he derived genuine aesthetic and spiritual pleasure from
visiting ancient village and grand urban churches. Instead, he prefers in
the imaginary landscapes of his novels to represent the power and glory of
religious faith as being primarily of an internal, psychological substance,
rooted within the self and the family.

For Waugh, the interdependent concepts of family life and dynastic
inheritance – with all their joys, vicissitudes and disappointments – lay
deeply embedded within his creative impulses. Unlike Greene, whose range
of distinguished upper-middle class ancestors and close relatives included
noted colonialists, bankers, educationalists and high-ranking civil servants
but no significant writers, the Waughs were and remain one of the most
productively diverse English literary dynasties. It was calculated in 2004
that nine of Arthur Waugh's descendants had produced over 180 books
between them – an inheritance which has proved both a source of pride and
a personal challenge to successive generations of the family.[8]

The Waugh family

Evelyn Waugh's paternal great-great-grandfather, the Revd Alexander Waugh (1754–1827), fondly denoted within the family as the 'Great and Good', was a leading non-conformist preacher of the Secession Church, a co-founder of the London Missionary Society, a vocal abolitionist and a friend of Thomas Carlyle. He first established the family's public literary profile by publishing, like many churchmen of his day, some now long-forgotten theological writings, including *Pastoral Care: a Sermon* (c.1792) and *Messiah, the Son of Righteousness: a Sermon* (1800). Alexander's son, George, rose in the commercial world to become pharmacist to Queen Victoria. Two of his daughters, Fanny and Edith, married – in succession and contrary to the Deceased Wife's Sister Act – the Pre-Raphaelite painter, Holman Hunt. Another, Alice Gertrude (d.1912), married Hunt's friend, the sculptor Thomas Woolner. Attracted by both the anarchy of their private lives and the stunning visual textures of their paintings, the Pre-Raphaelites remained an abiding interest for Evelyn. His father's library housed a high-backed armchair once owned by Rossetti and Evelyn's first published book was his biography, *Rossetti* (1928b). He also later planned a life of Holman Hunt and remained an avid admirer and collector of Pre-Raphaelite and Victorian narrative art. He purchased in 1938 for £10 Rossetti's chalk drawing, 'Spirit of the Rainbow' (now in the Lord Lloyd-Webber collection), to which he later added Holman Hunt's 'Oriana' and a version of Arthur Hughes' 'The Woodman's Child'.

Another of the Revd Alexander's sons, James Hay Waugh, also became a churchman and served as Rector of Corsley, Somerset, for forty-four years. He was an enthusiastic participant in amateur theatricals, an interest sustained in later generations by his son, Alexander, his grandson, Arthur, and great-grandson, Evelyn. As Evelyn's grandson, Alexander, pointedly remarks: 'Theatricality has proved itself the besetting sin of the fathers in my family for at least six generations'.[9] On his maternal side, Evelyn's great-great-grandfather, Henry, Lord Cockburn (1779–1854), a Scottish judge and friend of Sir Walter Scott, was a regular contributor to the *Edinburgh Review*. He also published in 1852 an acclaimed biography of his friend, the lawyer and literary critic Francis, Lord Jeffrey (1773–1850). His two most significant works, an autobiography, *Memorials of his Time* (1856), and his private *Journal* (1874), were both published posthumously and remain illuminating sources of first-hand reflections upon society and politics of the period.

James Hay's son, Dr Alexander Waugh (1850–1906), was a tyrannically short-tempered figure within his own family while enjoying local esteem as a genial general practitioner within the environs of Midsomer Norton, near Bath. His various petty cruelties towards his wife and children, symptomatic of a bullying nature bolstered by the false god of Victorian authoritarian paternalism, were aptly castigated within later generations of the family through his nickname, the 'Brute'. He married Annie Morgan, whose childhood had been dominated by the strict, pleasure-repressing codes of the Plymouth Brethren. In later life her latent artistic talents were expressed through skilfully executed cut-outs, watercolours and sketches of local scenes. Her mother, Anne Gosse, was the first cousin of Philip Henry Gosse (1810–88), whose father, Thomas (1765–1844), had been an itinerant miniaturist and portrait painter. Philip Henry was the father of Edmund Gosse (1849–1928), the poet, critic and translator of Ibsen whose renowned memoir, *Father and Son* (1907), traced the complex psychological background of a devout Plymouth Brethren household.

By the last decade of the nineteenth century, Edmund Gosse was an influential literary figure and he showed considerable kindness to his younger cousin, Arthur Waugh, whom he regularly invited to his Sunday salons at Maida Vale, frequented by Thomas Hardy, Rudyard Kipling, Bram Stoker, Henry James, W. S. Gilbert, Walter Sickert, Arthur Conan Doyle, Robert Louis Stevenson, J. M. Barrie, Arnold Bennett, Henrik Ibsen, Aubrey Beardsley and Max Beerbohm. *Father and Son*, tracing Gosse's gradual rejection of his naturalist father's anti-evolutionary theories and fundamentalist religious beliefs, provided an important precursor for the youthful Evelyn in his own dependent but often troubled relationship with his father. From his adolescence onwards Waugh shared with Gosse – whom he always professed to despise – the realization that sons can rarely grow up either to replicate their fathers or to live up to great (but often claustrophobic and irritating) paternal expectations.

Although in *A Little Learning* (1964) Evelyn minimized the literary influences of his father Arthur (1866–1943) and elder brother Alexander (Alec) Raban (1898–1981), both were of considerable significance in formulating his early tastes (even if their preferences often drove him in determinedly contrary directions) and his nascent ambitions as a writer. Selina Hastings observes:

> Arthur found writing both pleasurable and easy; he had the fatal facility of the second-rate, a facility inherited by his elder son Alec, and regarded with contempt by his younger son Evelyn, who referred dismissively to the 'deleterious speed' with which he composed both prose and verse.[10]

As a precocious child at Sherborne School in Dorset, Arthur had written poetry, edited the school magazine, *The Shirburnian*, acted in dramatic productions and drafted plays which were performed at home during holidays. He continued his dramatic compositions from January 1886 at New College, Oxford, by producing more plays and revues. The dramatic highlight of his university career was the staging of a burlesque tragedy, *Julius Seesawcer*, at the Holywell Music Room, for which he had written the libretto. Arthur graduated with a 3rd class degree but in 1888 proudly won the esteemed Newdigate Poetry Prize on the subject of 'Gordon of Africa' (a copy of the printed version was promptly sent by his mother to Gosse), previously awarded to John Ruskin (1839), Matthew Arnold (1843) and Oscar Wilde (1878).

Given his younger son's later distinction as a literary satirist, it seems fitting that Arthur's first published article after setting himself up as a London-based literary journalist was on 'The Decline of Comedy' for the American literary journal, *Lippincott's Monthly Magazine* (1890). In the same year he published a collection of six of his plays with performance notes, *Schoolroom and Home Theatricals*. Largely through Gosse's influence, he was employed as a reader at the newly founded publishing firm of William Heinemann. Again via Gosse, he also met Woolcott Balestier (later Rudyard Kipling's brother-in-law) who ran the London office of the American popular fiction publisher, John W. Lovell & Co., where he took up his first office job as a reader for the firm. Although Balestier's unexpected death triggered the closure of Lovell's London office in 1892, it provided Arthur with a timely opportunity to develop his literary career, with the *Illustrated London News* and the *National Observer* printing his articles and reviews. When Gosse declined Heinemann's offer to write the first major biography of Alfred Lord Tennyson, the commission was gratefully snapped up by Arthur. This rapidly compiled but perceptive volume, published in October 1892 only eight days after Tennyson's death, was a commercial success (running through six editions) and publicly confirmed Arthur's growing reputation as a productive and reliable journalist-biographer.

Following his marriage in February 1893 to Catherine (Katie) Raban (1870–1954), the great-granddaughter of Henry, Lord Cockburn and the step-daughter of a former army chaplain and Somerset parson, Arthur's literary journalism grew ever more prolific. He contributed to numerous magazines and newspapers, including the *Literary World*, *Daily Courier*, *Daily Chronicle*, *St James's Gazette*, *Outlook* and the *Sun* and wrote a regular London letter for the New York *Critic*. He was also employed as a sub-editor on *The New Review* (for which he secured serial rights on the early stories of his friend, W. W. Jacobs). Yet again through Gosse's influence, he contributed an essay, 'Reticence in Literature', to the first issue on 16 April 1894 of the notorious *Yellow Book*. In January 1896 he secured the position of assistant manager at Kegan Paul, Trench, Trübner & Co. and this well-salaried post acted as a catalyst for his self-confidence as an editor and biographer. During the next four years his publications were impressively diverse, including a six-volume edition of Johnson's *Lives of the Poets* (1896), a privately printed collection of bicycling poems called *Legends of the Wheel* (1898), rhymes for an illustrated children's book, *The Square Book of Animals* (1899) and a biography of Robert Browning (1900). The definitive moment in Arthur's literary career came when in December 1901 he was appointed as managing director of Chapman and Hall, the renowned publishers of Dickens, Thackeray, Trollope and Carlyle. Although much occupied by day-to-day commercial business, he continued

to churn out reviews and essays which were later collected together in two
volumes: *Reticence in Literature* (1915), dedicated to Alec, and *Tradition
and Change* (1919), dedicated to Evelyn.

From 1926 to 1936 Arthur served as chairman of his company, marking
this professional association in 1930 with his history, *Chapman and Hall,
A Hundred Years in Publishing*, and by becoming the first chairman of the
Publishers' Circle. He succeeded in attracting Arnold Bennett, Somerset
Maugham and H. G. Wells to his lists (partly as a means of compensating
for the loss of the Dickens copyright which expired in 1920). Throughout
this period, he also sustained a remarkable productivity as a journalist and
writer. From late-1906 to the early1930s he reviewed over 6,000 books for
the *Daily Telegraph*; provided introductions for new editions of Dickens
(1903–07) and Browning (1919); frequently collaborated with Ernest Rhys,
a close family friend and editor of the Everyman Library; and compiled
an autobiography, *One Man's Road, Being a Picture of Life in a Passing
Generation* (1931) which through its mingling of sentimental nostalgia
and astute literary analysis offers a touching psychological insight into its
author.

In the eyes of his sons, Arthur was a kindly (if sometimes deliberately
eccentric) enthusiast for numerous aspects of literature and the arts. He
enjoyed membership of a literary dining club, the 'Sette of Odd Volumes',
which his son Evelyn later mocked in *Brideshead Revisited*. He also chaired
meetings of the Dickens Fellowship (delighting in Ellen Terry's description
of him as 'dear little Mr Pickwick') and was an enthusiastic participant in
play readings hosted by the Shakespearean Society. He was passionate about
amateur dramatics and often cultivated an exaggeratedly theatrical persona
in his personal dealings and social life. He was also president of the 'Merrie
Andrews Dramatic Society' (MADS) which staged forgettable plays at the
Bijou Theatre, Bayswater. The Waugh family lived at Hillfield Road, West
Hampstead, from 1895 to 1907 when they moved to a newly built house,
Underhill (named after the lane at Midsomer Norton where Arthur had
first kissed his wife-to-be, Kate), in the then rapidly disappearing village
environment of North End, between Hampstead and Golder's Green. It is
understandable how, in retrospect, Evelyn and Alec compared their parents
to the Pooters of The Laurels, Brickfield Road, Upper Holloway, in the
Grossmith brothers' comic novel, *Diary of a Nobody* (1892), with Evelyn
ideally cast as their mischievously problematic son, Lupin.

Evelyn's childhood immersion in such a rich cultural background
attracted him towards the personal rewards of literary creativity and,
simultaneously, alienated him from the essentially conservative tastes of the
rest of his family. To make matters worse, it was always clear that Alec was
his father's favourite son. Arthur revelled in every major and minor triumph
of his schooldays, relishing their mutual passion for cricket and their shared
literary pursuits. Even more intensely, Arthur became fixated upon a quasi-
religious bonding between them, affirming that they possessed a spiritual

unity which transcended the material world. He became fascinating by the kind of crucifix displayed in some French cathedrals in which the figure of God the Father is also represented behind the Son on the Cross, sharing in his agony as the nails pierce both their hands. In similar fashion, he earnestly pledged in a letter of September 1911 to support Alec in all of life's vicissitudes and triumphs.[11]

Alec served with the Dorset regiment as a lieutenant in France during World War I and was posted as missing at Passchendaele during the Ludendorff offensive of spring 1918. Happily for his parents, he survived and after a grim period as a prisoner-of-war in Mainz returned home safely. In the previous year he had gained an unexpected literary notoriety. While waiting for his army commission, he rapidly drafted *The Loom of Youth* (begun late-1915; published July 1917). It was mainly a conventional memoir of his Sherborne schooldays at a fictional 'Fernhurst', inspired by *The Harrovians* (1913) by Arnold Lunn (who was later converted to Catholicism in 1933 by Father Ronald Knox). But, controversially, Alec's memoir also made daring reference to the prevalence of homosexual relationships between public schoolboys. Much to his father's shame, the headmaster had demanded in June 1915 Alec's withdrawal at the end of term, following his ensnarement in just such a relationship. This scandal led to the removal of both Alec's and Arthur's names from Old Shirburnian Society and rendered it impossible for Evelyn to follow his father and elder brother there. Thus Evelyn was deprived of his first chance of an entry into a lost golden world – a preoccupation which was to echo repeatedly throughout his later fictions.

In a fragment of a schoolboy novel, the hero Peter Audley expresses a complex mixture of admiration and resentment for his elder brother, Ralf, who returns home from war as the family's hero. The manuscript was dedicated to its own author, Evelyn Arthur St John Waugh, and its prefatory letter emotively expresses Evelyn's divided loyalties towards his relentlessly bookish heritage or, as he often denoted it, the 'family business'. If your family and most of their friends, Evelyn argues, earn a living from paper and print, then the youthful aspiring writer will inevitably be blighted by such an association:

Much has been written and spoken about the lot of the boy with literary aspirations in a philistine family; little can adequately convey his difficulties, when the surroundings, which he has known from childhood, have been entirely literary. It is a sign of victory over these difficulties that this book is chiefly, if at all, worthy of attention . . . Among books your whole life has been lived and you are now rising up in your turn to add one more to the everlasting bonfire of the ephemeral.

And all this will be brought against you. 'Another of these precocious Waughs,' they will say, 'one more nursery novel.' So be it. There is always a certain romance, to the author at least, about a first novel which no reviewer can quite shatter . . .Soon perhaps you will join the 'wordsmiths' jostling one another for royalties and contracts, meanwhile you are still very young.[12]

In later life Alec became a productive novelist, sometimes generously compared to Somerset Maugham and John Galsworthy. But he was obliged to accept that his childhood status as the preferred brother was rapidly reversed in early adulthood, with Evelyn consistently the more acclaimed writer and public figure from the late-1920s onwards. Nor has this kind of challenge diminished for later generations of the family.

The final chapter of this study will outline how the writings of Evelyn's son, Auberon (1939–2001), echoed and contrasted his father's central literary concerns over the challenges of family life and religious belief within a predominantly secular English society. Reference will also be made to the prolific literary outputs of other recent members of the Waugh family, including Auberon's wife, Lady Teresa Waugh (b.1940), his sisters Margaret (1942–86) and Harriet (b.1944), and three of his children, Sophia (b.1962), Alexander (b.1963) and Daisy (b.1967). This chapter will conclude with the philosophical, religious and family preoccupations of Evelyn's grandson, Alexander, three of whose publications, *Time* (1999), *God* (2002) and *Fathers and Sons* (2004), combine a wry analytical style with extensive textual and historical scholarship to explore multifaceted depictions of Time, God and the family – the trinity of literary subjects of primary concern to his grandfather.

1

The early years: 1903–28

Childhood and World War I

One of Arthur Waugh's favourite sayings was that all good men should revere the Bible, Shakespeare and *Wisden's Cricketing Almanac*.[1] Evelyn loathed cricket, his observations on Shakespeare were sporadic and he preferred the violence and mental disturbances of John Webster's revenge dramas. But the Bible and religious ceremonials were an entirely different matter. His parents were Anglicans and attended Sunday High Celebration at St Barnabas's, Golders Green, and then at St Jude's, Hampstead Garden Suburb. At least once a year Evelyn also visited the vicarage of his mother's step-father, the Revd Raban. Evelyn's childhood nurse, Lucy, was a devout chapel Christian who read the Bible daily from Genesis to Revelation on a six-monthly cycle, and took him on Sundays to the North End Rooms for low-church hymns. After her departure in 1910, Evelyn accompanied his parents to St Jude's where they took comic delight in the flamboyant gestures of its Anglo-Catholic vicar, the Revd Basil Bourchier, whose brother was the actor-manager Arthur Bourchier. Evelyn soon grew to regard his antics – switching on a bright red electric cross over the altar at Communion and sprinkling salt over his congregation and calling them the 'salt of the earth' – as memorably preposterous. The Revd Bourchier provided an early example of one of Evelyn's most familiar fictional character-types – an individual whose diligent professionalism is habitually imbued with unintentional farce.[2]

During his childhood and youth Evelyn alternated between pious seriousness and boorish Bohemianism. Religion may have first attracted Evelyn as a childish means of engaging more closely with his father since his elder brother Alec took no interest in such matters. Alexander Waugh explains: 'Whether wilfully, or subconsciously, Evelyn's early interest in religion helped him to feel a part of Arthur's world, not just an appendage to it'. At Evelyn's request, Arthur ensured that his family and servants met each morning for communal prayers until the outbreak of war in 1914. He was also a prolific compiler of devotional verses for his family and local churches. Sadly for the adolescent Evelyn, his father's religious devotions were already firmly fixated on Alec, whom he regarded as a unique and loving gift from God Himself. His letters to Alec when a schoolboy were often suffused with religious iconography and he churned out childish verses for elder son, such as 'A Boy's Prayer' (written 29 June 1906), which imagined Jesus always alongside his beloved eldest son.[3]

As he grew older, Evelyn's boyish devotions were nurtured by his relatives into a more genuine passion. When staying each year at Midsomer Norton with his father's maiden sisters, who ran Bible classes at their home on Sundays for the local children, he enjoyed accompanying them to Evensong at the local church. He befriended its young curate who taught him to be an altar-server and became aesthetically immersed in the rituals and church decorations of Anglicanism, sketching angels and saints in notebooks. He was delighted one year to be invited to decorate some carved angels in Clandown church, close to Midsomer Norton. Back home at Underhill, Evelyn designed in his bedroom a shrine with incense, statues and brass candlesticks so that he could theatrically play-act, like the Revd Bourchier, at being a priest. He proudly described this shrine in his diary as a twelve-year old and noted that he wanted his confirmation (29 June 1916) to be marked by the gift of a crucifix.[4] He also greatly enjoyed exploring country churches during holidays with his mother at Brighton and Westcliff-on-Sea.

For his father's fiftieth birthday (24 August 1916), Evelyn composed some precocious holy verses in tetrameters, 'The World to Come; A Poem in Three Cantos', modelled on Cardinal Newman's *Dream of Gerontius*, tracing the journey of a soul after death towards God. Arthur was delighted by his twelve-year-old son's poetic efforts and had several copies privately printed and bound. Although Evelyn's early devotions bear the signs of an earnest schoolboy's fascination with an all-absorbing hobby, he was beginning to cultivate more seriously the idea of becoming (like many of his relatives) a Church of England minister. Recalling the stifling vicarage piety of her own childhood, his mother Kate was overtly unsympathetic, as Alec recalled, only to be sternly rebuked by Evelyn that her besetting sin was a 'lack of faith in Catholic doctrine'.[5]

Coupled with this unusually intense absorption for a child in religious affairs was Evelyn's precocious ability, in terms of both word and image, with the pen. Thanks to his father, a naturally vivid imagination was nurtured by the wide range of his childhood fictional reading. He once earned a rare punishment from his father when, inspired by Jules Verne's *Journey to the Centre of the Earth*, he initiated secret excavations within a boot-cupboard at Underhill. Aged six, he began what he grandly termed his first novel, 'The Curse of the Horse Race', a racy tale, laced with violence and murder, warning against the pernicious effects of gambling. He also sporadically kept a personal diary from the aged of seven, with its first entry in September 1911 characteristically blending literary and religious matters in his observation that his father's office 'looks a offely dull plase' and his fears on such a blustery day: 'when I go up to Church I shall be blown away'.[6]

With some local children, Evelyn formed the Wyldesmead Underhill Dramatic Society (WUDS), for which he wrote various sketches and reviews, with titles such as 'The Sheriff's Daughter' and 'The Man from Downing Street', and designed the programmes with cast photographs. Always the leader in childhood games, he formed a militaristic 'Pistol Troop', with the avowed purpose of repelling any German invasion – a genuine fear prior to the outbreak of World War I. In 1912 the group's first magazine was 'published', typed by Arthur's secretary and bound in red morocco with a gold coat of arms specially designed by Evelyn stamped on the cover. Alec contributed a story about racing and Evelyn's six-page tale, 'Multa Pecunia', focused on a professional thief called Smith who masquerades as the butler in the household of a distinguished bibliophile, Sir Alfred James. Heroically, Sir Alfred's plucky son, Tom, foils Smith's crime and ensures that he ends up in Dartmoor.[7]

Despite a later disdain for his father's literary sentimentality, Evelyn remained an avowed admirer of his dramatic renditions of selections from Shakespeare, Dickens, Trollope, Browning and Tennyson, once remarking that only Sir John Gielgud was Arthur's superior in reciting poetry. From the age of eleven onwards, Evelyn also had to come to terms with his elder brother's literary triumphs. In 1914 Alec won, to his father's immense delight, the English Verse Prize at Sherborne. He habitually solicited advice on his poetry from his father who, in turn, had some of his best verses published. One of Alec's poems was accepted in August 1915 by the *Chronicle*, with others appearing in the *Poetry Review*, along with an article, 'The Public School in Wartime', in the *Evening Standard*. He passed into the Royal Military College Sandhurst, in August 1916 and his 'The Poet's Grave' (completed, January 1917) poignantly expressed his fears that probable death in the trenches would terminate his chances of literary immortality. The bereaved mourners stand around his grave and commemorate his illusory heroic reputation, taking consolation in the thought that even when the body dies, the soul lives on. But beneath the clay, the dead poet sadly smiles in the knowledge that he has left behind him only a world of cynical disillusionment. Alec's most powerful poem, 'Cannon Fodder' (originally 'Carrion' but revised at his horrified parents' request), was written in September 1917 at Flanders where he serving as a machine-gunner on the front-line at Passchendaele. It bitterly contrasts the proliferation of severed body-parts and rotting corpses, an everyday experience for Alec, with comforting delusions back home over the heroic nobility of a soldier's death.[8] These mournful poems, which the Waughs at Underhill would have read with horrified fascination, remain a sombre but now almost entirely overlooked influence on Evelyn's later fictional responses to the morally confused worlds of 1920s high society.

The superficial and callous activities depicted in Evelyn's early novels can be interpreted, on one level, as merely a satiric response to the vacuities of 'bright young things' during the 1920s. But the true origins of their underlying sense of social nihilism and human vulnerability may also be specifically traced back to the wartime experiences of the Waugh family. In late-summer

1914 Arthur was laid off by the *Daily Telegraph* as a reviewer, thereby losing virtually half of his annual income. This prompted him to cease morning prayers at Underhill because they now seemed pointless. By Christmas 1918, with Alec returning on 5 December from his prisoner-of-war internment after the horrors of the trenches, the world of middle-class England had irrevocably changed. Although just too young to be called up for military service, Evelyn and other near-contemporary writers – George Orwell (b.1903), John Wyndham (b.1903), Malcolm Muggeridge (b.1903), Graham Greene (b.1904), Anthony Powell (b.1905) and Samuel Beckett (b.1906) – spent the next two decades responding, both implicitly and explicitly, to the enormous social, political and religious upheavals engendered by the World War I. Christopher Isherwood's *Lions and Shadows* (1938) suggests that young men in this category, 'had experienced a sense of guilt and inadequacy at having missed the Test of Manhood'; and Alexander Waugh observes of his grandfather: 'Those, like Evelyn, who were too young to fight felt a greater estrangement from the previous generation than those who had seen action'.[9] In *Brideshead Revisited* 'Boy' Mulcaster laments to Charles Ryder during the 1926 General Strike that they had both been too young to fight in the last war but now they had a chance to show that they too could fight heroically. Ryder (born, like Waugh, in October 1903) agrees, insisting that he has come from overseas to defend his country in its 'hour of need' (198).

Like Evelyn – who aged thirty-five joined the Marine Infantry Brigade (as their oldest recruit) and then the commandos – these writers readily immersed themselves in their World War II service. Orwell, a Spanish Civil War veteran, was declared unfit for active service and instead worked in BBC propaganda; Wyndham joined the Royal Corp of Signals and the Normandy landings; Muggeridge, the Military Police, Intelligence Corp and MI6; Greene, the Ministry of Information and MI6; Powell, the infantry in Ulster and the Intelligence Corp; and Beckett, the French Resistance (receiving the Croix de Guerre). Evelyn's insistent preoccupations in his fictions with honour and dishonour, service and charlatanism and the essential randomness of mortality may be traced back to the teenage boy who avidly followed the unfolding of the World War I, the experiences of his elder brother Alec and the irreparable damage of the war to his own generation. In 1921 he wrote presciently of his desire to clarify the major influences over his generation, noting: 'I think that . . . I shall find that the war is directly responsible for most of us'.[10] For that select group of authors born between 1903 and 1906, the idea that the world remained in a perilous state of potential anarchy seemed an entirely logical concept.

Schooldays

Alongside his family's literary activities, Evelyn was also attracted as a youth to their accomplishments in the visual arts. Although irritated by Edmund Gosse's fussy old-worldliness, he was impressed by the artistic skills of his grandfather, Thomas Gosse, a miniaturist and portrait painter. Evelyn's grandmother, Annie (Morgan) Waugh, was a skilled watercolourist and his father's younger, seafaring brother, Alick (d.1900), produced exquisite watercolour sketches of various exotic locations, along with a series of naval charts which confirmed his skills as a cartographic draughtsman. As a child, Evelyn had developed his artistic eye by endlessly copying interesting images, whether from Froissart's *Chronicles* or his comics, and he came to view sketching, especially cartoons, as a pleasurable relaxation.[11] Indeed, many of the most vivid caricatures of his fictions, such as Apthorpe and Ben Ritchie-Hook in *Sword of Honour*, owe much to his early aptitude for creating essentially cartoon-like impressions of exaggerated human behaviour.

In later life Evelyn admired and collected Victorian narrative painting. But the chaotic social atmosphere engendered by World War I turned him, like many of his generation, towards a search for self-conscious newness and radical alternatives to all that now seemed outmoded and irrelevant in England's long-established artistic traditions. He eagerly espoused Clive Bell's modernist manifesto, *Art* (1914); and in 1917 the journal *Drawing and Design* published his precocious essay, 'In Defence of Cubism'.[12] With W. W. Jacobs's culturally voracious daughter, Barbara (later Alec's first wife), Evelyn eagerly visited galleries and exhibitions and developed a passion for all things 'modern', especially the Post-Impressionists and the Futurists. They studied together Filippo Tommaso Marinetti's *The Founding and Manifesto of Futurism* (1909), later satirically echoed in *Vile Bodies*, and converted the former day-nursery at Underhill into an artist's studio, boldly daubing their own cubist creations onto its walls.[13]

Marinetti, a fascist and later supporter of Mussolini, insisted that Art could only grow from violence, cruelty and injustice. He viewed war as the world's only true instigator of social hygiene, and advocated the closure and destruction of all libraries, museums and other institutions commemorating the past. The iconoclastic madness of such unquestioning modernity was soon rejected by Evelyn, who by the mid-1920s was publishing panegyrics of the Pre-Raphaelites. Nevertheless, Marinetti's relentlessly dehumanizing aesthetics left a lasting impression on his satiric vision as a novelist, chiming in perfectly with the barbarous architecture of Otto Silenus in *Decline and Fall*, who absurdly sees only factories as the perfect buildings since they cater for machines rather than for people.

Waugh's formal schooling continued the diversification of his artistic and literary interests. In September 1910, a month before his seventh birthday, he began attending a local preparatory school, Heath Mount, primarily because its headmaster, J. S. Granville Grenfell, had known his father Arthur at Sherborne. His father walked him to school each morning since it was on his route to Hampstead Tube Station. It was on these trips that Evelyn later claimed that he first began to get to know his father and enjoy his company. Through the influence of an enthusiastic English teacher at Heath

Mount, Aubrey Ensor, Evelyn discovered in the writings of H. H. Munro ('Saki') an attractive blending (later much in evidence in his own writings) of social satire, cruelty and the macabre. He also edited in 1916 a newly founded magazine, *The Cynic*, intended as a rival to the official *Heath Mount Magazine*. In May 1917 he started at Lancing College near Brighton, a High-Church establishment apparently chosen by Arthur in order to test out Evelyn's much professed Christian piety.

Lancing, with its gigantic gothic-revival chapel, recalls Paul Pennyfeather's 'small public school of ecclesiastical temper on the South Downs' (11) in *Decline and Fall*. At first, Evelyn marked himself out as a non-conformist oddity by his theatrical piety, kneeling at chapel during the Creed while others stood and at night kneeling deep in prayer in the dormitory. But, gradually, he was drawn into the diverse cultural life of the school. He joined the newly formed Dilettanti Debating Society and headed its Art section, reading on 11 November 1919 a paper on 'Book Illustration and Decoration'. He harboured vague ambitions of making a career as a draughtsman and won two first prizes for 'illuminated prayers' in school competitions. His housemaster, E. B. Gordon, granted him access to his own small printing-press and introduced him to a local aesthete, Francis Crease. He lived on a private income at nearby Lychpole and from January 1920 gave Evelyn lessons in calligraphy. These experiences were later reflected in his 1945 fragment, 'Charles Ryder's Schooldays' (published, 1982). His ever-supportive father responded by gaining some commissioned work for him from Chapman and Hall to design book jackets. He also arranged for Evelyn to visit Eric Gill's Roman Catholic arts and crafts community at Ditchling, close to Brighton, where he met the renowned calligrapher, Edward Johnston.

Evelyn's literary tastes at Lancing were considerably enriched as he delved into the works of late-Victorian and Georgian poets, including Walter Savage Landor, Hilaire Belloc, Ernest Dowson and A. E. Housman, each of whom fed his boyish appetite, respectively, for anarchy, Catholic controversy, decadence and classical poetry. Such literary eclecticism spurred on his own endeavours and he duly won the Lancing Poetry Prize and the Scarlyn Literature Prize, along with editing the *Lancing Magazine* and offering (unsuccessfully) samples of his poetry for *Public School Verses*. He was a member of the Shakespeare Society and joined the modern play-reading group (introducing him to George Bernard Shaw, Arthur Wing Pinero and John Galsworthy) of one of the school's most inspiring teachers, J. F. Roxburgh, a war-hero and later the first headmaster of Stowe School. Evelyn began in late-1918 his first (aborted) novel, with its hero, Peter Audley, based on himself. His satiric play, *Conversation*, was staged before the whole school in summer 1921 and, mocking the public-school ethos, included a parody of *The Loom of Youth* in its second act.[14]

In 1919 Arthur dedicated to Evelyn his second volume of collected literary criticism, *Tradition and Change*, in which he recognized that his younger son had been born into a period of radical changes and that it was only to be expected that he would be troubled and challenged by many of them. But he also shrewdly reminded him that personal contentment was often achieved by balancing the new with the old, just as an Old Master then hung over Evelyn's bed while he earnestly sketched Cubist designs in his living room.[15] While embracing the new social order, Arthur counselled, it was no less important for Evelyn to respect older traditions and beliefs. But such well-intentioned paternal observations went unappreciated by their recipient. To his younger son, Arthur seemed trapped in an archaic world of outmoded traditions and sentimentality, in which 'change' was viewed with either patronizing suspicion or incomprehension. In return, Evelyn sent his father an essay on 'Romance' in October 1919 which upset him by its overtly satirical tone.

The close proximity of his elder brother was also proving a mixed blessing. Alec had married Barbara Jacobs on 29 July 1919 and they were living at Underhill. He had been appointed as a part-time reader at Chapman and Hall and Evelyn continued his amicable artistic relationship with Barbara during the school vacations. They experienced together 'Vorticism', 'Futurism', *avant-garde* painting and the acclaimed revival of *The Beggar's Opera* at the Lyric Theatre, Hammersmith. Deeply frustrated by his office job, Alec continued to develop his freelance writing, publishing radical articles on the rights of the young, a verse-collection titled *Resentment: Poems* (1918) and an account of his war-time experiences, *The Prisoners of Mainz* (1919). Over the next four years, Alec's productivity as a writer was impressive, resulting in four works which drew heavily upon his own youthful past: a novel, *Pleasure* (1921), in which a soldier has a chance meeting with a former schoolboy infatuation; *The Lonely Unicorn* (1922b) and *Public School Life* (1922a), both dealing with male relationships at public schools; and a precocious autobiographical volume, *Myself When Young: Confessions* (1923). Privately, Alec was agonizing over his relationship with Barbara since their marriage remained unconsummated. While a liaison with a more experienced mistress soon resolved Alec's physical problems, they both realized their incompatibility and formally separated in January 1922, with a decree of annulment granted in January 1923. Alec's growing literary reputation, combined with their father's now venerable status in the London literary world, added an extra burden of expectation to the young Evelyn's hopes for the future. Somehow, he had to match them but, at the same time, to prove himself very different from them.

Evelyn was appointed as a junior sacristan in Lancing chapel and, when at Underhill, attended Sunday Mass at St Jude's, revelling in the Revd Bourchier's latest devotional fad, a festival marking 'The Coronation of the Blessed Mother of God'. But in 1921, prompted by a keenly argumentative divinity teacher, Mr Rawlinson, Evelyn's classroom religious discussions and periodic depressions led to a sense of personal agnosticism and, ultimately, a temporary loss of faith. His diary for 13 June records with an implicit sense of bravado:

> In the last few weeks I have ceased to be a Christian (sensation off!) I have realized that for the last two terms at least I have been an atheist in all except the courage to admit it to myself.

As he explained to his close friend, Dudley Carew, he had temporarily embraced agnosticism but was still ready to admit the existence of God as some kind of intangible force. He even founded a preposterous 'Corpse Club', with himself as its chief 'Undertaker', for those melancholy fellow pupils who felt entirely disillusioned with life. Agnosticism became for Evelyn yet another element in his growing loss of faith in twentieth-century English society.[16]

His editorship in his final year of the *Lancing Magazine* eloquently expressed his disenchantment with both school life and the inheritance of his own generation. His first editorial, a brief short story called 'The Community Spirit' (November 1921), defiantly deriding the much-prized communal ethos of public schools. His second editorial, 'The Youngest Generation' (December 1921), offered a prescient view of his own situation as a writer during the 1920s, noting that Rupert Brooke's generation had been broken and disillusioned by a war callously created by their elders. Instead, he hoped that the youth of 1922 would be clear-sighted, dispassionate and sharply analytic, gazing on a new world from a cynically comic perspective. These juvenile sentiments prefigure the essence of his narrative personae in his early novels, in which hard-headed, bitter satire is blended with anarchic, liberating comedy. This editorial ultimately offers 'an astute analysis of his own need to develop an aesthetic which would allow a realistic appraisal of the tawdry modern world while at the same time maintaining dissociation from it'.[17]

Oxford University and *The Scarlet Woman* (1925)

Evelyn sat the Oxford Entrance Examinations in early December 1921, writing in his 'General Paper' on Rupert Brooke, the Pre-Raphaelites and Arthur Symons's *Aubrey Beardsley: An Essay with a Preface* (1898). He was awarded a Senior History Scholarship at Hertford College and went up in January 1922, glad to escape the stressful atmosphere at home since his father was still anxious over the expiry in 1920 of Chapman and Hall's lucrative Dickens copyright and Alec was formally separating from his wife, Barbara. Evelyn happily occupied himself during his first two terms with making his maiden speech at the Union (opposing the motion, 'This House Would Welcome Prohibition'), drafting an entry for the Newdigate Prize Poem (won by his father in 1888 and referred to in *Decline and Fall* when hearties deface another student's entry), serving as Secretary to the Hertford Debating Society and working diligently for his History preliminary examinations.

But during his more riotous second year Evelyn grew to loathe Hertford's caustic history tutor (later its Dean and Principal), C. R. M. F. Cruttwell, who, in turn, regarded Evelyn as a suburban shirker with an inferiority complex. 'The dislike between Evelyn and himself' Alec remarked, 'was mutual, instinctive and as irrational as love'.[18] Cruttwell had enjoyed a distinguished student career at Oxford, leading to a first-class honours degree in History and election in 1911 to an All Souls' fellowship. He served during the war in the Royal Berkshires and in 1916 was severely wounded, experiences which seem to have affected his whole personality. Despite Alec's hardships as a prisoner-of war and his admiration for the war poets, Evelyn was not inclined to make any allowances for Cruttwell's awkward post-war temperament. In life-long revenge – and as an intriguing example of how minor facets of his Oxford life permeated the entire span of his literary career – numerous Cruttwellian caricatures haunt Waugh's fictions. These include the psychopathic criminal (*Decline and Fall*); a conservative MP (*Vile Bodies*); a social wastrel (*Black Mischief*); an osteopath (*A Handful of Dust*); a blowsy blonde ('Winner Takes All'); a bogus ex-brigadier salesman (*Scoop*) and an embezzling cub-master ('An Englishman's Home'). Even the disturbing tale of a homicidal lunatic's day out, 'Mr Loveday's Little Outing', was first titled 'Mr Cruttwell's Little Outing' (the name Loveday was borrowed from another war-veteran and director of Chapman and Hall).

As early as August 1923 Evelyn had published a dark short story, 'Edward of Unique Achievement', in the Oxford magazine *Cherwell* about a history undergraduate whose scholarship is revoked by Mr Curtis, a malicious tutor and sexual deviant, whom he loathes and eventually murders. A year later he satirized Cruttwell in a mock-panegyric tribute published in another student magazine, *Isis* (5 March 1924), accompanied by an unfortunate photograph of his victim attempting a genial smile.[19] In *Ninety-Two Days* (1934) Evelyn incidentally recalls Cruttwell's disapproval over his ignorance of the flow of the Rhine. Almost forty years later, another worthless history tutor, again called Mr Curtis (also murdered), appears in his final work of prose fiction, *Basil Seal Rides Again* (1963).

As an undergraduate Evelyn and another close Hertford friend, Terence Greenidge, had spread the scurrilous rumour that the bachelor Cruttwell sodomized dogs in his college rooms. They invented bawdy rhymes, made barking noises near his rooms and placed a stuffed whippet from a junk-shop in the quad under his window. This literary inheritance has also been reverentially preserved by later generations of Waughs. Evelyn's son, Auberon, gleefully claimed that the word 'Cruttwellism' had been coined as a definition of dog-sodomy. In another act of familial piety, Evelyn's grandson, Alexander, stood beneath Cruttwell's portrait at an academic conference held at Hertford College in 2003 to commemorate the centenary of Evelyn's birth. He recounts how 'great waves of family pride engulfed' him and, acknowledging that an 'ancient wound needed once more to be reopened', he led his distinguished audience in raising their glasses so that Cruttwell might 'for ever be remembered as a dog sodomist and a total shit'.[20]

Evelyn's indulgent and often drunken career as an Oxford undergraduate proved, on an academic level, uninspired. He achieved a 3rd class degree but failed to complete the required nine terms of residence necessary to receive it. Nevertheless, in terms of literary inspiration, Oxford provided him with a rich source of comic incidents and long-lasting character archetypes, along with some productive personal friendships. In *Decline and Fall*, for example, the riotous Bollinger Club echoes the high-society Bullingdon Dining Club; and an undergraduate at Balliol (who had unwisely confessed to having enjoyed beating small boys at his public school) lends his name to Philbrick, Dr Fagan's criminally minded butler. Similarly, in *Brideshead* the experiences of Charles Ryder constantly hark back to Evelyn's own university memories. Another close friend, Brian Howard, provided the primary archetype for one of his most memorable characters, Anthony Blanche (and also for Ambrose Silk in *Put Out More Flags*), and the urbane don Maurice Bowra inspired the ingratiating wit of Mr Samgrass.

Another influential personal contact Oxford was the independently wealthy aesthete, Harold Acton, whom he first met at the Catholic Newman Society when G. K. Chesterton was delivering a lecture. Acton introduced him to the poetry of Gertrude Stein and T. S. Eliot (declaiming parts of *The Waste Land* through a megaphone from a balcony) and to the novels of Ronald Firbank, whose distinctive cinematic prose style, with minimal descriptions and contemporary dialogue, was to exert a strong influence over Evelyn's early fictions. Acton accompanied Evelyn in June 1923 to the first performance of Edith Sitwell's *Façade* at the Aeolian Hall and then to the Sitwell's London home where he met Osbert, Lytton Strachey and Clive Bell. Acton and another friend, Robert Byron, were enthusiasts for the baroque style in art and they taught Evelyn how it drew together a cornucopia of ornament into an aesthetically rich and unified design, in contrast to the fragmentary disintegrations of modern art. These Oxford contacts were to play a crucial role in the formulation of Evelyn's later habit of providing a contextualized aesthetic for his fictional great houses. His discussions with Acton and Byron:

> fostered a sense of period styles in the arts as expressions of each age's fundamental moral and intellectual commitments, which would lead in the novels to a dense symbolic shorthand whereby the style of a building becomes a clue to the mind of its owner, artistic taste an index of moral character.[21]

The first edition of *Decline and Fall* was affectionately dedicated to Acton, in recognition of his generosity in encouraging Evelyn's literary and artistic ambitions at Oxford. Acton had commissioned from him two garishly stylized jacket-covers for his short-lived *avant garde* journal, *Oxford Broom*, and a macabre anti-romantic short story, 'Antony, Who Sought Things That Were Lost' (June, 1923).[22] This disturbing tale (perhaps reflecting the breakdown of his intense friendship with a fellow student, Richard Pares) tells how in the imaginary dukedom of St Romeiro, a Count Antony is voluntarily accompanied in his imprisonment by his beloved Lady Elizabeth but eventually strangles her. The proof of Evelyn's skills as a graphic artist offered by his journal covers for Acton led to other commissions for OUDS programmes, bookplates, dust-jackets for Chapman and Hall and the sale of some prints to the *London Mercury* and *Golden Hind*. Memorably, Evelyn produced for the *Cherwell* a series of disturbing woodcuts, 'The Seven Deadly Sins', including such idiosyncratic vices as 'The horrid sacrilege of those that ill-treat books', 'That grim act parricide' and 'That dull, old sin, adultery'. He also twice exhibited his work at the Oxford Arts Club and in 1924 was nominated to join its Hanging Committee.[23]

Evelyn's student journalism was also prolific, with reports on Union debates for the Conservative Carlton Club's *Oxford Fortnightly Review*, drawings and poems published under the pseudonym 'Scaramel' and regular subversive contributions to two student journals, *Isis* and *Cherwell*. He delighted in inserting into their pages mock adverts for insurance policies against examination failure and college fines. He honed his already distinctive satiric style through his acerbic film column, 'Seen in the Dark', and his 'Uncle Alfred' and 'Aunt Ermentrude' mock advice columns (with cartoons) in the 'Children's Corner' of *Isis*. This ephemeral student journalism, typified by his short story for *Cherwell*, 'Edward of Unique Achievement' (August, 1923, reprinted 1925), confirmed his talent for parodic dialogues and deadpan farce, qualities which later characterized the comic brilliance of his early fictions.[24]

For a young man who claimed at Lancing temporarily to have lost his faith, Oxford University during the early 1920s proved an intriguing religious environment. Although he felt that there was almost too much overt religion there, a liberally enquiring atmosphere prevailed among his student associates. Hertford did not enforce compulsory attendance at chapel and the regular presence at its services of Cruttwell, a devout Christian, hardly attracted Evelyn to its significance within college life. His co-persecutor of Cruttwell, Terence Greenidge, was drawn to the Oxford Movement during his first year before espousing a more sceptical attitude towards organized religion. Through Greenidge, Evelyn met the Catholic convert Douglas Woodruff, then President of the Oxford Union, editor of *Isis* and later the influential editor (1936–67) of the Catholic weekly, *The Tablet*. Two other friends, Richard Pares and Cyril Connolly, also regularly attended services at the Roman Catholic Westminster Cathedral in London.

As a brilliant undergraduate who eventually gained a 1st class degree and fellowship of All Souls, Pares was inducted into the social circle of Francis 'Sligger' Urquhart (1868–1934), the bachelor Dean of Balliol College and

Oxford's first Roman Catholic don since the Reformation. When Urquhart enforced the closure of one of Evelyn's favourite drinking societies, the riotous 'Hypocrites' Club' above a bicycle shop in St Aldates, a personal enmity inevitably developed, comparable to that with Cruttwell. Evelyn frequented Balliol at nightfall to sing loudly in the quadrangle, to the tune of 'Nuts in May': 'The Dean of Balliol lies with men!' – an ironic insult since his anger had been primarily triggered by his loss of Pares to Sligger's more decorously ephebic circle. Although Urquhart did not actively solicit his student friends to convert to Catholicism, he became a primary focus for Catholic affairs at Oxford. He played a leading role in the establishment of the university's Catholic Chaplaincy, ensuring in 1926 the appointment as its chaplain of his friend, Ronald Knox, whose biography Evelyn was later to write.[25]

By the mid-1920s Roman Catholicism had a distinct if discreet presence at Oxford, notably through the incorporation by statute in 1918 of the Jesuit Campion Hall and the Benedictine St Benet's Hall as private colleges of the university. A wide range of Evelyn's Oxford contemporaries and friends became converts to Catholicism, including the son of an Anglican bishop, Christopher Hollis (converted 1924), Alastair Graham (1924), Graham Greene (1926), Robert Speaight (1930) and Frank Pakenham (1940). Whether Evelyn was himself tempted towards Catholicism at this period remains uncertain but it is clear that Oxford heightened his awareness of the dichotomy between worldly sensuality and religious asceticism.

Such a dichotomy was embodied in Evelyn's final-year intimacy with another undergraduate at Brasenose College, the dreamily bookish Alastair Graham, whom he calls Hamish Lennox in his later autobiographical writings. Alastair's widowed mother, Jessie, was a dynamic lady from Savannah, Georgia, later fondly satirized as Lady Circumference in *Decline and Fall* and as Mrs Kent-Cumberland in 'Winner Takes All'. The Grahams lived in an early-nineteenth-century country house at Barford, midway between Warwick and Stratford-upon-Avon, and Evelyn's relationship with Alastair and his family evolved into an early precursor of the Arcadian friendship between Charles Ryder and Sebastian Flyte in *Brideshead*. So much so, that in the manuscript of the novel, the name Alastair is sometimes written instead of Sebastian. In August 1924 Evelyn travelled to Ireland with Alastair for a walking tour, visiting numerous Catholic churches and staying for two nights at Mount Melleray monastery. During this trip Alastair finalized his decision to become a Roman Catholic and on Saturday 13 September he was received into the church at Oxford by Father Cyril Martindale, S. J., himself a convert in 1897. On the following day, Evelyn met Alastair in London, accompanied him to Mass at Hampstead and was presented with a Bible bound in green morocco to commemorate Alastair's conversion. On the Monday Evelyn travelled back to Oxford with him for Communion and breakfast with Father Martindale. But this idyllic friendship was soon to end abruptly when Alastair departed for Kenya in mid-September 1924 to stay with his sister and her husband.[26]

An auction of Evelyn's more valuable books and pictures was held in his college rooms in early 1924 to alleviate severe debts occasioned by his busy social life since 'his taste for excellence was rarely hindered by common sense'.[27] This did not bode well for his parents' hopes that he would find some congenial employment after university in a literary or artistic environment. But Evelyn was still focused enough on the family profession to begin in mid-1924 the first chapter of a film-script style novel, 'The Temple at Thatch'. Heavily laced with melodrama and mental derangements, it focused on a young man who inherits a country house estate where only its eighteenth-century folly survives and in which he practises black magic. It seems to have been most influenced by the morbidity of *The Cypress Grove* ('the living talk of those gone away as of so many shadows, or fabulous paladins') by the seventeenth-century Scots poet and friend of Ben Jonson, William Drummond of Hawthornden.

Soon after leaving Oxford, Evelyn enrolled at Heatherley's Art School, off the Tottenham Court Road. But he found that it was aimed more at providing basic training in commercial artwork than fostering creative endeavour and in late-October he stopped attending classes. Instead, through Alec, he began in 1924 to frequent a private club, the Cave of Harmony, in Charlotte Street where he met a young cabaret performer, Elsa Lanchester (1902–86), who married in 1929 the actor, Charles Laughton. The club was run by Elsa's then partner, Harold Scott, who often staged radical plays and cabaret sketches which would have been unlikely to gain a licence from the Lord Chamberlain for public performances.

Enthused by the heady atmosphere of these underground pursuits, Evelyn persuaded Lanchester to take part in a cinematic film which he had scripted, with Terence Greenidge (the founder of the Oxford Cinematograph Club) as its director. This bizarre short film, *The Scarlet Woman: an Ecclesiastical Melodrama*, was a skit on D. W. Griffith's silent films and told of the Dean of Balliol's madcap plot to convert the king of England to Catholicism. It provided a cinematic debut for Lanchester, who a decade later became renowned for her roles as Mary Shelley and in James Whale's the *Bride of Frankenstein* (1935). Greenidge, his brother John, Alec, Evelyn and another college friend, John Sutro (later a film producer) – all former members of the 'Hypocrites' Club' shut down by 'Sligger' Urquhart – each put in £5 to finance the film which was shot between July and September 1924 at Oxford, Hampstead Heath and in the garden at Underhill. Evelyn played the parts of both Urquhart and the impecunious Lord Borrowington, and Lanchester was Beatrice de Carolle, an evangelical cabaret singer of dubious morality (a precursor to the evangelist Mrs Melrose Ape in *Vile Bodies*). Other parts were taken by Sutro as Cardinal Montefiasco (with Alec as his ancient mother who 'necks' with the Pope) and John Greenidge as the Prince of Wales (later King Edward VIII) who offers homosexual temptation to 'Sligger'.

The film was first shown in late-1925 at the Oxford University Dramatic Society, with musical accompaniment by Lennox Berkeley, and a second viewing was arranged at Campion Hall. Its master, Father Martindale, was so amused by the film that John Greenidge inserted a mock-licence as a sub-title: 'Nihil Obstat – projiciatur – C. C. Martindale, S. J.'. At the same period Evelyn (under the acting pseudonym of Wycliffe Hall) also took a part in another lost film directed by Terence Greenidge, *The Cities of the Plain*, in which he played a lascivious black clergyman. These experiences clearly fed into *Vile Bodies* and its account of a bizarre biopic of the life of John Wesley, the founder of Methodism, and his relationship with Selina, Countess of Huntingdon – 'the most important All-Talkie super-religious film to be produced solely in this country' (144) – on Colonel Blount's country estate near Aylesbury.[28]

While Catholicism in *The Scarlet Woman* was utilized primarily as a rich source of farce, Evelyn's association from 1924 onwards with two other Oxford undergraduates, the brothers Richard and David Plunket Greene, was of considerably more significance in terms of the development of his own religious affiliations. Following their parents' separation, the brothers lived in London at Hanover Terrace with their mother Gwen and sister Olivia and Evelyn was soon captivated by their bohemian family circle. Mrs Greene was intensely religious and converted to Catholicism in 1926. She was strongly influenced by her uncle, the Austrian Catholic theologian Baron Friedrich von Hügel (1852–1925), who had married her aunt, Lady Mary Herbert, the daughter of Sidney, first Baron Herbert of Lea. Hügel had been awarded in 1920 an honorary Doctorate of Divinity by Oxford University, the first honorary degree to be granted to a Roman Catholic since the Reformation. Evelyn grew infatuated with the cultured but heavy-drinking Olivia, a manically promiscuous white-faced waif, once memorably described as 'a ghost with a glass of gin in her hand'. Although she delighted in his social company, Olivia consistently rebuffed his attempts at a more intimate relationship. This situation became a source of intense personal frustration for Evelyn who remained especially close to her brother Richard, acting as his best man at his wedding on 21 December 1925.

Olivia's personal dissipations were matched by her new-found devotion to Roman Catholicism, especially the agonized writings of St Teresa of Avila and St John of the Cross. She was inspired in such spiritual matters by her mother, who in 1928 published a collection of her uncle's correspondence, *Letters from Baron Friedrich von Hügel to a Niece*, which she had previously lent to Evelyn in manuscript. While these religious interests certainly influenced Evelyn (not least her decision to seek mortification of the flesh through a vow of chastity), the actor Robert Speight (himself a convert to Catholicism) wisely dismissed her adopted role as a saintly flapper as self-deceptive, noting that it was foolish to limit one's reading to *Vogue* and St John of the Cross. Capturing Olivia's paradoxical combination of ascetic sensuality, Evelyn designed for her a bookplate, which he mischievously described as an 'Impietà, depicting her dancing naked beside a horn gramophone while brandishing the head of John the Baptist.[29] Despite their eccentricities and personal vices (David was a heroin addict), Evelyn's involvements with the

Plunket Greene family were to play a major role in his eventual conversion to Roman Catholicism.

School-mastering, the Pre-Raphaelites and *Rossetti* (1928)

Still searching for gainful employment and beginning what Harold Acton called his Dostoyevsky period, Evelyn attempted in December 1924 to start a printing and design apprenticeship with James Guthrie, the owner of the Pear Tree Press, near Bognor Regis, for which his father, Arthur, had paid a £25 indenture. But when he arrived, he found that most of the business depended upon the use of zinc intaglios taken from photographs which were then hand-printed to resemble drawings. He left after only a single night's residence with the Guthries. The remaining career option left open to him was the ignominious world of school-teaching and, following an interview in London, he received an offer of employment as a teacher of History, Latin and Greek for £160 per annum from a school in Denbighshire, North Wales, called Arnold House at Llanddulas (inspiration for Llanabba Castle in *Decline and Fall*), to which he dolefully travelled on 23 January 1925.[30]

The mundane circumstances in which Evelyn now found himself did not diminish (and, indeed, stimulated) his literary ambitions. He wrote enthusiastically to Acton about his ideas for a volume on Silenus, the drunken Greek god who accompanies the wine-deity Dionysius, recast as a sentimental idyll to recall Falstaff within green English pastures.[31] This subject seemed entirely appropriate to his current lifestyle since, soon after the end of his first term and back in London, he was arrested with a friend, Matthew Ponsonby (the son of the former Under Secretary of State for Foreign Affairs), for being incapably drunk while the equally inebriated Matthew tried to drive the wrong way around a traffic island on the Strand. Alec was also trying to fix Evelyn up with a plum job in Pisa as the personal secretary of Charles Scott-Moncrieff (1889–1930), who, like Alec, had served at the Western Front during World War I and had written about homosexual relationships between schoolboys in his 'Evensong and Morwe Song' (1907, reprinted 1923). Scott-Moncrieff was then in the midst of the first English translation of Proust, *Remembrance of Things Past* (1922–30).

Such creative employment could have proved genuinely stimulating to Evelyn and, even though he later regarded Proust as a mental defective, his influence is evidenced by chapter-titles (1: 'Du Côté de Chez Beaver'; 6: 'Du Côté de Chez Todd') in *A Handful of Dust* (1934). Buoyed up by these prospects, Evelyn began to turn his mind to new literary work but then experienced two major setbacks to his confidence. Acton had agreed to read through 'The Temple at Thatch', only to categorize it condescendingly as a piece of trivia. He viewed it as 'an airy Firbankian trifle', worthy only of a private printing 'in a few elegant copies for the friends who love you'. Evelyn immediately destroyed the manuscript in the school furnace but then also learnt that his hopes for a job in Italy had dissipated, even though he had already handed in his notice at Arnold House. He later claimed to have attempted suicide by swimming out to sea but he was stung by a jellyfish and decided to abort this half-hearted attempt at self-extinction.[32]

Evelyn sought alternative employment by writing to art magazines and various galleries, including the National Gallery, but without any success. Fortunately, Richard Plunket Greene was then teaching at a small 'crammer' at Aston Clinton, Buckinghamshire, and alerted him to a vacancy for an English, History and Art teacher at £160 per year. Appointed to this dreary but convenient post, Evelyn found little to inspire him in the school's mundane ethos, although he did take over its Literary Society (inviting Alec to address it), staged a scene from *The Tempest* and designed a cover for the school magazine. During November 1925, while recuperating at Underhill from a drunken fall, he began to read about the Pre-Raphaelites and noted in his diary that he might 'write a book about them'.[33] He also went briefly to Paris in late-December with the actor-manager, Bill Silk. The trip was notable for a sleazily disappointing trip to a male brothel and Evelyn's solitary but more productive wanderings around the Louvre, becoming 'glutted' with its renowned collection of Poussins, including '*Les bergers d'Arcadie*' – a painting of central importance to *Brideshead Revisited*. Back at Aston Clinton for the spring term, he began to read widely, from Plato's *Republic* and Kenneth Graham's *The Wind in the Willows* (a life-long favourite) to Eliot's 'The Waste Land'. He was also strongly influenced by Sir Joshua Reynolds' *Discourses* which advocated the primacy of English historical painting, as later practised by Royal Academicians and the Pre-Raphaelites – views shared by Evelyn in later life as a keen collector of nineteenth-century narrative art.[34]

He completed on 26 August 1925 a self-reflective short story, 'The Balance: A Yarn of the Good Old Days of Broad Trousers and High Necked Jumpers', about a young art student, Adam Doure, who is dumped by his flapper girlfriend, Imogen Quest.[35] Adam unsuccessfully attempts suicide and finally consoles himself with the thought that a commitment to his art is ultimately the way to preserve his appetite for life. Exploring the need for a balance between the senses and reason (and recycling elements from 'The Temple at Thatch'), it is the first surviving example of Evelyn's use of his fiction as a means for self-analysis. It contains nostalgic references to Oxford and a country house ('Thatch') and has distinctly cinematic qualities, later developed to great effect in *Decline and Fall* and *Vile Bodies*. It also tries out several literary devices later used in his early satiric novels, including an innocent male protagonist and his self-obsessed love interest enduring the vicissitudes of blind fate within a sophisticated but amoral society. Although first rejected by three other publishers, it appeared in the 1926 Chapman and Hall annual, *Georgian Stories*, edited that year by Alec, alongside contributions by Aldous

Huxley, Gertrude Stein and Somerset Maugham. 'The Balance', with its brittle social world, comic irony and sharp dialogue exerted a significant influence over *Vile Bodies*, which reuses the names 'Adam' and 'Imogen Quest'.

During July 1926 Evelyn was asked by Alastair Graham, who owned a small printing press and was then apprenticed at the Shakespeare Head Press, to compose something for publication. When at Lancing, he had once planned a paper on 'The Failure of the Pre-Raphaelites' and, enthused by his family relationship to Holman Hunt (who married two of his great-aunts), he took up again the notes on the Pre-Raphaelites made at Underhill in November 1925. He completed in just over four days, while also correcting examination scripts, an essay titled, *P.R.B.: An Essay on the Pre-Raphaelite Brotherhood 1847–54*. It was privately published by Graham as a twenty-five page pamphlet (mainly on Millais and Hunt) and provided productive groundwork and several passages for recycling in his first published book, *Rossetti: His Life and Works* (1928b).

Evelyn continued to diversify his literary activities during the autumn term of 1926 at Aston Clinton, drafting an essay, 'Noah, or the Future of Intoxication', based on his earlier interest in Silenus, for Kegan Paul's light-hearted series, *Today and Tomorrow*. He also read essays on art and aesthetics by Herbert Read and periodically sought escapism in Edgar Wallace's crime fiction. Given the humdrum nature of his school life, he welcomed a chance to visit Alastair Graham at Athens, where he was about to take up a posting as an honorary attaché to the British Legation. He left London for Marseilles on Christmas Eve 1926 aboard the *Patris II* and spent much of the voyage out reading *The Varieties of Religious Experience* (1902), originally delivered as the Gifford Lectures on Natural Theology at Edinburgh University by the Harvard philosopher and psychologist, William James (brother of the novelist Henry James). Of special interest to Evelyn were James's theories that religious beliefs and mysticism were intrinsically important aspects of human existence and his view that a belief in things which cannot be proven empirically is essential to the happiness and fulfilment of the individual. James's theories on humanity's powerful 'need to believe' and the psychology of conversion, were clearly of significance both to Evelyn's own spiritual journey during the late-1920s and to his abiding conviction of the centrality of the Catholic faith to his often discordant and confrontational lifestyle.

Although pleased to see Alastair again, Evelyn was alienated by his self-indulgent paederasty with young Greek boys and, after only a week, headed off on his own to Olympia (where he admired the Hermes of Praxiteles, then housed in a shed), Corfu (where Mrs Beste-Chetwynde owns a villa in *Decline and Fall*) and Rome. He arrived back at Underhill on 22 January 1927 and found there a letter from Kegan Paul, rejecting his manuscript essay on 'Noah, or the Future of Intoxication' which he then destroyed. This disappointment was mitigated by a ten-guinea commission from the *New Decameron* for a short story. His return to Aston Clinton was short-lived since he was promptly sacked, apparently both for drunkenness and for making a pass at the school's

matron (previously at Lancing) as she came out of the bathroom. Back yet
again at Underhill, and with the threat hanging over him of an interview with
the Bishop of Bath and Wells about becoming an Anglican clergyman, Evelyn
wrote in his diary on 21 February: 'the time has arrived to set about being a
man of letters', an assertion prompted as much by despair as ambition.[36]

To tide himself over, Evelyn accepted employment at a state school in
Notting Hill for one term before securing (via Osbert Sitwell) a three-month
probationary post in Fleet Street, working for the *Daily Express*. He was
further lifted by the news that his short story, 'The Tutor's Tale: A House of
Gentle Folks' – a black comedy about an undergraduate, who is sent down
from Oxford and becomes tutor to a lunatic juvenile Marquess – had been
accepted for the *New Decameron* (1927).[37] More significantly, he received a
£50 commission from Duckworth's (with Anthony Powell's assistance) to write
a biography of Rossetti for publication in 1928, the centenary of his birth. He
also noted in his diary for 7 April 1927: 'I have met such a nice girl called Evelyn
Gardner' (known to his friends as She-Evelyn), the daughter of the deceased
Liberal politician, Herbert Gardner, Lord Burghclere (d.1921).[38] She lived with
her mother, Lady Burghclere, the biographer of the first Duke of Ormonde
and second Duke of Buckingham, whose brother, the Fifth Earl of Carnarvon
(d.1923), was still renowned for his sponsorship of Howard Carter's discovery
in 1922 of the tomb of Tutankhamen. Evelyn only lasted from April to May
1927 at the *Daily Express* before being sacked just before beginning work on
Rossetti. He managed first to squeeze in a short holiday in the south of France
with his parents and Alec, who had resigned from Chapman and Hall and was
about to leave for Tahiti and the Far East. On the last night, the two brothers
explored the red-light district of Marseilles, an adventure which formulated
Paul Pennyfeather's farcical excursions there in *Decline and Fall*.

By 1 July 1927 Evelyn was drafting his *Rossetti* biography, under the
working-title, 'The Last Born of Eve'. He based himself during August at
the Abingdon Arms at Beckley which allowed him to travel regularly into
Oxford to work in the Union library. He also wrote a short introduction
to a private printing of *Thirty-Four Decorative Designs* by Francis Crease,
indulgently stating that only Ruskin was fit to preface Crease's exquisite
artistry.[39] Always a diligent researcher, Evelyn made a trip to Barford to
see Mrs Graham who took him to William Morris's house at Kelmscott,
Oxfordshire. There he met one of Morris's daughters, May (1862–1938),
who showed him two childhood crayon portraits of herself and her sister
Jane by Rossetti, sketches of their mother, Jane Morris (with whom Rossetti
had an intense relationship) and studies for the *predella* of 'Dante's Dream'.
He also travelled to London to meet the novelist and critic, Sir Hall Caine
(1853–1931), who as a young man had lived with Rossetti during his final
months. He provided Evelyn with a wealth of eye-witness anecdotes about
Rossetti, his wife Elizabeth Siddal (in whose coffin he had buried a journal
containing unique copies of his poems, later having them dug up again) and
his housekeeper and lover, Fanny Cornforth.

Rossetti demonstrates an impressive facility for transmuting scholarly research and complex relationships into accessible reassessments of the private lives and artistic outputs of the Pre-Raphaelite Brotherhood. Evelyn provides informed and sensitive interpretations not only of Rossetti's paintings, watercolours and drawings but also of his poetry and his developing sense of a mid-Victorian social aesthetic. His narrative is judiciously sympathetic to the often chaotic aspects of these artists' private lives (hardly surprising given his own recent lifestyle) and characteristically laced with comic touches, such as his caricature of the bombastic historical painter Benjamin Haydon as Mr Toad from *The Wind in the Willows*.

Remarkably in such an early work, Evelyn offers an implicit but insistent focus upon teasing out connections between Rossetti's religious and artistic ethos, underlining his growing conviction that artistic creativity had to be nourished by an energy fostered within the individual's inner spirituality. This belief prompts his concluding assessment of Rossetti's conspicuous failings as a man who lacked an *'essential rectitude'* and, therefore, as an artist suffered from a 'sense of ill-organization' and a 'spiritual inadequacy' (226–7). Again, Evelyn was using the writing process as a self-reflective exercise, testing out against the creative lives of the Pre-Raphaelites his own artistic uncertainties and ambitions. 'The biography was in many respects a reflective portrait. Rossetti's was a parallel case and he used him to rationalise his own discontents', Martin Stannard observes, noting that it also 'offers intriguing clues as to the theological direction his mind would take less than three years later'.[40]

Rossetti is first defined not as an artist but rather as a 'mystic without a creed; a Catholic without the discipline or consolation of the Church' (13–14). Similarly, his father Gabriele is categorized as a 'Catholic' who lost his faith through the 'raw free-thinking of his youth' and, instead of embracing orthodoxy, had fashioned a personalized religion from Swedenborg and the 'sacred books of the Brahmins' (14–15). Rossetti's early friendship with the moralistic painter, Ford Madox Brown, is also interpreted by Evelyn as a key element in fostering the interdependence of spirituality and artistic creativity in his work. There was a personal reason for Brown's prominence in Evelyn's biography. It is noted that his renowned painting of emigrants, 'The Last of England', had been inspired by the departure for Australia of his friend, the impecunious sculptor Thomas Woolner, who later married one of 'three handsome sisters called Waugh' (35), Evelyn's great-aunts. But, more significantly, it was Brown who first introduced Rossetti to the intensely spiritual values of the Romantic Nazarene school of painting of the German colony at Rome:

> They taught that the religious faith of the artist and his purity of life were vital factors in his art. Many of their followers adopted a monastic life and monastic clothing. They have much in common with the Dominican movement centring around Mr. Eric Gill today'. (28)

Distinctively Catholic elements increasingly surface in Evelyn's biographical narrative. He explains how Rossetti was heavily influenced by the 'Catholic revival' (29) within the Church of England; and then details how another member of the Brotherhood, James Collinson, converted to Catholicism, thereby preventing his marriage to Rossetti's sister, the poet Christina. He also notes how early in Rossetti's career, the two paintings which made the most impression on the public, 'The Girlhood of the Virgin' and 'Ecce Ancilla Domini', were 'both devotional, full of ecclesiastical symbolism and sadly Romish' (51), with the latter eventually having to be renamed 'The Annunciation' to remove any 'taint of Popery' (63).

Other members of the Brotherhood reminded Evelyn of his own youthful high-Anglican churchliness. William Morris and Edward Burne-Jones met at Oxford while studying for the Church and together 'visited neighbouring churches and took rubbings from the brasses'. When Morris inherited an income of £900 a year, he considered 'devoting his fortune to the foundation of a monastery from which, in celibacy and communal life' his artistic colleagues could engage in a 'Crusade and Holy Warfare against the Age'. Although the Brotherhood soon became 'thoroughly secularised' (79–81) – primarily through complex sexual relationships with their models, mistresses and wives – Evelyn's assessment of Rossetti's greatest artistic achievements insistently returns to his religious and biblical work. He describes with obvious relish 'Fra Pace', a delicate 'watercolour of a monk copying a mouse in an illumination' (82–3); and commends one of his entries for the famous Pre-Raphaelite Exhibition of 1857 – a pen-and-ink sketch of 'Mary Magdalene' (known as 'Mary at the Door of Simon Peter's House') which inspired one of his most famous oil paintings. Along with Rossetti's powerfully stylized portraits of Elizabeth Siddal and Jane Morris, Evelyn also carefully assesses the range of Rossetti's less successful works, such as his triptych of 'The Seed of David' (1855, completed 1864) for Llandaff Cathedral which, although Rossetti himself considered it seriously flawed, still offers intriguing perspectives on his biblical work. Through seeking to make sense of Rossetti's energetic but often chaotic life and failings as an artist, Evelyn seems to have formulated a clear vision of an essential aesthetic bonding of spirituality with creativity which was to become central to his own career as a writer. At this stage, before Evelyn's conversion to Catholicism, art seems to have become a kind of personal theology or even surrogate religion for a writer still unsure of his route in life.

Decline and Fall (1928)

For the remainder of 1927 Evelyn still had to focus upon earning a living. His father obtaining for him occasional paid reviewing for *The Bookman* and he took a part-time teaching post at a school in Golder's Green. More interestingly, he agreed to produce a drawing of God for a symposium, planned by his Oxford friends, Robert Byron and Brian Howard. This image (inspired by St John's revelations but never completed) sought to convey an abstract impression of the Divinity.[41] In a more practical vein and inspired by Ruskin and Morris, he enrolled at the Central School of Arts and Crafts (Holborn Polytechnic), seeking to channel his creative skills into cabinet-making. He enjoyed this learning process, although it still did not seem to offer any definitive route to a lasting or lucrative career. Nor was his lifestyle any more economical since his relationship with She-Evelyn was growing more serious. When in mid-December 1927 she was planning a trip to Canada, he unexpectedly proposed marriage during a dinner at the Ritz. Next morning, she telephoned to accept his offer and his *Rossetti* was published in April 1928 with a dedication to 'She-Evelyn' (removed from later editions). They were married on 27 June 1928 at St Paul's, Portman Square, by the curate (two guineas cheaper than the vicar) before a makeshift altar made from a table covered in black velvet.

In his diary for 3 September 1927 Evelyn noted: 'have begun on a comic novel'.[42] On the next day he browsed through his old Lancing diaries and wrote to Tom Balston, Anthony Powell's senior at Duckworth's, about this project. At Underhill he read aloud to Powell selections from his working manuscript, although he claimed later to have burnt these earliest drafts. By January 1928 he had completed about fifty pages which he read to Dudley Carew. To complete the novel by late-April 1928, he took rooms first at The Bell at Aston Clinton and then the Barley Mow in Colehill, Dorset, close to where Evelyn Gardner was then staying. It was titled, variously, 'Untoward Incidents' (recalling Wellington's off-hand dismissal of the peacetime destruction of the Turkish fleet), 'Facing Facts: a Study in Discouragement', 'Picaresque, or the Making of an Englishman' and finally, echoing Gibbon, *Decline and Fall*. Evelyn proudly dedicated the final version to Harold Acton but Duckworth's (influenced by Lady Burghclere's distaste for her prospective son-in-law since Gerald Duckworth was married to Evelyn Gardner's aunt), began to raise editorial problems. Specifically, they quibbled over the novel's passing references to lavatories, incest, knocking-shops, Welsh sheep-shagging, headmaster debagging and paedophile homosexuality. Evelyn was requested to make some textual emendations. Outraged, he withdrew the novel and took it to his father's firm, Chapman and Hall, where it was accepted for publication (diplomatically while Arthur was away in France on annual leave).[43]

Much has been written about the satiric brilliance of *Decline and Fall* and its subversive mockery of the British establishment. It is unnecessary to re-cover such critical ground here, just as it is readily evident that the novel's inspiration is richly autobiographical. Hertford College is resurrected as Scone College; Arnold House as Llanabba Castle; its rampantly homosexual teacher, Dick Young, recast as the irrepressible Captain Grimes; Mrs Jessie Graham as Lady Circumference; and the hated Cruttwell appears as the castrator of a Harley Street abortionist. Of more significance to this study, is how the novel – albeit through a zanily comic framework – reflects facets of Evelyn's thoughts about institutional religion and the English Church,

alongside his stark depiction of the essential meaningless of a world devoid
of moral and spiritual values. In this sense the timeless farce of the novel
frames the first sustained fictional exposure of Waugh's maturing moral and
religious aesthetic.

The novel opens in an undistinguished Oxford College with the riotous
antics of the Bollinger (Bullingdon) Club reaching a glass-breaking climax.
Mr Sniggs, the Junior Dean, hopes that the chapel will be attacked since
Founder's vintage port is served at high table when high student fines have
been levied. Recalling Evelyn's time at Lancing and his own short-lived
aspirations to become a clergyman, Paul Pennyfeather is from a minor
public school of 'ecclesiastical temper' (11) and is reading for the Church.
He is randomly debagged by the college hearties and unjustly sent down for
indecent behaviour. The chaplain demands the return of his copy of Dean
Stanley's *Eastern Church*, offering the consolation that it was better now
to confirm his unsuitability for the priesthood. Like Evelyn's father, Arthur
Penrhyn Stanley had won the Newdigate prize and in 1839 was elected to
a fellowship at University College after entering Holy Orders. He became
a respected historian and the leading liberal theologian of his generation.
He published in 1844 an acclaimed life of Thomas Arnold, his former
headmaster at Rugby School, and was appointed in 1856 to the Regius
Chair of Ecclesiastical History, leading to his *Lectures on the History of the
Eastern Church*. In *Rossetti* it is recorded how the young William Morris and
Edward Burne-Jones delighted in reading 'aloud to each other' (79) from this
work when students at Oxford. In 1863 Stanley succeeded to the Deanery
at Westminster and married Lady Augusta Bruce, the sister of Lord Elgin,
Governor-General of India. When he died in 1881 he was buried in the royal
chapel of King Henry VII at Westminster, with the Duke of Westminster and
the poet Matthew Arnold (who commemorates him in his poem, 'Westminster
Abbey') among his pallbearers. Dean Stanley's academic life and glittering
church career represented to the young Evelyn an idealized but now hopelessly
unobtainable establishment lifestyle to which he had once himself innocently
aspired. Oxford's High Church Anglicanism became the archetypal precursor
to various other lost Edenic worlds later embedded in his fictions.

The predominantly secular landscapes and farcical incidents of *Decline
and Fall* are, with surprising frequency, heavily tinged with religious and
ecclesiastical references. As he is unjustly sent down from Scone College,
Pennyfeather utters an uncharacteristically forthright curse: 'God damn
and blast them all to hell' (14). He seeks educational employment via the
ecclesiastically named scholastic agents, 'Church and Gargoyle' (16), but,
in contrast to the alluringly monastic colleges of Oxford, Llanabba Castle's
ostentatious medievalism offers a dismally secular take on Waugh's lifelong
preoccupation with antiquity and country houses. Its superficially ancient
grandeur is exposed as merely the manorial fiction of a Lancashire mill-
owner who had converted it into a castle by exploiting the labours of
unemployed mill-workers during the 1860s cotton depression. Along

with Captain Grimes, a drunken pederast and Old Harrovian, Llanabba's teaching staff includes the timid and bewigged Prendergast, who a decade earlier had been a Church of England clergyman, about to take up a living in Worthing and with modest aspirations for a rural deanery. But his church career had floundered when he was suddenly beset by doubts over why God had made the world, a question which his bishop had been unable to answer. Paradoxically, only the utterly amoral Grimes reveals the vestiges of an innate sense of spirituality, when he echoes Browning's famous phrase, 'God's in his Heaven–/All's right with the world' (from *Pippa Passes*), as an explanation for his unwavering optimism, despite constantly being 'in the soup' (34).

Apart from Grimes, who believes that his paradoxical blending of carnal lusts and spirituality places him in harmony with the 'primitive promptings of humanity' (35), the barbarian culture of Llanabba Castle habitually reduces the traditions of Anglican devotions to farce. The headmaster, Dr Fagan (inevitably recalling Dickens' Fagin) begins morning assembly with a random biblical reading of conspicuous violence and a half-hearted recitation of the Lord's Prayer, immediately followed by various banal school announcements. Similarly, Pennyfeather's regular organ lessons in the parish church with a precocious pupil, Beste-Chetwynde, effortlessly slide from the sublime into the ridiculous, as the '*vox humana*' stop (traditionally associated with the voice of a devotional soloist) is utilized for a lively rendition of '*Pop goes the Weasel*'. Even snippets of religious news from Oxford, communicated in a letter from Pennyfeather's boring college friend, Arthur Potts, carry reports of crazy papers on 'Sex Repression and Religious Experience', delivered to the Oxford Student Christian Union.

The school sports-day brings to a climax the novel's habitual blending of overt religiosity and secular farce. The devout greetings of the local Welsh Silver Band, 'the Lord bless and keep you', is subversively undermined by their sub-human, feral appearance: 'low of brow, crafty of eye, and crooked of limb . . . with the loping tread of wolves, peering about them furtively as they came' (64). Another hapless pupil, Tangent, is accidentally shot in the foot with the starter-gun by a drunken Prendergast who had been excitedly discussing the Abyssinian Church's apostolic claims with the local vicar. He, in turn, wisely observes that secular interest in church matters is 'often a prelude to insanity' (72).

The flamboyant mother of Pennyfeather's pupil-organist, Mrs Beste-Chetwynde, then arrives with her latest beau, Sebastian Cholmondley, known as 'Chokey'. His character was based on the black American musical entertainer, Leslie Hutchinson ('Hutch'), who had arrived in England in 1927. Alec's then girlfriend, Zena Nayler, had been one of his lovers. Chokey is innocently moved by the aesthetic beauty of English church architecture. When he sees its cathedrals his 'heart just rose up and sang' (79), and he now wants to visit all the great country houses. Even the concept of God is reduced to the level of a mere fashionable commodity when Mrs Beste-Chetwynde notes that Chokey wants to talk to the vicar since he views religion as 'just divine' (82). The lacing of Chokey's tastes with a recurrent church motif emphasizes in *Decline and Fall* how the barbarians have irrevocably breached the traditional values of English society. They have now appropriated to their own self-indulgent and superficial tastes the time-honoured dignity and authority of great English churches and country houses.

The next chapter, ominously titled 'Post Mortem', opens with Chokey, Prendergast and Philbrick (Dr Fagan's felonious butler) arguing over a minor detail of ecclesiastical architecture since Chokey suspects Prendergast of lacing his comments on rood-screens with implicit colour-prejudice. Growing ever madder, Prendergast rants about infant baptisms and (as a former clergyman) the Church's hostility towards lay advisors, before seeking mental solace through caning twenty-three boys. He then recounts, in quasi-hagiographical style, one of Philbrick's many fantasy life-stories. He tells how Philbrick, masquerading as a Roman Catholic, had once confessed to a priest that he had killed a Portuguese Count in an honour-duel and, as his penance, had been instructed to renounce his wealth and dwell among the 'lowest of the low' (92) (i.e., at Llanabba). When Pennyfeather is unexpectedly invited by Dr Fagan to marry his unprepossessing daughter, Florence (known as Flossie), and to become a partner in Llanabba Castle school, Prendergast sombrely debates the three reasons given in the Prayer Book for marriage while Grimes philosophically ponders the point of human existence. It is as though they have become Pennyfeather's deranged spiritual advisors in this morally inverted world where trickery and fantasy have usurped truth and tradition.

In *Decline and Fall* the dignity of the Sacraments and religious traditions are consistently displaced by comically fraudulent deceptions. The bigamous marriage of Grimes and Flossie is celebrated at Llanabba Parish Church with a moving address from the vicar on 'Home and Conjugal Love' (106). The police then arrive at the school to arrest Philbrick for impersonation and false pretences. One of the detectives recalls a similar case in Somerset when a felon masqueraded as the Bishop of Bath and Wells (the real one had recently interviewed Evelyn about becoming an Anglican priest) and had piously confirmed various children. Horrified by his own wedding, Grimes interrogates Prendergast over whether Divine Retribution is most likely in this or the next world and soon secretly decamps to take up employment as travelling salesman for a brewery. He fakes his own suicide, leaving his clothes on the seashore and a note (parodying Romans 8:5): 'THOSE THAT LIVE BY THE FLESH SHALL PERISH BY THE FLESH' (114) – words which draw to a close Part One of *Decline and Fall*.

The focus shifts at the opening of the second part to Margot Beste-Chetwynde's two great mansions: her William and Mary London house, once regarded as the most beautiful residence between Bond Street and Park Lane; and her country estate in Hampshire, King's Thursday. The latter had been since Queen Mary's reign the seat of the Earls of Pastmaster and, prior to Margot's ownership, untouched by later building fashions. Once regarded as England's finest example of Tudor domestic architecture, complete with its Catholic priest's hole, King's Thursday offered to its privileged visitors a mirror unto a lost golden age of English traditional country life. But, as with many other great houses after World War I, running costs and death duties rendered King's Thursday ruinously expensive. Lord Pastmaster had decided to sell up and decamp to the French Riviera. After an abortive plan to transplant and re-erect it in Cincinnati, it was purchased by Lord Pastmaster's mysterious sister-in-law, Margot, whose ominous view that timbered Tudor architecture was 'bourgeois' and 'awful' (118) rings the death knell for its traditional historic splendour.

Although Evelyn was no personal enthusiast for Tudor domestic architecture, in attacking the mindless iconoclasm of the modernists he creates one of his most memorable comic characters. 'Professor' Otto Friedrich Silenus – whose abstemiously prim tastes ludicrously clash with his namesake, the Bacchic satyr Silenus – is appointed by Margot to rebuild King's Thursday. She commissions something square and clean, even though his only prior experience comprises rejected designs for a chewing-gum factory in Hungary and the *décor* for a cinema film shot without human characters. Silenus epitomizes the dehumanizing barbarism of the modernist architectural aesthetic in his desire to eliminate all human elements from considerations of structural form. He believes that only factories can aspire to be regarded as perfect buildings since they are for machines not humans. His Swiftian disgust at common humanity bursts forth in his demeaning parody of Hamlet's 'What a piece of work is man' speech. He loathes man as a self-destructive and immature 'mischief' who merely prances his 'half-formed, ill-conditioned body' on the evolutionary stage. He admires the instinctive responses of animals and the unwavering productivity of machines but views man as alien both from Nature's '*being*' and the machine's '*doing*', viewing him instead as a 'vile *becoming*!' (121).

The sheer beauty of the pre-Silenus King's Thursday is poignantly visible when Pennyfeather first arrives there, as the 'temperate April sunlight' plays on the budding chestnut trees, revealing green glimpses of 'park-land and the distant radiance of a lake' (123). Springtime brings out the 'dreaming ancestral beauty' of the English countryside as Evelyn's implicit anxiety over society's potentially irredeemable fall into chaos is encapsulated within its timeless landscape. Its ancient chestnut trees stand for something 'enduring and serene in a world that had lost its reason and would so stand when the chaos and confusion were forgotten' (124). Pointedly, Pennyfeather has as his bedtime reading at King's Thursday Sir James Frazer's *The Golden Bough*, in which religion was treated as a cultural and anthropological phenomenon rather than as a theological concept. Its title recalled when Aeneas and the Sibyl give a golden bough to the gatekeeper of Hades to gain admission – an ominous literary echo for Pennyfeather's innocent entry

into the hellishly pagan world presided over by Margot Beste-Chetwynde
and Silenus. In another bedroom, Silenus lies silently like a soulless machine
draining away the vitality of human life and creativity, with his brain silently
ticking over, sucking in 'more and more power' (127). Under his influence
King's Thursday is transmuted into a 'new-born monster to whose birth
ageless and forgotten cultures had been in travail' (137).

In the next chapter of *Decline and Fall*, 'Resurrection', the supposedly
drowned Grimes resurfaces, having been offered a job in one of Margot's
Argentinean brothels. Dr Fagan also reports in a letter to Pennyfeather that
Prendergast has rediscovered his vocation as a churchman through reading
articles by a progressive bishop who argues that Anglican clergymen no
longer need commit themselves absolutely to orthodox religious belief.
Pennyfeather is innocently drawn into Margot's white slave racket when
he is sent to Marseilles to sort out the transit problems of some Rio-bound
girls. This leads to his arrest by Inspector Bruce of Scotland Yard and, in the
third part of the novel, his trial at the Old Bailey with his former Oxford
friend Potts as the chief witness for the prosecution. Margot flees to Corfu
while he begins a sentence of seven years penal servitude at Blackstone Gaol.
The end of the novel neatly echoes its beginning, as his prison turns out to
be merely a darker version of Llanabba Castle school.

Pennyfeather first meets there the fantasist Philbrick, now the reception
bath cleaner, and Prendergast who is the prison chaplain, a position considered
by his bishop as more suited to the modern cleric than conventional parish
work. The benignly self-deceiving governor, Sir Wilfred Lucas-Dockery
(previously Professor of Sociology at a Midland university), had been
personally recommended for the post by the Labour Home Secretary because
of his appendix on penology in a report on 'Conscientious Objectors'. He
hopes to establish a theology class at the prison and is a firm exponent
of psychoanalysis. He regards Prendergast as commendably broad-minded
and believes that virtually all crimes are the result of the felon's 'desire for
aesthetic expression' (167) being repressed, thereby unwisely denying the
existence of genuine evil and mental derangement. In his cell Pennyfeather has
the Bible, a copy of the Rev. Septimus Bead's *Prayers on Various Occasions*
(Edinburgh 1863) and, as one of Lucas-Dockery's edifying innovations, a
typewritten 'Thought for the Day': '*SENSE OF SIN IS SENSE OF WASTE*'
(169). Thus removed from a degenerate and uncaring society, in a Pauline
paradox, Pennyfeather finds his solitary confinement some of the happiest
weeks of his life. His only hardship lies in his daily visit to the prison chapel
daily, where he has to listen to Prendergast, 'blaspheming' (170) against the
beauty of sixteenth-century biblical language.

The tragi-comic 'martyrdom' of Prendergast provides a fitting climax
to this section of the novel in a chapter titled, 'The Death of a Modern
Churchman'. At afternoon exercise Pennyfeather meets a deranged religious
fanatic obsessed with the Second Coming who had formerly been a cabinet-
maker (a profession to which Evelyn once aspired). He recounts how he

had 'gone into captivity' at Blackstone Prison after visions of a flaming angel, extorting him to 'Kill and spare not. The Kingdom is at hand', and advising him that he had been appointed as the 'sword of Israel'. This 'mystical homicide' (177–8) then tells Pennyfeather, whom he now regards as a father-confessor figure, that he has experienced another vision of the prison, drenched in crimson blood as though 'carved of ruby, hard and glittering' (179). Two days later at chapel, where the organ is played by a prisoner who was formerly an assistant cathedral organist, Pennyfeather learns that Prendergast has had his head sawn off by this deranged visionary. His murderer is dispatched to Broadmoor Criminal Lunatic Asylum (now Broadmoor Psychiatric Hospital) and Pennyfeather is transferred into the Hardyesque world of Egdon Heath Penal Settlement.

The novel's final phase sustains its characteristic blending of farce laced with ecclesiastical references and concludes with a comic, life-affirming paganism. On the train journey from Blackstone to Egdon Heath, two warders respectfully discuss the new stained-glass windows in the chapel, representing the angelic release from prison of St Peter and St Paul. Hypo-critically, Margot even presents Egdon Heath prison chapel with a new carved alabaster pulpit. When he visits the chapel, Pennyfeather encounters not a Godly presence but, yet again, the irrepressible Grimes, now imprisoned for bigamy. Predictably, Grimes escapes and the hounds follow him to the edge of Egdon Mire (recalling Grimpen Mire in *The Hound of the Baskervilles*). It seems that he has died horribly in the marshy bog but Pennyfeather finally realizes that Grimes' sheer comic energy grants a secular resurrection and immortality. In a parody of Walter Pater's eulogy of the *Mona Lisa*'s face reflecting all histories, Paul knows that Grimes still lives on as a 'life force' as one of the 'immortals' who would 'rise again somewhere at some time' (199).[44]

The ending of *Decline and Fall* becomes relentlessly cyclical in both structuring and imagery. Pennyfeather is sent to a nursing home, Cliff Place at Worthing, where he is meant to undergo a spurious appendix operation during which he will reputedly die and leave all his estate to Margot. Yet again, it is another version of Llanabba Castle school since it is run by Dr Fagan and his daughter 'Dingy'. He obtains a fraudulent death certificate for Pennyfeather before he is spirited away, in yet another chapter titled 'Resurrection', to Margot's Corfu villa. There he meets up again with Otto Silenus who philosophically compares their lives to those who visit the crazily spinning wheel at Luna Park, categorizing humanity as those who either seek the excitement of spinning perilously somewhere on the wheel or those who merely sit in the viewing gallery watching these zany antics.

Pennyfeather's life spins full-circle as he returns to Scone College to study theology, pretending to be his own distant cousin. He befriends a studious theologian called Stubbs from Hertford, buys a copy of *Mother Wales* by Augustus Fagan and places it alongside Dean Stanley's *Eastern Church* on his bookshelf. He and Stubbs then complete another cyclical movement by visiting Oxford gaol to sing to the prisoners. He glimpses Pilbrick in an open Rolls-Royce and, dipping into the fraudulent ways of the world, casually advises Stubbs that it is the author Arnold Bennet. Pointedly, Bennett's name is misspelt, despite him being a close friend of Arthur Waugh. They then attend (in a passage added by Evelyn after the manuscript was completed) a lecture about a bishop of Bithynia who had denied the Divinity of Christ, the immortality of the soul, the existence of good, the legality of marriage, and the validity of the Sacrament of Extreme Unction – a cleric who could fit readily into the world of Prendergast, Philbrick and Grimes.

In the 'Epilogue', set one year after the final chapter, Pennyfeather recaptures his essential innocence from the novel's 'Prelude'. He offers Stubbs his copy of Von Hügel, (edited by the mother of Evelyn's friends, the Plunket Greenes), and settles down in his chair, just as the 'ascetic Ebionites' (216) turned to Jerusalem to pray. He eventually goes quietly to bed, untroubled by whatever future carnivalesque events await him. As Evelyn noted in a 1937 essay in Graham Greene's *Night and Day*, Pennyfeather's adventures established the essential elements of his comic novels for the rest of the 1930s. They usually centre upon a modest hero who is drawn into bizarre circumstances and company before returning to his humdrum habits – a form which lends itself equally to romance, farce, sentimentality, satire or melodrama and, if well handled, never fails.[45] The key difference between *Decline and Fall* and the later satires is that it is Evelyn's only major fictional work untouched by his conversion to Catholicism. It is also the only one in which he is unambiguously on the side of the anarchic vigour of a world defined by trickery, self-interest and deception.

2

Catholicism and the professional writer: 1928–34

She-Evelyn and *Labels* (1930)

Living with She-Evelyn in a borrowed flat in Islington, Evelyn began in late-summer 1928 a life of John Wesley for Duckworth and was also trying his hand at a detective story. In September *Decline and Fall* was published to considerable acclaim, with Arnold Bennett describing it as 'uncompromising' and a 'brilliantly malicious satire' and Cyril Connolly praising its 'delicious cynicism'. With the novel in a third impression by December 1928, Alec introduced him to his own influential agent, A. D. Peters, who was also a friend of Arthur and acted for J. B. Priestley, Rebecca West, C. S. Forester, C. S. Lewis and V. S. Pritchett. Through Peters's influence, Evelyn was soon being commissioned to write for major newspapers, such as the *Manchester Guardian*, *Evening Standard* and *Observer*. He even planned a detective serial about the murder of a popular writer (mischievously based on Alec) and an article on 'Youngest Generation's View of Religion' but, sadly, neither was completed.[1]

She-Evelyn's health was still delicate after a bout of German measles and so her husband was delighted to receive an offer, negotiated by Peters, of an all-expenses paid Mediterranean cruise in return for publicity for the shipping-line and a series of travel articles, also to be published as a book. They left London on 10 February 1929, with Evelyn even half-hoping that his artistic sketches from their travels might prove successful enough to allow him to abandon writing in favour of painting. They boarded the *Stella Polaris* at Monte Carlo but She-Evelyn's health declined so dramatically that she had to be taken off at Port Said with double pneumonia and pleurisy, resulting in a month's recuperation at the British hospital. By 1 April they were able to move into a comfortable hotel near Cairo, where the drafting of Evelyn's travel essays, titled *Labels*, finally prospered. He was also keen to learn more about the artefacts discovered in Tutankhamen's tomb in 1923 by She-Evelyn's uncle, Lord Carnarvon. They rejoined the *Stella Polaris* at Malta, met up with Osbert, Sacheverell and Georgia Sitwell at Constantinople and passed through Venice, Monte Carlo, Barcelona, Gibraltar and Lisbon before arriving back at London in late-May 1929.[2]

There is little hint in *Labels* (working title, 'Quest of a Moustache') of the personal tribulations which lay behind the voyage. Alec also published a travel book, *Hot Countries* (1930b), at this period and both brothers used the same device of attributing their own experiences to fictional characters. In Alec's volume, one of his own love affairs is so disguised while in *Labels* Evelyn created the characters of Geoffrey, a small young man with a curly moustache, and his ailing wife, Juliet. Evelyn also utilized the drafting of *Labels* as a means of analysing his personal situation, especially his rapidly developing religious sensibilities. He points out in the Author's Note, appended to the first edition that this account had been written eighteen months earlier: 'Since then my views on several subjects, and particularly on Roman Catholicism, have developed and changed in many ways' (4).

At first, however, *Labels* treats Catholic issues merely light-heartedly and in keeping with the spirit of comic farce of *Decline and Fall*. Evelyn recalls how when at Oxford he and the President of the Union went up for a spin in a dilapidated Avro biplane with a former RAF officer. The flight proved so terrifying that two days later his hearty companion was secretly received into the Catholic Church, as were three other passengers, with the pilot wryly described as a 'good ally' (10) of the Jesuits and Campion House. Similarly, when the ailing Juliet is found a bed in a *couchette*, its other occupant turns out to be a youthful priest who flees in terror, preferring to spend the night in the freezing train corridor. As *Labels* heads eastwards towards the Holy Land, Evelyn also gently mocks Hilaire Belloc's ideal of the Catholic pilgrim, clad in shabby clothes, with a big stick and a haversack, cheerfully singing songs in 'dog Latin' (36) as he strolls along.

Comedy continues to cloak a gradual movement in *Labels* towards more serious perspectives on Catholicism. At Naples Evelyn finds various Englishwomen determinedly seeking out the Protestant church and, instead, decides to visit the city's cathedral for Catholic Mass. On the way he manages to thwart the local taxi-driver's attempts to take him to a house of ill-repute but even at Mass one of his fellow-worshippers offers to show him racy Pompeian dancing girls after the Mass ends. When Evelyn primly rejects this offer with 'Protestant aloofness' (46), the man merely crosses himself and resumes his prayers. Nevertheless, he is fascinated by the strongly sensual element in Italian Catholic devotions. When he visits the Neapolitan Church of Sansevero he wonders at the subtle artistic sensuality of Antonio Corradini's statue, 'La Pudicizia', a female figure clad in muslin drapery marvellously carved in marble. He is then led down into the crypt by a charming bare-footed girl to view two dark-brown bodies, partially mummified by the arid atmosphere and stood upright, naked in rococo coffins. The disturbing contrast between the timeless beauty of the 'all but living' (49) marble and these desiccated corpses provides a stark parallel to the renowned two-tier Renaissance 'transi-tombs' in which a dignitary is depicted on the upper level in all their earthly pomp and below as writhing, worm-eaten skeletal remains. Evelyn's travels in Italy in 1929, coupled with his wife's near fatal illness, taught him the central lesson of both Roman stoicism and Christianity (and, ultimately, *Brideshead Revisited*): 'Memento mori' ('Remember you must die').

Evelyn's onward itinerary embraces a brief tour of the Holy Land, taking in Nazareth, Tiberias and Mount Carmel. At Cana in Galilee he is amused by a little girl selling 'original' wine jars from the miracle of the wine and fishes; and he visits other notable holy places, including Mary's Well and the Church of the Annunciation. He is shown the reputedly original cave-like sites of the Annunciation and Joseph's workshop by a friendly Irish monk who is openly sceptical of the Holy Family's supposed cave-dwelling. He also notes the importance of the Carmelites as one of the most important Latin orders in the East since they remain responsive to the tolerant liaison between Christianity and paganism so often found within the Eastern Churches. At Malta, expecting it to be undemonstratively Protestant, he finds the 'most ardently Catholic people in Europe' (109), with priests, nuns, monks and novices everywhere and one third of the island owned by the Church. He is also impressed by the ancient hybrid identity of the Knights of Malta, an 'international aristocracy' (112) combining the careers of monk and mercenary. As the comic mode in *Labels* is steadily displaced by a more reverential tone, he is deeply moved by the baroque frescoes on the barrel vaulting of the roof of the Cathedral of St John, with its high altar by Bernini, a Caravaggio on its walls and reliquaries holding, reputedly, a fragment of the True Cross and a thorn from the Crown of Thorns. By this mid-point in *Labels*, Evelyn's profound fascination with the sensory potency and timelessness of Catholicism is unmistakeable.

As he moves on to visit Athens, Evelyn recalls how on his earlier trip there in 1926 he had spent much of the voyage reading William James's *Varieties of Religious Experience*, which argued for the necessity of religious belief and explored the psychology of religious conversion. Still under James's influence when arriving in Venice, his sense of the fundamentally Catholic identity of Italy is overpowering. He recognizes the disadvantages of Protestant Englishmen attempting to interpret its culture and art, reflecting how 'unlike most men of letters, Ruskin would have led a much more valuable life if he had been a Roman Catholic' (138). At Barcelona he is enthralled by its gothic cathedral and entranced by the sheer 'glory and delight' (150) of Gaudi's architectural creations there. He is deeply moved by his (still incomplete) Church of the Holy Family and devotes several pages of *Labels*, with photographic illustrations, to its description, intending one day to write a monograph about it. By the time the *Stella Polaris* headed westwards back to England, Evelyn was preoccupied by the thought that to remain an insular English Protestant would effectively isolate him from the age-old spiritual and artistic heritage of the Mediterranean regions. Certainly, by the time he reached Seville, his description of its cathedral exudes a tone of genuine reverential commendation for the uplifting spirituality of its high gothic architecture.

Along with his exposure during this Mediterranean trip to the timeless religious cultures of Italy and Spain, the other major factor which seems to have been a catalyst in Evelyn's conversion to Roman Catholicism on 29 September 1930 was his discovery of his wife's infidelity with one of their friends, John Heygate, an Old Etonian BBC news editor and youngest son of a baronet. Certainly, Alec regarded She-Evelyn's behaviour as a key moment in Evelyn's conversion and he recalled an anguished discussion in which he asserted: 'The trouble about the world today is that there's not enough religion in it. There's nothing to stop young people doing whatever they feel like doing at the moment'.[3] After the manuscript of *Labels* was completed and four brief extracts were published in the *Fortnightly Review* – but prior to its book publication in late-August 1930 – Evelyn added a penultimate concluding paragraph, ominously describing the fog-horn of the *Stella Polaris* as they approached Harwich:

> a very dismal sound, premonitory, perhaps, of coming trouble, for Fortune is the least capricious of deities, and arranges things on the just and rigid system that no one shall be very happy for very long. (178)

Vile Bodies (1930)

An equally stark transition in tone is also traceable in the manuscript (Brotherton Library, University of Leeds) of Evelyn's next satiric novel, *Vile Bodies*, exactly at the point in early July 1929 when, at the opening of the seventh chapter, he learnt of She-Evelyn's affair. He had begun *Vile Bodies* (Philippians 3:21: 'the Lord Jesus Christ who shall change our vile body, that it may be fashioned like unto his glorious body', from the Anglican Burial Service) in June 1929, working in the country at Beckley during the week and only meeting up with his wife at weekends. Even before he became aware of She-Evelyn's infidelity, Waugh's farcical plot focused on an anarchically chilling view of 1920s society, blending the slangy and superficial worlds of Ronald Firbank and P. G. Wodehouse with the mental derangements of Lewis Carroll. His characters seem rootless and fixated on the ultimate futility of life, trapped in a vortex of chaos from which there is no hope of escape.

Nothing remains sacrosanct in this fallen world. Even Roman Catholicism is endowed with a double-edged worldliness, through the slippery omniscience of Father Rothschild S. J. As he boards the ferry from France with 'Asiatic resignation' (9), his self-interested watchfulness silently absorbs anything that might potentially be of use to him and he seems miraculously endowed with an ability to detect 'falsehood and exaggeration' (37). No less striking is Mrs Melrose Ape, a profiteering female evangelist, and her motley harem of choric 'angels' (9): Faith, Charity, Fortitude, Chastity, Humility, Prudence, Divine Discontent, Mercy, Justice and Creative Endeavour, the last almost missing the ferry through meeting a chatty gentleman on the train. Pointedly, 'Hope' is missing from her choir, even though it represents the key Christian virtue which Mrs Ape supposedly offers to her audiences.

Soon afterwards, Adam Fenwick-Symes, an unsuccessful young writer, encounters Father Rothschild who precisely recalls their previous meeting five years earlier at a luncheon given by the Catholic Dean of Balliol, 'Sligger' Urquhart, whom Evelyn had delighted in antagonizing. But, as the crossing becomes rougher, so these superficial social interactions dissolve into comic chaos. Passengers are overcome with seasickness which they hope to counter with champagne while Mrs Ape's angels give a wildly discordant rendition of her uplifting spiritual, *There ain't no flies on the Lamb of God* (16). Only the Jesuit priest can take temporary spiritual refuge from these physical discomforts in his familiar Catholic devotions, contemplating the 'sufferings of the saints' and the 'mutability of human nature' (15), while reciting penitential psalms. The visual separation on the page of these religious thoughts into a segregated five-line subsection of the chapter serves to confirm how alien traditional religious practices have become within this godless novel, masquerading under such a biblically inspired title.

Like Paul Pennyfeather, Adam is habitually vulnerable to the vicissitudes of cruel fate. He is rendered penniless by a suspicious Customs officer at Dover who confiscates and burns the typescript of his autobiography as 'downright dirt' (25), which he had hoped would be a best-seller. Much of the plot then revolves around whether he will be financially secure enough to marry his beloved (but fickle) Nina Blount, an on-off relationship which seems to echo elements of Evelyn's own marriage. Against a shifting backdrop of farcical incidents – the Honourable Agatha Runcible is mistaken for a jewel smuggler and strip-searched at Customs while some post-party revellers find themselves having breakfast with a bewildered Prime Minister at 10 Downing Street – the pathos of Adam's essentially innocent love for Nina steadily escalates. He dutifully visits her half-mad father, Colonel Blount, at his dilapidated residence, Doubting Hall (echoing Bunyan's Doubting Castle, the home of Giant Despair), near Aylesbury. The estate encapsulates the now crumbling traditional world of English county society. Its driveway is 'bordered by dripping trees and a dilapidated stone wall . . . [a] lofty Palladian façade stretched before them and in front of it an equestrian statue pointed a baton imperiously down the main drive'. (68)

In its latter half *Vile Bodies* becomes a much darker novel than *Decline and Fall*. In particular, the treatment of both sexual relations and religious issues shifts from the merely superficial or ludicrous into more disturbing, darker contexts. Nina finds her first sexual encounter with Adam painfully distasteful and Margot Metroland cynically recruits Mrs Ape's Chastity for one of her South American brothels, noting that such a pretty girl shouldn't be wasting time 'singing hymns' (95). The failed gossip columnist, the Earl of Balcairn ('Mr Chatterbox' of the *Daily Excess*), files by telephone from his flat a fictitious account of Margot's party for Mrs Ape at her Mayfair mansion, describing its *'wild religious enthusiasm . . . reminiscent of a negro camp-meeting in Southern America'* (104–5). He claims, in an exposé which fulfils his dream of becoming a front-page journalist, that various social luminaries publicly confessed an outrageous range of past sins, with jewels, heirlooms and blank cheques steadily piling up on the parquet flooring as guilt offerings. He then finishes his cocktail and gasses himself in his squalid kitchen oven. Mrs Ape confirms Balcairn's fictions before fleeing the country with her angels, intent upon spicing up the 'religious life of Oberammergau' (109).

Adam takes over as 'Mr Chatterbox' in Chapter 7 (when Evelyn learnt of his wife's infidelity) and is soon filing equally inventive fantasies about fictitious people, such as his account of a Lord who claims to have composed the Ten Commandments and personally delivered them to Moses on Sinai. But then a serious discussion on marriage between Adam and Nina abruptly intrudes into the narrative, in which he plaintively asserts that a 'marriage ought to *go on* – for quite a long time' (123). This interchange is followed by a passage (added after the completion of the manuscript) of near-Swiftean disgust at the endless round of savagely frivolous parties attended by the Bright Young Things of the 1920s. They are dismissed as a pathetic troupe of Dionysiac revellers and soulless 'vile bodies', moving endlessly around dismal fancy-dress parties and other pointless entertainments. Father Rothschild concludes the novel's jarring shift into high seriousness by offering a stern sermon on the moral folly of the 1920s young generation:

> They had a chance after the war that no generation has ever had. There was a whole civilization to be saved and remade – and all they seem to do is to play the fool . . . I don't think people ever *want* to lose their faith either in religion or anything else. I know very few young people, but it seems to me that they are all possessed with an almost fatal hunger for permanence. (131–2)

Eventually, Nina dumps Adam and marries a rich polo-playing friend, Eddy 'Ginger' Littlejohn (also first introduced in the personally angst seventh chapter). In a nightmarish dream of disillusionment, the final chapter (ironically called 'Happy Ending') finds Adam as a soldier lost from his platoon on a prophetically described World War II battlefield. There he meets a character, encountered earlier in the novel as a drunken Major who promised to put Adam's gambling winnings on a horse. He is now a monocled General who has lost his entire division and staff car. They eventually relocate his Daimler stuck in the mud with Chastity in its rear seat, fast asleep and wearing a French army grey-coat. This 'woebegone fragment of womanhood' (222) has been trafficked by Margot Metroland from Buenos Aires and then back to Europe to work as camp-following prostitute. As they sit together drinking looted champagne and sheltering from the threatening sounds of approaching battle, *Vile Bodies* concludes on a note of absolute futility and nihilism.

What next? Roman Catholicism

Evelyn's work on *Vile Bodies* had been abruptly halted in early July 1929 by his tribulations with She-Evelyn but he sporadically resumed writing and managed to complete it by October. In early September he filed for divorce, thereby initiating seven years of a rootless and wandering existence. Ironically, he was then commissioned by the *Daily Mail* to write an article, 'Let the Marriage Ceremony Mean Something', and was wryly amused that its publication would coincide with his divorce proceedings becoming public knowledge. It appeared on 8 October, arguing that the social efficacy of marriage could only be achieved if it was regarded as a permanent state. Despondently, however, he admitted that most marriages could only aspire to an illusion of permanence. His own decree nisi came through on 17 January 1930 but She-Evelyn's infidelity still rankled and in an article, 'Tell the Truth About Marriage', he lamented that overblown female expectations of marital sexual relations were also often responsible for couples heading for the divorce courts.[4]

The early 1930s marked a major transition in the respective literary reputations of the Waughs. Arthur retired as managing director of Chapman and Hall (but remained as chairman of the Board of Directors) and he completed an informative history of the company, *A Hundred Years of Publishing* (1930). He was also hard at work at his nostalgic reminiscences, *One Man's Road* (1931). But he now viewed his own writings as distinctly secondary to the pride which he took in his sons' literary achievements. Alec was still the more publicly renowned of the brothers. Between 1924 and 1930 he had published several novels, including *Card Castle* (1924), *Kept: A Story of Post-war London* (1925), *Love in These Days* (1926a), *Nor Many Waters* (1928a), *Three Score and Ten* (1929) and *"Sir!" She Said* (1930a); a collection of essays, *On Doing What One Likes* (1926b); and a travel-book, *The Last Chukka: Stories of East and West* (1928b). In June 1925 Alec had undertaken a nine-month tour around the world, travelling first by steamer from Marseilles, via the Suez Canal, Ceylon, Malaya and Singapore, to Tahiti (returning there again in 1926), which provided the foundations for his lifelong interest in travel writing and exotic settings for his novels. He briefly went to Africa in February 1930, the year in which his immensely successful *The Coloured Countries* (1930b; US title, *Hot Countries*) also appeared, based on his travels to Tahiti. It was chosen as a book of the month for May 1930 by the American Literary Guild, guaranteeing lucrative sales.

To Arthur's delight, Evelyn's career was also blossoming. Following largely celebratory reviews, *Vile Bodies* was reprinted eleven times during 1930 and publishers and newspapers competed to get a share of his new outputs. There were rumours that he was planning a biography of Jonathan Swift and an American agent breathlessly reported that the prestigious American publisher, Little, Brown, were 'crazy to get Waugh' and would 'crash through a swell offer for the Swift biography'. London newspapers and magazines also vied for his contributions and he signed lucrative contracts for feature articles for the *Daily Express* and *Daily Mail* and a regular book-review column for the *Graphic*. Even *Harper's Bazaar*, having previously rejected serialization rights for *Vile Bodies*, requested a short story.[5]

The growing self-confidence which came with this literary success fed directly into Evelyn's renewed determination, readily assisted by some of his closest friends, to reform his spiritual and personal life. He delighted in the company of the Pakenhams, especially Frank, later Lord Longford, who converted to Catholicism in 1940. Their warm family life and huge moated gothic mansion, Pakenham Hall, in Westmeath, Ireland, greatly impressed him. He also developed a passing but unreciprocated passion for another devout Roman Catholic, Teresa 'Baby' Jungman. But the ever-supportive Plunket Greene brothers were most influential, including their mother Gwen (who had been converted in 1926 by Bede Jarrett) and sister Olivia (also a recent convert). Olivia recommended Father Martin D'Arcy, S. J., later master of Oxford's Campion Hall, who was as urbane as the fictional Father Rothschild and Evelyn's kindred spirit in 'looking back with nostalgia to a romantic and dignified past as represented by the great houses and ancient lineage of the old Catholic nobility'.[6] In late-August 1930 Evelyn wrote to D'Arcy with a clear sense of spiritual conviction, affirming his belief that only Roman Catholicism represented the true nature of Christianity and that it was, and always had been, essential, to Western-European culture.[7] On 29 September 1930 he was received into the Catholic Church by Fr D'Arcy at the Immaculate Conception, Farm Street with his Oxford friend, Tom Driberg, also invited. Although a High Anglican, Driberg was then 'Dragoman' of the *Daily Express*'s gossip column and, therefore, a convenient means of publicly announcing Evelyn's conversion.

In a newspaper article, 'Converted to Rome: Why it Has Happened to Me', Evelyn promoted his view that mere sectarian tensions between Catholicism and Protestantism were no longer as significant as the global clash between Christianity and chaos. Without the spiritual influence of the Church – and, specifically, Catholicism in its most coherent and universal identity – civilization was under threat since it lacked in itself the potency to survive. It now seemed to him impossible to embrace civilization without also acknowledging the supernatural foundations upon which it must surely rest and he lamented:

> the active negation of all that western culture has stood for. Civilization
> . . . has not in itself the power of survival. It came into being through

Christianity, and without it has no significance or power to command allegiance. The loss of faith in Christianity and the consequent lack of confidence in moral and social standards have become embodied in the ideal of a materialistic, mechanized state, already existent in Russia and rapidly spreading south and west. It is no longer possible . . . to accept the benefits of civilization and at the same time deny the supernatural basis upon which it rests . . .

That is the first discovery, that Christianity is essential to civilization and that it is in greater need of combative strength than it has been for centuries.

The second discovery is that Christianity exists in its most complete and vital form in the Roman Catholic Church.[8]

Evelyn's Catholic conversion completed his sense of personal and aesthetic identity and, henceforth, he adopted in his fictions the historical concept of Christendom as a central spiritual anchor for society. This perspective enabled his satirical 'Catholic' novels to be imbued with negative moral implication, thereby condemning those superficially glittering worlds in which the essential values of the Church and family life were ignored. His faith remained largely unchanged for the rest of his life and on Easter Sunday 1964, two years before his death, he wrote in his diary that when he joined the Catholic Church he was attracted not by its sense of the ceremonial: 'but by the spectacle of the priest as craftsman. He had an important job to do which none but he was qualified for'. For Evelyn, this conjunction of the priest and the artist-craftsman endowed his writings with an innate sense of moral worth since he believed that the priest and the writer were dedicated to comparable and commensurate tasks. He also affirmed from 1930s onwards his unquestioned faith and, as he explained in an April 1962 interview with Julian Jebb (Hilaire Belloc's grandson), he still reverenced the Catholic Church 'because it is true, not because it is established or an institution'.[9]

Escape abroad: Abyssinia

While staying at Pakenham Hall, Westmeath, Evelyn heard about the forthcoming coronation of Ras Tafari, as Emperor Haile Selassie ('The Power of the Trinity') in Addis Ababa, Abyssinia. Keen to escape from England, he decided to travel there and, with the help of Douglas Woodruff and Tom Driberg, gained accreditation as a correspondent for *The Times* (and also surreptitiously with the *Graphic* and *Daily Express*), to cover his expenses for the coronation. He left Marseilles in mid-October and arrived ten days later at Djibouti, French Somaliland, from where he travelled by train to Addis Ababa along with other invited dignitaries, including the Duke of Gloucester. His experiences and observations until his departure

from Cape Town on 17 February and his arrival at Southampton on 10
March 1931 were described in his travelogue, *Remote People* (1932; US
title, *They Were Still Dancing*) which blends his novelist's eye for the bizarre
and exotic with a journalist's concern for geographical and social accuracy.
Stylistically, *Remote People* and its spin-off novel *Black Mischief* (1932),
both interrogating white colonial imperialism, remain key transitional works
between the farcical semi-surrealism of *Decline and Fall* and *Vile Bodies* and
the more sombrely realistic contexts of *A Handful of Dust*, *Brideshead* and
the *Sword of Honour* trilogy.

At Westmeath, his amused interest was stimulated by the claims of
his diplomatic-service friend, Alastair Graham, that Pontius Pilate had
been canonized by the Abyssinian Church and their bishops' heads were
consecrated with spit. An ancient encyclopaedia in the Pakenham's library
suggested a society not dissimilar to that of *Vile Bodies* since, although
nominally Christian, drunkenness and polygamy were reputedly rife among
the Abyssinians and even in their monasteries. Arriving at Addis Ababa on
26 October, Evelyn was captivated by its 'crazy enchantment' and 'peculiar
flavour of galvanized and translated reality' (200), delineating its alien and
often incomprehensible culture as a kind of preposterous *Alice in Wonderland*
environment. Nevertheless, he took his journalist's accreditation seriously
and strove in his articles and cables to provide an informed impression of
Abyssinian society.[10]

His growing fascination with Ethiopian religious culture is often apparent
in *Remote People*. *Decline and Fall* had made passing mention (derived
from Dean Stanley's *Eastern Church*) of the debatable 'Apostolic Claims
of the Church of Abyssinia' (72); and *Remote People* defines its religious
faith as one of the two great strengths of Abyssinia, the other being the
warlike bravery of its hills-men. On an aesthetic level, Evelyn marvels at
the hereditary skills of ecclesiastical fresco painting in Abyssinian churches
in which designs are copied and recopied down through the generations.
He encounters at the coronation (2 November) an American Byzantine
specialist and has great fun with his obvious confusion over Coptic rituals
as he struggles even to identify when the gospel, epistle and the Mass itself
are beginning. Together they visit the Coptic monastery at Debra Lebanos,
a renowned centre of Abyssinian spiritual life, but are disappointed to
discover little of interest in its supposedly richly endowed library where a
previously unknown version of Ecclesiastes had recently been discovered.
Later they view a shawl wrapped around a reputed fragment of the True
Cross acquired from Alexandria. They also attend a two-hour Mass with
an utterly unintelligible liturgy, at which Communion is given to babies but
no-one else.

Despite such strangeness, Evelyn gains through his confusing experiences
at this monastery a spark of spiritual insight into his own newly embraced
religious beliefs and the central function of Christian devotional ceremonies.
He had previously wondered why Western Christianity 'alone of all the

religions of the world, exposes its mysteries to every observer' but at Debra Lebanos he realizes that its grand basilica and open altar may be regarded as an inspiring achievement, a 'triumph of light over darkness'. Drawing upon Dean Stanley's analysis of Abyssinian devotions, theology is viewed as a 'science of simplification' (248) through which abstract and intangible ideas are rendered intelligible, culminating in the 'great open altars of Catholic Europe, where Mass is said in a flood of light, high in the sight of all' (249).

At the Arab city-state of Harar, to the east of Addis Ababa, Evelyn focuses on the missionary zeal of the Catholic Church in Abyssinia. He visits a leper settlement run by an old French priest and Harar's cathedral where he meets its renowned bishop, Monsignor Jerome, who resembles an 'El Greco saint' (260). He had worked as a missionary in the country for almost fifty years and could recall the decadent Catholic French poet, Arthur Rimbaud, at Harar during the 1880s. Rimbaud, a hero figure for Evelyn's Oxford generation, had traded as a gunrunner and became a close friend of the town's governor, Ras Makonnen, the father of Emperor Haile Selassie. Evelyn then moves on to Zanzibar where he notes how British imperialism had always possessed primarily an 'evangelical' rather than a 'military or commercial' (308) impetus. Unfortunately, the spirit of colonial imperialism, even when supported by Anglican or Protestant zeal, is seen by Evelyn as one which has almost destroyed traditional native values, replacing it only with a 'mean and dirty culture' rather than a 'Christian civilisation' (310).

This debate over the efficacy of Christian missions in Africa culminates during his time at Kampala, Uganda, where he seeks to provide a balanced assessment of the opposing arguments. Some people, he appreciates, regard missionaries as merely the 'vanguard of commercial penetration' (341), while others deplore the displacement of native carvings with plaster statues of the Sacred Heart. Even loyal churchmen, he notes, can harbour resentments towards the vast sums of money raised each year for dubiously defined overseas aid in 'remote corners of the globe'. But his tone then shifts into one of confident conviction, insisting that every soul saved through Baptism, whether in a 'black or white body' (342), confirms the enduring efficacy of missionary work. These evangelical views also fed into the religious zeal of his biography of Edmund Campion, the culminating text of his 1930s literary output in terms of its triumphant assertion of the centrality of religious faith and missionary work to the human condition.

Characteristically, a key link between twentieth-century Catholic missions to Africa and Jesuit missions to Elizabethan England lies within Evelyn's blending of literary comedy and fantasy. In a dreamlike short story, 'Out of Depth' (1933), a middle-aged lapsed-Catholic American, named Rip Van Winkle after Washington Irving's eponymous hero, is dining at Margot Metroland's London house. There he meets a magician, Mr Jagger (Dr Kakophilos in later versions), who transports him five hundred years into the future where he finds himself stranded in the desolate wreckage of what was once London. The plot was inspired by John Gray's novel *Park* (1932), itself influenced by Evelyn's reports of Haile Selassie's coronation, in which black Catholics have become the dominant civilizing force. Rip eventually locates a notice-board with the single word 'Mission' painted onto it and a black Dominican friar greets him with the concluding words of the Roman Rite of the Catholic Mass: '*Ite, missa est*'. Suddenly waking back in 1933, Rip guiltily confesses to a priest that he has experimented in black arts and returns to the Faith. Underlining the temporary nature of civilization, Martin Stannard explains the story's religious symbolism as 'Waugh's first overtly apologetic work of fiction' – a mode prefiguring that of *Brideshead* twelve years later:

> In one sense it is a Christmas story reaffirming the continuity and lucidity of Catholic teaching. Rip's return to the Church from the apathetic sleep of agnosticism signals his unconscious recognition of the link between civilisation and faith.[11]

Black Mischief

After returning home in March 1931, Evelyn attended a Holy Week retreat at Stonyhurst, the Jesuit school in Lancashire. He then went with his parents and Alec to the south of France in June before completing the manuscript of *Remote People* at a monastery near Grasse. It was published by Duckworth on 3 November to only moderate reviews. But he remained determined to continue to profit from his travels and began a new novel, under the working-title 'Accession', which later became *Black Mischief*. Its composition coincided with his growing friendship with the three Lygon sisters, Sibell, Mary and Dorothy, whose brothers, William (Viscount Emley) and Hugh, he had known at Oxford. Their bisexual father, the Earl of Beauchamp, was married to a sister of the thuggish Bendor, Duke of Westminster, who – recalling Oscar Wilde's persecution in the 1890s by the Marquess of Queensbury – had ensured the flight abroad of his brother-in-law (or, as he called him, 'bugger-in-law') when he learnt of his homosexual encounters with servants. Socializing with the Lygons who affectionately endowed him with the masonic nickname 'Boaz', Evelyn was captivated by their huge moated red-brick manor house, Madresfield Court, Worcestershire, and it exerted a strong influence over the formulation of his fictional preoccupation with the great houses of the English aristocracy. Parts of *Black Mischief* were written there (with the sisters posing for his line drawings) and elements of the Lygon's family life and Madresfield – including its mid-1860s arts and crafts chapel, its patriarch exiled to Italy and its vibrant family tinged with melancholia – provided direct inspiration a decade later for *Brideshead*.[12]

Black Mischief (completed, June 1932) is set within the imaginary African island of Azania (off the Somali coast) and metropolitan London, two contrasting but equally decadent centres for Evelyn's continuing preoccupation with the triumph of self-interested chaos over social order. Azania's young and idealistic ruler, Seth (based on Ras Tafari, Emperor Haile Selassie), appoints his Oxford acquaintance, an amoral and rakish racketeer called Basil Seal (based on Evelyn's Oxford friend, Peter Rodd, later the feckless husband of Nancy Mitford), to head his recently established Ministry for Modernization in an attempt to impose western civilization on his backward country. Predictably, high farce ensues when his starving army gratefully eat their newly issued boots. A birth-control advert also backfires, with a weary-looking woman with multiple children being viewed by male Azanians as the ideal hard-working wife while a relaxing mother with a single child is regarded as idly unproductive.

Basil's modernization programme in Azania merely cloaks its endemic corruption, brutality and squalor; and London's urbane but frivolously pointless social life seems no less reprehensible in its moral vacuity. Basil repeatedly describes London as an urban hell and his charmingly malignant influence in Azania only serves to foster its own nightmarish qualities, where even murder and cannibalism seem comically unremarkable. Various echoes of earlier writings occur, when the ever-avaricious Margot, Lady Metroland, briefly drifts into view and a parasitic Toby Cruttwell fills Basil's empty place at his mother's dinner-party. The admirable Mr Bergebedgian, the proprietor of the Lion d'Or hotel in *Remote People* becomes the wily Armenian fixer, Krikor Youkoumian. The monastery of Debra Lebanos is recast as the that of St Mark the Evangelist with its ludicrous array of holy relics, including the stone fired by David to kill Goliath, Adam's rib from which Eve had been fashioned and a wooden cross which had mysteriously fallen from the heavens during a Good Friday luncheon. *Black Mischief* was published on 1 October 1932 (its first chapter had appeared in the June issue of *Life and Letters*) and, like *Remote People*, received only mixed reviews. There was a growing sense among critics that, although Evelyn's touch as a comic stylist was unwavering, his moral perspectives on both Western-European and African society seemed increasingly despondent and destructive. He now offered to his readers only a world without hope as it drank and danced its way towards irreversible anarchy and chaos.

The only glimmer of spiritual solace lies in the novel's sporadic focus on the civilizing work of Christian missionaries. Seth's grandfather, Emperor Amurath the Great, had been educated by Nestorian monks of the Eastern Church and idealistically began the modernization of his country. He had introduced railways (although many of his subjects were killed by these strange mechanical monsters), abolished slavery and deemed Christianity as the official religion of his empire while retaining freedom of conscience for Mohammedans and pagans. He keenly encouraged western missionaries, resulting in Anglican, Catholic and Nestorian cathedrals in Debra Dowa, as well as Quaker, Moravian, American-Baptist, Mormon and Swedish-Lutheran missions. Conveniently, such influences attracted lavish funds from Christian countries abroad and enhanced his international reputation as a progressive and enlightened ruler. But a note of discord creeps into this idealized landscape when Amurath brutally orders the hanging in front of the Anglican Cathedral of two alleged murderers of a foreign businessman, along with some witnesses who had not provided satisfactory evidence for the prosecution. A punitive half-European force then arrives to teach Amurath the error of his primitive tribal ways. But it is readily repulsed and five of its captured European officers are summarily hanged on the battlefield. In honour of this dubious triumph, Amurath offers to the White Fathers a 'silver altar to Our Lady of Victories' (13). Beneath the veneer of civilizing Christianity in Azania still lies, it seems, the murderously brutal instincts of a godless dictatorship presiding over his jungle empire.

Amurath's supposedly benign religious toleration leads not to civic harmony but to an escalating potential for conflict and social discord. In the evening the city reverberates with prayers led by the *muezzin* in the mosque proclaiming Allah while the Angelus and '*Ecce ancilla Domini*' echo from the mission church. But later, the night becomes 'alive with beasts and devils and the spirits of dead enemies' (26) as the country's dark and ancient paganism effortlessly overwhelms the hopeful spiritual light of modern faiths. Even the Christian missionaries seem far from perfect as the reader encounters a 'vast Canadian priest' (38) in a white habit casually assaulting a native sergeant-major of the Imperial Guard after Mass whom he had found scoffing his breakfast. Later, Basil has a desultory conversation with an old colonial type over tensions between the 'Arabs and the christianized Sakuyu' (68). Their interchange yet again underlines the essential duality of Azania's religious identity, combining Arab and Christian, Eastern and Western Churches, and native paganism and missionary zeal.

The novel concludes with Seth abdicating and being replaced by Amurath's long-lost son Achon, Evelyn then recycles his experiences described *Remote People* during the coronation of Haile Selassie but within a heightened comic framework. The Nestorian Cathedral, its walls decorated with holy frescoes and images of Amurath the Great, heaves with frenetic activity as the coronation finally arrives. Three choirs accompany an endless litany of 'psalms, prophecies, lections and many minor but prolix rites of purification' (202). Leviticus is recited from ancient manuscript rolls and deacons beat out hypnotic rhythms on a silver gong and hand-drums. But these grandiose devotions shift disturbingly into farce when, just as the aged Achon is crowned and pledges to protect the faith of his people, he drops dead. Seth, it is discovered, has also been murdered and Basil brings his body back to Moshu for public cremation. At a great native feast held to mark Seth's passing, tribal paganism enjoys an unchallenged resurgence in Azania. As he passes out through intoxication, Basil realizes that he has cannibalistically shared the remains of his casual mistress, Prudence, the daughter of the head of the British legation. Her body had been found by the natives after the plane, supposedly taking her back to civilization in London, had crash-landed in the forest.

The final chapter of *Black Mischief* neatly balances the anarchic worlds of London and Azania. Basil returns to England, having 'had enough of barbarism for a bit'. He visits friends who tell him about the General Election and the Gold Standard crisis, prompting even the most adept of survivors, Margot, Lady Metroland, to flee to America. His friends are weary of tales of Basil's outlandish adventures in far-flung climes and instead recommend that he should just write a book about them since, like some of Evelyn's reviewers, they are well and truly tired of 'travel experiences' (232). Back in Africa Azania is declared a joint Anglo-French protectorate and yet another frenetic bout of colonial improvements begins, with new civic buildings and roads hastily built and a nationwide inoculation campaign underway. Traditional prayers still echo from both the mosque and the mission churches but two passing Arab gentlemen sadly conclude: 'Things were better in the time of Seth. It is no longer a gentleman's country' (233). The novel closes with two British policemen striding through the native quarter as the vapid sounds of Gilbert and Sullivan's, 'Three little maids from school are we', echo from a gramophone in the Portuguese Fort at Matodi. It is implied with unsentimental pessimism that another (and no doubt doomed) colonialist attempt to bring civilization and progress to Azania is now well underway.

Escape abroad again: British Guyana

During 1932 Evelyn was drawn into the social circle of Lady Diana Cooper, daughter of the Duke of Rutland and wife of the Tory parliamentarian, Duff Cooper. Lady Diana (the model for Mrs Stitch in *Scoop*) enjoyed amateur dramatics and earlier that year had appeared at the Lyric Theatre in Max Rheinhardt's production of *The Miracle*, a bizarre mimed imitation of a medieval morality drama. She had to stand motionless as the Madonna, while a fallen nun was pursued around the stage by an evil seducer. Evelyn saw the play in April and thought it an impious travesty but, captivated by Lady Diana's company on a trip to Venice in August, he agreed to accompany its northern tour during the autumn. His experiences read like a benign version of Paul Pennyfeather's exploits, including reading *The Wind in the Willows* aloud to Diana as she rested between shows, travelling with her to view Chatsworth, Hardwick, Belton and Belvoir (her family home) and accompanying her aged mother, the Duchess of Rutland, on the Scottish leg of the itinerary. Evelyn soon became infatuated with Diana's personal charms and earnestly sought to convert her to Catholicism.[13] But Evelyn's own ardent faith now ensured that this attractive married woman could never be more than a platonic friend and his involvements in the Coopers' frenetic social life only aggravated his personal sense of social isolation.

Alec's advantageous second marriage in October 1932 to an Australian, Joan Churnside – she inherited £250,000 in 1934 and purchased a large Queen Anne mansion, Edrington, on the Hampshire-Berkshire border – and his unrelenting literary productivity which culminated in the success of *Hot Countries* (1930b), further accentuated Evelyn's depressive state. Following his brother's lead, he planned another escapist trip abroad, this time to British Guiana (Guyana) and Brazil. He explained in the Preface to the resulting travelogue, *Ninety-Two Days*, how he and Alec had light-heartedly agreed to carve up the world between them, with Evelyn taking Africa and parts of Asia in return for Alec's exclusive rights over the Polynesia, North America, and the West Indies.

After early morning Mass at St James', Spanish Place, Evelyn left Tilbury on 2 December 1932 on board the SS *Ingoma*, an old, bug-infested cargo ship. His depressed spirits did not lighten until his ship arrived in the Caribbean, stopping briefly just before Christmas at Antigua with its cathedral recently rebuilt after an earthquake (383); Barbados, rendered picturesque by its 'castellated churches' (384); and Trinidad where he coincidentally stayed at a hotel previously criticized by his brother. There is a melancholy (even penitential) aspect to the published account of his experiences and its dour title sounds like a ninety-two-day prison sentence. His first sight on 23 December of the harbour at British Guiana, reeking of sugar, offered a dismal perspective: 'hope dried up in one at the sight of it' (387). Georgetown, the drab capital of British Guiana with an unfinished concrete cathedral, was also far from prepossessing, although its governor and his wife proved generously hospitable.

As with Evelyn's earlier travel writings, the reassuring presence of missionaries offers a sense of navigable possibilities within this alien and hostile environment. At Georgetown his spirits momentarily rise as he recalls his letter of introduction to a Jesuit missionary near the Takutu River. But they sink again when he travels there with an asthmatic, half-creole district commissioner, Mr Bain. He recounts endlessly fanciful stories, including one about a horse which could swim under water and a talking parrot who scouted routes for an Indian guide. He also turns out to be obsessed with theology and metaphysics, insistently offering his judgement on a wide range of moral issues, including marriage and God's love. They briefly rest at the ranch of an old and very pious black man with white hair called Mr Christie whose eccentricities and religious mania surpass even those of Mr Bain. He solemnly advises Evelyn that he was expected since he had seen him approaching in a vision. Mr Christie assures his visitors that he regularly communes with the heavenly choirs and is privileged to be able to view the Elect. Asked if he believes in the Trinity, he replies that the 'mistake the Catholics make is to call it as mystery. It is all quite simple to me.' (435). As his exhausted guest gradually falls asleep, he continues to drone on endlessly about his visions and 'mystic numbers' (436). He later inspired the maniac in 'The Man

Who Liked Dickens' (completed at Boa Vista in February 1933), and Mr Todd in *A Handful of Dust*.

With evident relief, Evelyn's party pressed on up-country to the Jesuit mission of St Ignatius where he met a self-effacing missionary, Father Mather, hard at work at his carpentry. He offers an inspiring example of a humble artisan-priest, a 'skilled and conscientious craftsman' who makes his own furnishings and 'loves and studies all natural things' (444). The priest-carpenter-writer trinity was still intensely meaningful to Evelyn since his identity as an artist-manqué was finally being replaced by that of the writer. At the beginning of *Ninety-Two Days*, he compares the writer who cannot leave any 'experience in the amorphous, haphazard condition in which life presents it' to a carpenter who planes rough timber into useful objects. A writer should put experience into 'communicable form' (378), just as missionary priests like Father Mater bring to life the essential mysteries of Faith, the Mass and the Sacraments for their flocks.[14]

Father Mather's mission is only externally identifiable from an ordinary ranch by its river-bank Calvary; and the close proximity of its small corrugated iron church, basic school-house and workshop confirms the spiritual and practical efficacy of the missionary's role as an artisan-priest. Each day began systematically with Mass at seven, followed by coffee and work in Father Mather's workshop, concluding with washing in the river at sundown. During the day Evelyn rested and read Robert Cunninghame Grahame's study of the heroism of Jesuit missionaries in Paraguay, *A Vanished Arcadia* (1901). His simple statement that Father Mather was 'one of the happiest men I met in the country' (446) and that these were 'peaceful and delightful days' (447) delicately conveys one of the most reinvigorating of all the elusive Edens described in Evelyn's writings.

The next stage of the journey took Evelyn to the grim town of Boa Vista in Brazil, where he had a letter of introduction from Father Mather to an emaciated Swiss-German Father Alcuin at its Benedictine priory. The starkness of this unwelcome geographical shift from an Eden-like pastoral to a fallen urban environment is encapsulated by an implicit comparison between the holistic vigour of Father Mather and the silent, feverish melancholia of the non-English speaking Father Alcuin. At Boa Vista the natives are violent and 'naturally homicidal' in a place where gangsters prevail and murder is regarded as 'mildly regrettable' (462). The locality seems to exude an 'antagonism to anything godly or decent' (464) but, surprisingly, the local church is well attended, with nuns shepherding in neatly dressed children to sing sugary hymns. Even the men-folk stand respectfully in the church-porch, leaving occasionally to smoke cigarettes. With only an old copy of Bossuet's sermons and a few saints' lives in French to read Evelyn sinks into a deep sense of ennui and despondency.

His departure from Boa Vista takes him due East across the Takutu River and then back to Bon Success and the St Ignatius Mission. With inadequate horses and provisions, the gruelling journey assumes a nightmarish, almost visionary, quality so that even a passing peasant seems to have a 'face like El Greco's St Ignatius' (479). Foolishly, Evelyn decides to press on alone and soon becomes hopelessly lost. Recalling a St Christopher medal given to him in London, he prays desperately for 'supernatural assistance' (482). Miraculously on cue, he immediately stumbles upon not only a creek of drinkable water but also a friendly English-speaking Indian heading for Bon Success who gives him plentiful food and drink at his nearby home. Stunned by this chance survival, Evelyn calculates that in this remote region of British Guiana the odds against meeting such an individual were about one in 54.75 million and he happily accepts the experience as proof of St Christopher's efficacy as the patron-saint of travellers.

He arrives safely at the St Ignatius Mission where he meets Father Keary, a tough and cheerful ex-army chaplain with the 'eyes of a visionary' (485), who is setting out on his rounds of local villages. Evelyn recuperates by reading Dickens, writing letters home and planning the next stage of his itinerary to Kurikaburu, the most distant village on the mission's regular cycle of visits. Setting out on 5 March he enjoys on route the hospitality of a devout American rancher, Mr Hart, who assembles his whole household so that they can together recite the Rosary by moonlight. As he travels on, he muses on the falsity of oft-made accusations that Christian missionaries habitually seek to clothe the nakedness of natives, insisting instead that a combination of 'modesty' and 'ostentation' (497) prompts the females to welcome gifts of clothing, for which they are happy to be baptized, confirmed and taught the Ten Commandments. He finally catches up with Father Keary at Tipuru and they agree to travel on together. He becomes fascinated by the all-pervasive native fear of the supernatural concept of *Kenaima*. This malevolent sense, he feels, corresponds to Western-European religious concepts of evil which can be exploited by sinful individuals. The latter stages of *Ninety-Two Days* cast its author as a zealous Christian anthropologist who is testing out how the central tenets of Catholicism sometimes overlap with other supposedly primitive forms of superstitious belief.

Evelyn remains silently impressed by Father Keary, who habitually recites the Rosary as he travels, says Mass with his portable altar in native houses and conducts multiple weddings and baptisms. This final leg of the journey proves especially arduous, with Waugh stricken by lameness just as the rainy season arrives. Father Keary leaves him at the riverside camp of a gold and diamond prospector, Mr Winter, who proves a genial and uplifting host. He relaxes by reading *Martin Chuzzlewit* and in early April returns to Georgetown, from where he sails to Port of Spain, Trinidad, staying at a Benedictine monastery there for Holy Week. He arrives back at his parents' house, Underhill, on 1 May 1933. Although Evelyn claims at the end of the travelogue that his experiences in British Guiana should not be regarded as a 'spiritual odyssey' (543), he now clearly regards himself as a writer whose Catholicism provides the central anchor for his spiritual and anthropological world view.

Controversy, divorce and *A Handful of Dust*

It was now impossible to minimize the public importance of Evelyn's private religious beliefs, which soon became became apparent when he was drawn into a specifically Catholic controversy. On 7 January 1933, while he was still abroad, Ernest Oldmeadow, editor of the *Tablet*, a Catholic weekly owned by Cardinal Bourne, had denounced *Black Mischief* as an immoral and sacrilegious work, unbefitting a Catholic author. Twelve prominent Catholics wrote in Evelyn's defence, stating that they regarded Oldmeadow's words as beyond the 'bounds of legitimate criticism' and an 'imputation of bad faith'. These included the publisher Tom Burns, the Jesuit Fathers Martindale and D'Arcy, Father Bede Jarrett OP (the Prior of Blackfriars and friend of Graham Greene), two renowned Catholic artists, Wyndham Lewis and Eric Gill, and two of Evelyn's closest Catholic friends, Christopher Hollis and Douglas Woodruff.[15]

Shocked and angered by Oldmeadow's accusations, but also encouraged by his influential supporters, Evelyn drafted in May a scathing pamphlet in the form of an 'Open Letter to H. E. the Cardinal Archbishop of Westminster', meticulously refuting these aspersions against his writings and Catholicism. Although never published, Waugh had copies privately printed and kept the bound manuscript in his library. This debacle demonstrated that Evelyn's Catholicism was now an integral element of his public literary identity. He also later exacted a characteristic form of revenge on the cardinal in his 1959 biography of Ronald Knox, casting Bourne as dim-witted, retrogressive philistine.[16] His 'Open Letter' provides a revealing insight into the consolidation of Evelyn's hard-line perspectives as a Christian writer. He identifies a moral chaos lurking beneath the surface veneer of western civilization and feels morally obliged as a Catholic to highlight these dangers. His intention had been unambiguously didactic in highlighting the encroachment of barbarism on society and the pessimistic conclusion of the novel implied the impending collapse of civilization. *Black Mischief* and the controversy prompted by Oldmeadow's denunciations marks a momentous transition in his public identity as a writer from that of a secular social satirist to a Christian satiric moralist.

The rest of 1933 was filled with drafting *Ninety-Two Days*, frenetic article writing to replenish his finances and an autumn Hellenic cruise with Father D'Arcy and some Catholic friends. This led to an idyllic stay at Altachiara, an elegant villa at Portofino near Genoa (the model for 'Castello Crouchback' in *Men at Arms*). It was owned by Mary Herbert, the widow of the MP and scholar Aubrey Herbert (whose biography was later written by Evelyn's daughter, Margaret), the model for Sandy Arbuthnot in John Buchan's *Greenmantle*. The villa was named after the Berkshire seat, Highclere, of their relatives, the Earls of Caernarvon. Evelyn first met here in September Mary's youngest daughter, Laura (a 'white mouse' aged seventeen), who was a first cousin of Evelyn Gardner and would later become his second wife.

During 1933 he began annulment procedures for his first marriage on the grounds of 'lack of real consent', with the case falling under the jurisdiction of Cardinal Bourne and the Diocese of Westminster. After inordinate delays caused by the dilatoriness of the church authorities in London, prompting a personal visit by Evelyn to Rome in December 1935, the annulment was finally granted by the Holy See on 4 July 1936.[17]

By early November he had completed the typescript of *Ninety-Two Days* at West House, a small Regency villa near Bognor Regis, lent to him by Diana Cooper. Worn out by these labours, he left for Fez in Morocco on 28 December 1933 to draft his new novel, with the working title 'A Handful of Ashes' (after the earth thrown onto a coffin at burial), later revised to 'Fourth Decade' (the hero, like Evelyn, turns thirty in the novel), in which he tried for the first time to write about ordinary people rather than eccentrics. While there he visited Rabat, Marrakesh and Casablanca, purchased the sexual services of a young Moroccan girl, dined occasionally with the British consul, gloomily watched silent films at the local cinema and read a biography of the soldier and explorer Charles de Foucauld who eventually became a Trappist monk (as later described in *Work Suspended*).[18]

Back in England by late-February 1934, Evelyn diligently worked on completing his novel, now called *A Handful of Dust*. Its lucrative pre-publication serialization rights were negotiated with *Harper's Bazaar* but with a different ending to that of the novel itself. This was because he had decided to reuse the concluding fantasy scenario of 'The Man Who Liked Dickens', first published in America in *Hearst's International* (September 1933) and then in England's *Nash's Pall Mall* (November), as a means for the tragic-comic stranding the hero, Tony Last, in an exotically alien clime. Seeking excitement and release from the drudgery of writing, in early July 1934 he met Sandy Glen at the Lygons' London house. He impetuously agreed to join his imminent trip with Hugh Lygon to Spitsbergen above the Arctic Circle as part of an advance party for the Oxford University Arctic Mission (1935–6). It proved an unexpectedly arduous and dangerous expedition and led to only a single dismissive article, 'Fiasco in the Arctic'.[19] Henceforth, Evelyn regarded travel merely for its own sake, rather than as a means of stimulating artistic and intellectual creativity, as pointless and potentially self-destructive.

He incorporated this challenging idea into the disturbing ending of *A Handful of Dust* (published, 3 September 1934). It recounts the tragic-comic mishaps and betrayals of Tony Last, a harmless country gentleman, who represents the plight of a civilized man trapped among metropolitan savages, led by his faithless wife, Brenda, and her opportunist, amoral lover, John Beaver. Tony loves his wife, his son, John Andrew, and his great mid-Victorian gothic-revival house, Hetton Abbey (partly based upon the Lygons' Madresfield). But Brenda callously betrays her loyal husband (echoing Evelyn's own abandonment by his first wife) and while she makes a rewarding second marriage, Tony loses everything. In the novel's nightmarish ending, lifted from 'The Man Who Loved Dickens', he ends up in a Brazilian jungle as the prisoner of the deranged Mr Todd (based on Mr Christie from *Ninety-Two Days*, the inspiration for the entrapment of Paul Henty by the insane Mr McMaster in the original short story).

Although a defenceless victim of the savagery surrounding him, Tony is not without personal faults. Like Paul Pennyfeather, he is cast as an innocent abroad but one who, in contrast to the benignly comic landscapes of *Decline and Fall*, finds himself in a more malignant and destructive world. Tragically, he lacks the imagination or maturity to defend himself from an all-encompassing chaos and, in particular, seems complacently satisfied with his dull Anglican conformity. Even when his son is accidentally killed in a hunting accident, he is embarrassed by the vicar's kindly meant words of consolation, remarking: 'the last thing one wants to talk about at a time like this is religion' (115). Accentuating this sense of awkwardness, Brenda responds to this tragic news with momentary horror when she thinks that it is her worthless lover, John Beaver, who has died rather than her only son. Through the ramifications of this grotesque incident, Tony's superficially civilized world, centred upon his beloved Hetton, is steadily drawn into an amoral vortex of self-destruction. Devoid of hope or moral direction, he drifts away from the callously indifferent Brenda. Seduced into pointless travel to South America with the self-deluding Dr Messenger in search of a quasi-mythical lost city, Tony ends up in the clutches of the diabolical Mr Todd, trapped in his hellish world of endlessly reading Dickens aloud.

Hetton Abbey (also partly modelled on Lancing College) encapsulates much of the social and moral ennui of both the novel and 1930s England. Extensively redesigned during the mid-nineteenth century to incorporate all that was anachronistic and self-deluding in later Victorian architecture (as opposed to Evelyn's genuine admiration for early-English Gothic Revival styles), it stands essentially as a grandiose fake, with its faux mediaevalism and comfortless bedrooms named after characters from *Morte d'Arthur*. It is Tony's private fantasy world and personal temple, encapsulating a world of arrested childhood cocooned in Victorian tastelessness. He lovingly admires:

> the general aspect and atmosphere of the place; the line of its battlements against the sky; the central clock tower where quarterly chimes disturbed all but the heaviest sleepers; the ecclesiastical gloom of the great hall, its ceiling groined and painted in diapers of red and gold, supported on shafts of polished granite with vine-wreathed capitals, half-lit by day through lancet windows of armorial stained glass . . . the dining-hall with its hammer-beam roof and pitch-pine minstrels' gallery; the bedrooms with their brass bedsteads, each with a frieze of Gothic text . . . where the bed stood on a dias, the walls were hung with tapestry, the fire-place was like a tomb of the thirteenth-century. (14–15)

When his divorce from Brenda necessitates its sale, he mournfully laments that a 'whole Gothic world had come to grief' (151). In contrast, Brenda hates Hetton's outmoded pretensions and commissions the appalling Mrs Beaver, a fashionable decorator and mother of her feckless lover, to vandalize its interiors with modernist chrome and sheepskin. Yet despite its garish qualities, Hetton still encapsulates the elegiac theme of the lost city of Jerusalem which resurfaces in Charles Ryder's moving recollection of *Lamentations*: 'Quo*modo sedet sola civitas [plena populo]*' ('How doth the city sit solitary [that was full of people]') (331), in the Epilogue to *Brideshead*.

The original title, 'A Handful of Ashes', was replaced by T. S. Eliot's phrase from 'The Waste Land', when one's shadows at morning and evening prompt only 'fear in a handful of dust'. These words offer a potent commentary upon the human condition, especially for self-deluding characters like Tony. During life we seek to convince ourselves of our own mortal significance by seizing upon the insubstantial presence of our morning and evening shadows. But, if this is the only proof that our existence is meaningful, then we are tragically deluded. All we can hope for – if we live without a more nourishing moral, social and spiritual framework – is a pathetic confirmation of the endless cycle of mortality, from mere 'ashes to ashes' and 'dust to dust'. Ultimately, *A Handful of Dust* becomes Evelyn's first ardently Catholic novel in its mocking rejection of secular humanism and its insistence upon the essentially fallen nature of humankind.

Evelyn regarded the spiritual history of England as Catholic for 900 years, Protestant for 300 and agnostic for the previous century, leading ultimately to an amoral void at the centre of so-called civilized society. The domestic history of Hetton neatly encapsulates this historical English fall from Grace, as its once grand monastic buildings were secularized at the Reformation but remained 'one of the notable houses of the county' (14). This essential link with the past stood until Tony's great-grandfather demolished the old house and in 1864 erected a meaningless mock-gothic edifice as deceptively fake as Llanabba School. From this perspective, the mercantile utilitarianism of the Victorians casts them as the chief instigators of villainy in the novel, ruthlessly sweeping away the historical and aesthetic continuities of the past. They seek to disguise their philistine crimes by superimposing on traditional country residences an illusory fake-medievalism which fails to mask their self-inflicted cultural vacuity. This underlines how the Victorians tended to substitute cloying sentimentality for the rigours of true Faith. It is, therefore, entirely appropriate that Tony ends up reading aloud the works of that ultimate purveyor of Victorian sentimentality and idealized family life, Charles Dickens.[20]

Mrs Beaver, cynically pimping her own son, also rents out to Brenda a small London flat in Mayfair where she can secretly continue her adulterous affair. The stark contrast between the rambling intimacy of Hetton and the hard-edged functionality of this flat, becomes a key element in the alternative ending, 'By Special Request', provided for the novel's serialization as 'A Flat in London' in *Harper's Bazaar*. In this version, after discovering his wife's infidelity, Tony leaves for a luxury cruise in the West Indies rather than Brazil and eventually returns as calculating and self-interested as his wife with whom he is nominally reconciled. Unbeknown to Brenda, he keeps on the London flat, for his own intended infidelities as he now conforms to the general moral degeneracy of English society.[21]

A Handful of Dust is often judged to be Evelyn's prose masterpiece. Certainly, it proved a pivotal work in facilitating an enriching transition in his writings from the fantastic and semi-surreal comedy of his earlier novels to the more literally realized worlds of *Brideshead* and the *Sword of Honour* trilogy. This transitional shift generated the novel's deft balance between its lighter tones of riotous immorality and its darker elements of impending tragedy. The duality and shape-shifting nature of Evelyn's writings at this period is aptly illustrated by *A Handful of Dust* possessing two starkly contrasting endings. In one, Tony's fate is one of darkest tragi-comedy as he finds himself trapped in the jungle domain of a Dickens-addicted madman. In the other, he is transformed into an urbanely amoral man of the world, now using the London flat to indulge in meaningless affairs of the flesh. Paradoxically, redemption may still somehow prove possible for the Tony who is imprisoned by Mr Todd but the comfortably sophisticated Tony of 'The Flat in London' seems to have irrevocably fallen into a hellish metropolis from which there is no escape.

3

Campion, second marriage and war: 1934–45

Catholic hagiography

The first half of 1934 proved immensely productive for Evelyn. In late-February he advised his agent, A. D. Peters, that he was planning a life of Gregory the Great (Pope, 590–604) after completing *A Handful of Dust*; and on 15 April *Ninety-Two Days* was published to generally positive reviews.[1] The subject matter of his new and eminently Catholic project rapidly shifted from Pope Gregory to the Elizabethan Jesuit missionary and martyr, Edmund Campion. This change was prompted by various Jesuit friends (especially Father D'Arcy) and inspired by his privileged access to extensive biographical notes on Campion compiled by a recently deceased priest from Farm Street. He was further intrigued by his friend, Douglas Woodruff, purchasing the house where Campion had been taken prisoner. This project also enabled him to develop his fascination with missionary zeal, as demonstrated in *Remote People* and *Ninety-Two Days*. By the end of August Evelyn had signed a contract with the Catholic publisher, Sheed and Ward, in association with Longmans. Both the writer's and the publisher's proceeds were granted in perpetuity to the Jesuits at Oxford since their lease on Campion Hall in St Giles (where Father D'Arcy was now Master and English Provincial) had almost expired, with a new house under construction off St Aldate's to designs by Sir Edwin Lutyens.

The biography's composition occupied most of Evelyn's time from September 1934 until May 1935, the longest period he had ever spent on a single book, indicating just how personally significant this project had become. He writes in *Edmund Campion* not only as a well-briefed historian but also as a fervent devotee of Roman Catholicism. His depiction of Campion as a prototype English Jesuit martyr (he had taught at Douai the first of the seminarian martyrs, Cuthbert Mayne) is a potent and, at times, lyrically written hagiography. But it also seeks to provide a wider readership, and not just an exclusively Catholic one, with a sense of the essential character and fortitude of the man. It was published to considerable acclaim in September 1935, receiving in June 1936 the prestigious Hawthornden Prize (£100) for the best work of imaginative literature by a young British author. *Campion* confirmed Evelyn's public identity during the mid-1930s as a major literary figure whose commitment to Roman Catholicism provided a clear moral and intellectual framework for his interpretations of human and social behaviour.

In the 1946 preface to the second edition of *Campion*, Evelyn recalls his motivating debt of gratitude to Father D'Arcy, 'to whom, under God, I owe my faith', and reaffirms how his biography seeks to offer a true story of 'heroism and holiness'. He emphasizes how it has grown increasingly relevant to the first half of the twentieth century when the Catholic Church and personal religious beliefs are being ruthlessly persecuted and suppressed in various global regions. He admired the 1867 authoritative biography of Campion by Richard Simpson (like himself an Anglican convert), but argues that a fresh consideration of Campion was timely because the twentieth century had proved far less tolerant than the Victorian period, bringing Campion much nearer to his own age. He notes how the martyrdom in 1927 of Father Pro in Mexico (described in Greene's *The Lawless Roads*) had faithfully re-enacted Campion's:

> We have seen the Church drawn underground in country after country. In fragments and whispers we get news of other saints in the prison camps of Eastern and South-eastern Europe, of cruelty and degradation more savage than anything in Tudor England, of the same, pure light shining in darkness, uncomprehended. The haunted, trapped, murdered priest is our contemporary and Campion's voice sounds to us across the centuries as though he were walking at our elbow. (5)

Evelyn's biography is unashamedly partisan in its desire to utilize the facts of Campion's life and martyrdom as a means of asserting the essential truths of the historical and moral potency of the Catholic Church. Consequently, his account begins by implicitly undermining the efficacy of the Tudor regime. It focuses not on the glories of the Elizabethan age but rather on the pathetically squalid death in March 1603 of its once-great queen, propped up on the floor with cushions and superstitiously wearing a gold talisman around her neck to prevent her dying. So ends, he muses, the great Tudor dynasty and its spirit of secular humanism which had led to a 'new aristocracy, a new religion, a new system of government' (8), following the 'ruin of countless gentle families' (65). He then tracks back some forty years to the mid-1560s and outlines Campion's stellar university studies and the attractions of what would have undoubtedly been a distinguished court career. Pre-Reformation Oxford, he proposes, epitomized the 'spacious, luminous world of Catholic humanism' (13). But as the dictates of rigorous Protestant conformism rapidly spread following

Elizabeth's accession in 1558, so Oxford lost a historically English quality offered by Catholicism. Protestantism also isolated England's aesthetic sensitivities from the cultural richness and artistic developments of the rest of Catholic Europe. Evelyn developed these historical perspectives from Hilaire Belloc's *How the Reformation Happened* (1928) which depicted the Reformation as a 'diversion of the main stream of the Renaissance into narrower, incongruous channels, flowing in a different direction from that which the mighty stream of rediscovered culture would have followed, had it been left undisturbed'.[2] At the same time, Evelyn also highlighted major limitations on the Catholic side in, for example, his delineation of the naiveté of the unworldly Dominican friar, Pope Pius V, in his politically inept excommunication of Queen Elizabeth in 1570.

Campion's departure from a spiritually diminished Oxford is recounted – even though his college, St John's, was still strongly Catholic – leading to his revitalization first at Dublin with the cultured Stanihurst household and then at Douai where young men were trained as 'missionaries and martyrs' (35). Evelyn places emphasis upon the still-surviving copy of the *Summa* used by Campion at the college, with the word '*Martyrium*' annotated in Campion's own hand against an argument on baptism by blood. He then travelled pilgrim-like to Rome where he became a Jesuit; and then to Bohemia and Prague where he began his priestly ministry before crossing heroically and joyfully back to certain death in England. Implicitly, constructing this historical narrative of the suppression of Catholicism in Tudor England exerted a major effect on Evelyn's later fictional writings. Henceforth, a sense of profound loss over Protestant England's alienation from European historical and cultural continuities underlies his later fictional depictions of dispossessed aristocratic families and their great houses, culminating in the nostalgia for a lost Catholic world in *Brideshead* and the *Sword of Honour* trilogy.

Like the protagonists of Evelyn's earlier satiric novels, Campion is a victim of a cruel world but, unlike them, he also becomes a triumphant hero, confirming the efficacy of individual endeavour and commitment. Campion's last year of life, travelling in disguise between numerous English recusant households becomes his personal *via dolorosa* (Jesus's route through Jerusalem when carrying his cross to crucifixion) before his capture, imprisonment, torture and grisly execution. Campion is cast as an inspirational activist and counter-revolutionary hero whose actions are imbued with the timeless significance of a man expressing absolute obedience to the Divine plan. Despite its horrors, Campion's triumphant death affords an evangelical contrast to the demise of Elizabeth which opens the biography. Framed by the grotesque death of a Protestant queen and the glorious self-sacrifice of a Catholic saint, *Edmund Campion* preaches that the Protestant reformation was a national catastrophe for England, encumbering its people with false bishops and an heretical Prayer Book, rendering the Anglican Church merely insular and isolating its congregations from the nourishing spirituality of Western-European culture, civilization and religious debate. Because of the Reformation, Evelyn suggests, it was only via hatred and bloodshed that the true faith was 'one day to return to England' (30).

The final chapter, 'The Martyr', traces Campion's last days following his capture at a recusant house, Lyford Grange, in Berkshire. It recounts how he was brought into London to the Tower, pinioned on horseback, his elbows tied behind his back, his wrists in front and his ankles strapped together under the horse. A scrap of paper on his hat read: 'CAMPION THE SEDITIOUS JESUIT' (95). He was incarcerated for four days in the notorious 'Little Ease', a cell so small that a man could not stand erect or lie with limbs outstretched. He was then taken for a meeting with the Queen and his former patron, Robert Dudley, Earl of Leicester. They invited him to renounce his Catholic faith and re-enter the Protestant Church but his firm rejection of this offer led to a warrant for him to be tortured on the rack. He was interrogated by four conferences of legal experts and churchmen, accompanied by the Governor of the Tower and his rack-master, at which he was denounced as a traitor and apostate 'unloyal to his Prince' (107). Condemned to death by hanging, drawing and quartering, Campion exultantly warned: 'In condemning us you condemn all your own ancestors – all the ancient priests, bishops and kings – all that was once the glory of England, the island of saints' (116). He and the other condemned men then recited the *Te Deum* as they were led back to their cells.

Eleven days later Campion is dragged on a hurdle through the mud and rain to Tyburn, where he insists with the noose around his neck that he remains a Catholic and a priest who intends to die for his Faith. Although Evelyn notes that his heroic martyrdom generated many thousand converts to Catholicism, he concludes by focusing on the response of a single witness. A young Cambridge scholar, Henry Walpole, was so close to the execution that he was splashed by the blood from Campion's entrails as they were torn from his body and thrown into boiling water:

> In that moment he was caught into a new life; he crossed the sea, became a priest, and thirteen years later, after very terrible sufferings, died the same death as Campion's on the gallows at York. (121)

Campion underlines the unending continuity of the priestly vocation, stretching from Campion and Walpole down to twentieth-century missionary martyrs such as Father Pro in Mexico and the dedication by the present-day Oxford Jesuits of their new college to Campion's honour. It also stridently confirmed Evelyn's personal commitment to the global family of Catholicism and prompted his tentative plans in early 1935 to write a follow-on biography of Mary Stuart, for which he hoped (ultimately, without success) that his agent would obtain a contract from Chapman and Hall.

Abyssinia (again), *Mr Loveday* and second marriage

Campion was completed when Evelyn's social contacts with Laura, the daughter of Aubrey (the second son of the Earl of Carnarvon) and Mary Herbert (only daughter of Lord Vesci), were maturing into a meaningful relationship. He enjoyed staying at the Herberts' home, a comfortably spacious Georgian mansion at Pixton near Dulverton, Somerset. The family was strongly Catholic, following Mary's conversion after her husband's early death in 1923. Regular visitors included Hilaire Belloc and an old laundry had been converted into a private chapel where Fathers D'Arcy and Knox often officiated. Perhaps seeking to echo the intrepid exploits of Laura's late father, Evelyn set out once more for Abyssinia on 7 August 1935, this time as a war correspondent for the *Daily Mail* to cover Mussolini's invasion. Through the influence of Tom Burns, he also signed a lucrative contract with Longman to produce a serious political book on the Abyssinian war.

Evelyn's inexperience as a foreign journalist put him at a considerable disadvantage to other reporters but his paper still ran over sixty of his cables between 24 August and 20 November. He assumed a contrary position to the popular view in England that the innocent and noble Abyssinians, seeking protection for their borders from the League of Nations (mocked in *Decline and Fall*), were being overwhelmed by fascist imperialism. Instead, he represented them as savages having civilization forcibly offered to them by Mussolini. In contrast to the pessimistic conclusions over *Black Mischief*'s fictional Azania, real life seemed to be providing, via the Italians, a rare chance for order to triumph over barbarity in Africa, as he explained in a provocative newpaper report, 'Abyssinian Realities: We Can Applaud Italy'.[3] In this article, he seems to subscribe to Belloc's idiosyncratic Catholic view of world history that no country could be considered civilized which had not previously been under Roman dominion. Mussolini's Italians were cast as offering such opportunities to the Ethiopians and *Waugh in Abyssinia* concludes with newly constructed roads symbolizing beneficent imperialism down which:

> will pass the eagles of ancient Rome, as they came to our savage ancestors in France and Britain and Germany, bringing . . . the inestimable gift of fine workmanship and clear judgement – the two determining qualities of the human spirit, by which alone, under God, man grows and flourishes. (712)

Although such words inevitably raised suspicions that their author was a Fascist sympathizer, by 1936 Mussolini seemed to Evelyn and other fellow Catholics to offer the only means of preventing the godless Nazis from annexing Catholic Austria. Hence, it seemed foolhardy to oppose his potentially positive modernizing plans for such a lawless and globally insignificant country as Abyssinia since such hostility would merely serve to drive him closer to an allegiance with Hitler.

Evelyn left Abyssinia in December 1935 and headed for the Holy Land, hoping to spend Christmas at Bethlehem, a trip which laid the seeds for a desire to write about St Helena. He also visited Baghdad and Damascus before travelling to Rome where he was granted a secret audience with Mussolini at the Palazzo Venezia. He then returned to London in early January 1936 and began the contracted Longman book, under the punning title, *Waugh in Abyssinia*, about his African experiences. He made concerted efforts in April and May 1936 to complete it but, following Haile Selassie's flight from Abyssinia, more primary material was needed and he had to arrange a hasty return visit there. He travelled to Rome in late-July to secure a visa and financial support for his trip from the Italian government and reached Djibouti on 18 August. Contrary to his hopes, the Italian invasion had led to chaos, bombing and poison-gas attacks by the Italians on their helpless opponents. He was relieved to return home promptly via Cairo, Tripoli and Rome. A disillusioned plan to call his book, *A Disappointing War*, was vetoed by Tom Burns for marketing reasons and it remained a deeply unsatisfactory work to complete. Divided into three sections, the first focused on a concise historical survey of the country's political problems. The second recounted Evelyn's own experiences there (from which comic materials for *Scoop* were derived) and the third unwisely attempted to celebrate the Italian invasion and its supposed benefits to the country. He remained far from happy with the book and in a later edition of his travel writings, *When the Going Was Good* (1946), most of the first and all of the third parts were silently dropped. By the time *Waugh in Abyssinia* was published on 26 October 1936 (after part-serialization in the *English Review*), English attention had shifted to Hitler's occupation of the Rhineland and the Spanish Civil War. His agent failed to find any American firm interested in publishing it.

Of more lasting importance, and certainly more enjoyable to complete, was an opportunistic collection of his previously published magazine short-stories, *Mr Loveday's Little Outing and Other Sad Stories* (July 1936). The title-story had originally been called 'Mr Cruttwell's Little Outing' in memory of his much derided Hertford tutor (who, ironically, died insane). It told the whimsical tale of a meek psychopath who is let out of his lunatic asylum only to commit exactly the same kind of murder which had first led to his incarceration there. He later reworked this theme of an escaped lunatic in his short-story, 'The Sympathetic Passenger', in which an innocent driver picks up a homicidal madman who (like Evelyn) loathes the radio. Another darkly comic story, 'On Guard', recounts how a possessive poodle, Hector (based on a spaniel owned by Teresa Jungman), bites off his beloved mistress's exceptionally cute nose in an attempt to deter an endless line of besotted suitors. The collection also included 'By Special Request', the alternative ending to *A Handful of Dust*, 'Bella Fleace Gave a Party' set in an Irish country house, and a brief account of expatriate life in Abyssinia, 'Incident in Azania'. Another story, 'Winner Takes All', playfully distorts Evelyn's relationship with Alec by focusing on the dilemmas of Tom, an overlooked younger son whose wealthy Australian fiancée is stolen by his elder brother Gervase. Tom's mother arranges for him to marry a previous girlfriend, Gladys Cruttwell, a blowsy clerk from a Midlands car factory, so that they can be packed off to Australia and conveniently forgotten.[4]

By the end of 1936 a distinctive blending of social comedy and Catholic commentary was firmly rooted in Evelyn's creative imagination. He also recognized that he had become a writer who was expected to occupy a prominent position as both an accomplished literary stylist and Catholic moral commentator. He was now the most acclaimed member of his own family literary dynasty, a distinction rendered all the more poignant when during a brief visit to his parents' new home at Highgate in late-January 1935 he accidentally set fire to his father's treasured library, which housed hundreds of signed first-editions from eminent English writers of Arthur's generation.[5]

In early July 1936 Evelyn undertook an arduous pilgrimage to Lough Derg, Donegal, requiring barefoot walking over sharp rocks and two nights spent in prayer and fasting on a bleak island in a lake. Arriving back in London on 7 July, he finally received his long-awaited annulment of his first marriage. On the following morning he joyfully met up with Laura Herbert and her mother, Mary, at Mass at Farm Street to announce his good news which offered a fresh start for both his private life and literary career. He had been firmly convinced for over a year of his desire to marry Laura and she had responded positively. In mid-June he attended the opening of the new Campion Hall at Oxford and was awarded the Hawthornden Prize at the Aeolian Hall on 24 June for his biography. He was by then hopeful that Laura's devout Catholic mother would be suitably impressed with his Catholic credentials. But his agent, A. D. Peters, did not attend this award ceremony. Instead, he had to attend court, attempting to prevent Evelyn's potential imprisonment for debt. This embarrassment was avoided only by the arrival of some American royalties and a £1,000 advance from Chapman and Hall for a five-novel contract. With money and marriage now much on his mind, Evelyn's financial position was further improved by the publication in 1937 of his first collected works by Chapman and Hall and by Penguin Books bringing out a sixpenny paperback of *Decline and Fall*, thereby providing him with a much wider and potentially lucrative readership.

As a soon-to-be married man with anticipated family responsibilities, Evelyn churned out a weekly *Spectator* column and regularly contributed to the *London Mercury*, *Morning Post*, *Tablet*, *Nash's Magazine* and *Night & Day* (an English version of the *New Yorker*, edited by Graham Greene). He became a director of Chapman and Hall and planned various future books, including under the working title 'In the Steps of Caesar', an anti-pacifist

take on Belloc's admiration all things Roman, and others on either saints
or Renaissance explorers. He even completed in April 1937 a script for
Alexander Korda for a projected film about show-girls, titled 'Lovelies
from America' or 'Lovelies Over London', which, fortunately, never reached
production.[6]

Laura's grandmother, Lady de Vesci, financed, through a gift of £4,000,
the purchase of Piers Court, at Stinchcombe between Stroud and Bath in
Gloucestershire, as a wedding present. Finally attaining his own country
seat, an elegant Georgian fronted manor-house in golden Cotswold stone,
enhanced Evelyn's preoccupations in his fictions with great English houses
and their families. He also ensured, after detailed discussions with the College
of Heralds, that the Waugh family coat of arms was carved on the pediment
of his new home. On 17 April 1937, after early morning Mass at Farm
Street, Evelyn and Laura were married at the Church of the Assumption
in Warwick Street by its curate, Father O'Ferrall, with Fathers Gilbey and
D'Arcy assisting. The honeymoon was spent first at Portofino and then
Rome, Assisi and Florence, before returning to Portofino where by 10 May
Evelyn had resumed work on his next novel, *Scoop* (begun on 15 October
1936), based upon his Abyssinian adventures. With Piers Court still under
refurbishment, they moved into their new family home in late-August but,
with so many domestic distractions, as well as Laura's first pregnancy with
their daughter (Maria) Teresa (born, 9 March 1938) and his new role as a
country gentleman, *Scoop* was not finished until February 1938 (published,
7 May).[7]

Piers Court rapidly became the secure rural centre of Evelyn's domestic
and literary affairs but his public status now increasingly drew him into
problematic public debate. Unlike most of his contemporary writers who
supported the republican rebels, Evelyn and the Herberts sided with
Franco's nationalists in the Spanish Civil War and his sister-in-law, Gabriel
Herbert, like Cordelia in *Brideshead*, volunteered as a medical assistant on
Franco's side. His essays and reviews of the period insistently highlighted,
often controversially, how self-interested free-thinking humanism, combined
with the deceptive veniality of the press and the ruthless repressions of
international politics, were inevitably leading western civilization towards
another global catastrophe.

Scoop, Budapest and Mexico

As the first major literary product of his married life with Laura, *Scoop*
remains one of Evelyn's most carefully crafted and amusing novels. The
novelist (and adapter of Waugh for the screen) William Boyd stated: '*Scoop*
is, in my opinion, Waugh's real masterwork. It has a classical and deeply
satisfying shapeliness, but also contains sequences of hilarious comic writing
unrivalled in English literature'.[8] It blends through its adoption of a thinly

disguised Abyssinian background, the sombre realism of *A Handful of Dust* with increasingly farcical plot developments, centred upon an innocent protagonist, a kindred spirit to Paul in *Decline and Fall* and Adam in *Vile Bodies*. But unlike his hapless predecessors, this naive hero, William Boot, is unharmed by his experiences within the corrupt and dangerous world of war journalism and a happy resolution to this light-hearted satire is eventually achieved.

William resides contentedly with a motley group of eccentric relatives and staff, led by his rakishly deranged Uncle Theodore who constantly sings the doleful refrain: 'Change and decay in all around I see'. Their family's country seat, Boot Magna Hall is based on the Herberts' Pixton Hall and P. G. Wodehouse's Blandings Castle. This ramshackle mansion is surrounded by 'immense trees' laid out by 'some forgotten, provincial predecessor of Repton' and looks down on a lake 'moved by strange tides' (17) since the only estate worker who could work its sluice gates had died fifteen years earlier. William regularly contributes a trivial nature column, 'Lush Notes', to the *Daily Beast* (modelled on the *Daily Express*) but he is torn from his comfortable rural domesticity by the paper's ruthless proprietor, Lord Copper (mocking Lord Beaverbrook), who instructs his foreign editor, the creepily subservient Mr Salter, to send the unwilling William to report on outbreak of war in the fictional Ishmaelia. Summoned to Lord Copper's Megalopolitan Building (echoing Beaverbrook's Fleet Street headquarters), William is mistaken for another fashionable young writer, his cousin, John Courtney Boot (the protégé of the dynamically manipulative socialite, Julia Stitch, based on Lady Diana Cooper), whose career up to 1936 closely reflects Evelyn's. William is packed off to Ishmaelia on an inflated wage and lavish expenses, even though his non-existent knowledge of foreign war reporting matches Evelyn's own inexperience in Abyssinia.

The comic brilliance of the novel, echoing Evelyn's reverence for Wodehouse's sharp dialogue and lively caricatures, lies in its transmuting of the mature deceit, callousness and idleness of hard-bitten journalists into a more endearing form of childish egocentricity and one-upmanship. The group of hacks covering the war – William, his friend Corker, their associates Shumble, Whelper and Pigge, and the distinguished fraud, Sir Jocelyn Hitchcock (modelled on Sir Percival Phillips of the *Daily Telegraph*) – habitually make up copy, steal each other's telegraph cables and spoil their rivals' stories. Even Evelyn's habitual reverence for missionary work provides yet more comic material in his description of the fate of nineteenth-century missionaries in Ishmaelia:

> None returned. They were eaten, every one of them; some raw, other stewed and seasoned – according to local usage and the calendar (for the better sort of Ishmaelites have been Christian for many centuries and will not publicly eat human flesh, uncooked, in Lent, without special and costly dispensation from their bishop). (74)

Finally, William accidentally stumbles upon a major scoop, returns home as his paper's hero, 'Boot of the *Beast*' (219), and happily resumes his 'Lush Notes' column. Unlike Evelyn's other picaresque innocents abroad, William's innocence protects him from the savagery and chaos of the outside world. Boot Magna Hall, locked in a time-warp of ancient respectability, remains a genteelly decaying haven of Eden-like tranquillity. It is as though William begins the novel, and remains throughout, unstained by Original Sin. Although he apparently lacks any mature religious or spiritual dimension, his simple childlike qualities ensure his protection from an otherwise vicious and self-destructive world.

Although missionaries and other western colonialists receive short shrift in *Scoop*, an implicit strand of truth in this otherwise lightly satirical novel lies in its reminder that the only true defence for the individual against the general venality, chaos and decay of the wider, fallen world lies in the timeless securities of religious faith:

> *Scoop* like all Waugh's previous novels ultimately preaches, through satiric exposure of a series of false faiths, the need for the absolute standards of a true one, a universal faith that does not change. Like *Black Mischief* and *A Handful of Dust*, *Scoop* is full of sly references to false churches and gods, especially Anglican.[9]

Despite generally positive reviews, Evelyn remained uncertain of the intellectual scope and moral substance of *Scoop*. He had experimented in the novel with giving his central characters a greater psychological range, establishing Boot's subconscious through his daytime musings and dreams. Although only tentatively developed in *Scoop*, these techniques proved of increasing importance in subsequent works such as *Put Out More Flags* (1942a) and *Work Suspended* (1942b). Like John Plant, his commercially successful but privately dissatisfied detective-fiction writer in *Work Suspended*, Evelyn felt that he had reached by 1938 a 'climacteric' in his career as a writer and public figure. While the light comedy of *Scoop* pleased him well enough, he hankered after a more mature prose style which would allow him to move on from the anarchic and superficial fantasies which so delighted his British and American readership. So resolute was he in this respect that in his subsequent novels only *The Loved One* (1948) and *Basil Seal Rides Again* (1963) revert to youthful comic modes of writing.[10]

One readily available route during the late-1930s to assist Evelyn's development of a more weighty literary style and public identity lay in actively involving himself on an international level in Catholic political and theological affairs. To this end, he and Laura attended a Eucharistic Conference in Budapest in late-May 1938 as special correspondent (with his friend, Father Martindale) for the *Catholic Herald*, celebrating the ninth centenary of St Stephen, Hungary's patron saint. The English and Irish delegation numbered some 400 members led by Cardinal Hinsey and its progress to Budapest provided Evelyn with first-hand observations of the escalating European crisis. Their party, closely guarded by Nazi soldiers, had been denied access to Germany and was diverted through France and Austria where Hitler's anti-Semitic policies were being ruthlessly enacted. Restrictive visa requirements had effectively banned Catholic Germans and Austrians from attending and Evelyn angrily described in the *Catholic Herald* (3 June 1938) how Hungary's near neighbours had been denied their primary human right of freedom of worship. On a personal level, Evelyn revelled in the warmth of the international Catholic fraternity at Budapest. For him, the most important part of the pilgrimage lay in being able to share his Catholic devotions with like-minded people rather than being part of an often suspect religious minority in England. Furthermore, he came to the stark realization there that his fear of an impending global chaos, so insistently present in his comic fictions during the 1930s, was becoming a disturbing and terrifying reality through the political divisions engendered by German militarism.[11]

Just before his departure for Budapest, Evelyn was approached by the Cowdray Estate, which had lucrative oil interests in Mexico, to write a travel book about the country which would also expose the machinations of the communist government of General Lazaro Cárdenas. Legislation had been passed in March 1938, expropriating all foreign-owned assets including the Cowdray oilfields. This secretive arrangement (drawn up with Clive, a son of Weetman Pearson, Viscount Cowdray, an engineer who had drained Mexico City) provided Evelyn with a large advance and an all-expenses paid holiday with Laura in an exotic location. They sailed on the *Aquitania* for New York on 7 July and then travelled via steamer to Vera Cruz and overland to Mexico City. Poignantly, this was exactly the same route followed in 1926 when the Jesuit martyr Father Pro had secretly returned to his homeland. The resulting book was completed by mid-April and published in July 1939 with the pungent title for the English market, *Robbery Under Law: The Mexican Object Lesson*, and a toned-down title, *Mexico: An Object Lesson*, for its North American publication. Its text opened with the stark assertion: 'The succeeding pages are notes on anarchy' (3).[12]

Evelyn knew that Graham Greene was also producing an important exposé of the Mexican situation in *The Lawless Roads* (1939), which directly inspired his novel, *The Power and the Glory* (1940). Conscious of how Greene boldly penetrated inhospitable and dangerous Mexican regions (while he remained holed up in the Hotel Ritz apart from some brief excursions), Evelyn instead sought to provide in the first two-thirds of the volume a diligently documented history of Mexican politics. He traces how during the 1920s the repression of the Catholic Church was first instigated as an attempt by Presidents Obregon and Calles, to appease two powerful labour unions, the C.R.O.M. (a Marxist grouping) and its successor the C.T.M. syndicate. Despite being penned in his characteristically elegant prose style, the first two hundred pages of *Robbery Under Law* reads as a

doggedly factual history lesson. The execution of Father Pro and a revolt by
the Cristeros ('followers of *El Cristo Rey* – Christ the King') are only briefly
mentioned, in conjunction with the *Decline and Fall*-like end of General
Obregon, assassinated in 1928 by a 'religious cartoonist named Tocal' (57).

He then presses resolutely on with a damning account of the self-
interested and corrupt regimes of Calles and (from 1934) Cárdenas. The
intended central purpose of *Robbery Under Law* – from which a more
religious itinerary could only have distracted – comes when Evelyn records:
'In March 1938 he [Cardenas] took the grave step of confiscating the whole
oil industry' (58), a theft of the country's one profitable export which lay
Mexico open to the development of a fascist state. And so this potted survey
of recent Mexican politics continues for the next 150 pages, demonstrating
how the 'law of the jungle had taken over, just as the jungle had overtaken
Tony Last's civilized world in *A Handful of Dust*'.[13] But then, unexpectedly,
it seems as though Evelyn could himself take no more of these commercial
and political perspectives. In a marked shift of both subject matter and tone,
his personal preoccupations finally break through, radically redefining the
rest of the work.

It is within 'The Straight Fight', the seventh chapter in *Robbery Under
Law*, that Evelyn's Mexico finally comes to life and converges with the
religious preoccupations of Greene's *The Lawless Roads* and *The Power and
the Glory*. Beginning with a rhetorical acknowledgement of the common
charge that Catholics 'intrude their religion' into everything, he unashamedly
adopts the very same tactic. Having dutifully dealt at length with the oil
expropriation question, he can at last categorically insist that it is not politics,
oil or race but religion which is the 'single, essential question of the nation'
(206). Shaking off the shackles of the Cowdray Estate's financial interests,
he refers back to selected passages from Greene's delineation of Father Pro's
civilian disguise in his own description of a local priest: 'a dusty fellow in lay
clothes like an impoverished *ranchero* to look at' (212). He lavishes praise
on the pioneering work of early Spanish Jesuit and Dominican missionaries
among the Aztec natives and records how even many of those who had
supported the revolution admitted that the 'Jesuits were a fairly decent lot'
(214). He celebrates the establishing of a large seminary in Texas which
had supplied many priests in recent years to Mexico (like Campion's Douai
sending its students back to England) and notes that secret seminaries were
even beginning to spring up in Mexican cities.

Evelyn's greatest enthusiasm is reserved for his lengthy description of the
miraculous visitation and cult of the Virgin of Guadalupe – also reverentially
described by Greene in *The Lawless Roads* – which he represents, alongside
the martyrdom of Father Pro, as one of the two key gestures of irrepressible
Catholic resistance in Mexico: 'Pro is the inspiration of thousands through
whom the Mexican Church is still alive' (240). *Robbery Under Law*
postulates that the 'Church for her life, has to have a priesthood, an order
of men peculiarly educated and consecrated for a specific work' (245) and,

although originally commissioned as commercial propaganda, it concludes (like *Campion*) with a triumphant affirmation of the endless renewal of the missionary cycle.

Through his involvements in Budapest and Mexico, Evelyn was able to draw together Western-European fascism and South-American Marxist socialism as clear evidence of the ever-present human potential for the triumph of chaos over order and barbarism over civilization. A key element in his political perspectives during the late-1930s became an outright rejection of the familiar oppositions between the Right and the Left or Fascists and Communists, all of which were to be regarded as alternative totalitarianisms. The choice, it seemed, was no longer merely a political one between Franco's Catholic nationalists versus secular Republicans, or Marxist governments in Mexico versus the traditions of the Catholic Church in South America, or the National Socialist German Workers' Party versus the parliamentary Weimar Republic, but rather a choice between the insidious challenge of all forms of totalitarianism to the moral and spiritual value of the individual.

Home, *Work Suspended* and Alec Waugh

On his return to England in October 1938, following Neville Chamberlain's 'Peace in our time' speech on 30 September marking the Munich Pact, Evelyn again turned his mind to the twin practicalities of earning more money and developing his literary range as a writer. Tom Burns had earlier suggested that he should write for Burns and Oates a history of the Jesuits but this attractive proposal was quietly shelved due to its uncommercial nature. Although the *Daily Mail* rejected a series of his articles on Mexico, the *Tablet* accepted four under the title, 'Religion in Mexico. Impressions of a Recent Visit' (29 April–20 May 1939). He continued to be a prolific reviewer, delighting in outspoken judgements on contemporary writers including, in positive terms, Somerset Maugham (compared to an accomplished cabinet-maker), and negatively, H. G. Wells, W. H. Auden and Cyril Connolly.[14]

Reflecting on his experiences as the owner of Piers Court, Evelyn wrote an article on the pleasures and challenges of country life for *Harper's Bazaar*, 'The New Rustics' (July 1939), brazenly recycling material from an earlier *Spectator* article, 'The New Countrymen' (8 July 1938). Also of interest is a psychologically revealing short story, 'An Englishman's Home', for *Good Housekeeping* (August 1939). This self-reflective tale tells of the metropolitan Mr Beverley Metcalfe (the schoolmistress's name at Stinchcombe) who, after retirement from the cotton trade in Alexandria, establishes himself as a country gentleman in an idyllic village, Much Malcock. He defers to his genteel neighbours, headed by Lord Brakehurst, the county's Lord Lieutenant, and regards his taciturn gardener Boggett (based upon Prewitt, the gardener at Piers Court) with unquestioning admiration. He and his neighbours are conned by two devious brothers, the Hargood-Hoods, who purchase a small plot of land adjoining his estate and threaten to build there an experimental industrial laboratory. Eventually, Metcalfe meets their extortionate price of £500 to buy the land back and, in the process, proudly becomes the local potentate, with the local Brakehurst Arms pub renamed as The Metcalfe Arms. Ironically, the Hargood-Hoods turn out to belong to an ancient but impoverished country family who reside in an elegant house, with renowned topiary gardens. Built before the days of onerous property taxes, the brothers had developed their land-purchase racket for this harsher age in which they have to pay off annually extortionate Schedule A Tax Demands. Their latest success at Much Malcock even leaves some money over for cleaning their own fishponds, as they happily pore over an ordnance survey map of Norfolk in their Great Hall, identifying their next victims.[15]

During 1939 Evelyn was hard at work on an enigmatic new novel, through which he sought to reinvigorate his sense of direction as a writer. But it was clear that he could not finish it while on active service and he asked his agent Peters to see if the two completed chapters could be sold separately to a high-brow journal or newspaper as 'Work not in Progress' or 'Work Suspended'. A version of the first chapter, 'My Father's House' (later called 'A Death'), duly appeared in the newly established *Horizon* (November 1941), edited by Cyril Connolly, with both chapters published by Chapman and Hall in a limited edition of 500 copies on 21 December 1942 as *Work Suspended and Other Stories*.[16] These fragments offer a serious meditation upon his youthful family relationships (especially with his father) and future potential as a writer. They also focus upon his need to develop a more substantial and lasting prose style (ultimately facilitating *Brideshead* and *Sword of Honour*), conducive to his handling of serious issues of personal and public morality.

Work Suspended is the only one of Evelyn's fictions to use an intimate first person narrator. Its dissatisfied protagonist, John Plant, is a commercially successful thriller writer, who lives a self-contained and emotionless life at Fez in Morocco while working on his eighth novel (just as Evelyn had resided there in 1934 when writing his eighth book, *A Handful of Dust*). He is summoned home in the first chapter by the death of his father, an accomplished but now unfashionable painter of vast religious, historical and domestic genre pictures as favoured by the Royal Academy during the nineteenth century. These were just the kind of paintings which Evelyn was beginning to collect after establishing himself at Piers Court. Plant's father had also worked, more dubiously, as a 'restorer' of Old Masters for a West End Gallery:

> The truth was that, while excelling at Lely, my father could paint, very passably, in the manner of almost any of the masters of English portraiture and the private and the public collections of the New World were richly representative of his versatility. (254)

This father and son, although sketched at the opening of *Work Suspended* as markedly contrasting characters (very much like Evelyn and Arthur), both embody a melancholy sense that their respective talents have been thwarted from finding suitably rewarding artistic outlets. Plant's father had despised the modern movement of painters and, likewise, his detached and emotionally cold son feels alienated from the literary tastes of his own generation.[17]

Only in the second chapter, 'Lucy Simmonds' (later, 'A Birth'), does the younger Plant grow in vitality and hint that he may ultimately develop a more productive creative maturity. He falls in love with Lucy, the heavily pregnant wife of a socialist writer friend, Roger Simmonds, echoing Evelyn's infatuation with the pregnant Diana Guinness (Diana Mosley since 1936). But this second and last chapter of the novel ends gloomily with his alienation from Lucy after the birth of her child which, symbolically, also marks the arrival of a new social age. After Plant's return to England his family home, embodying the old Pre-Raphaelite ideal, is sold to a philistine property developer and demolished to make way for an ugly block of flats. Although a firm admirer of the Pre-Raphaelites, this destruction perhaps hints at the end of Evelyn's own often unhappy memories of his parents' house, Underhill, and its psychological replacement with a new-found contentment with his wife and young family at Piers Court.

Plant is haunted by a boorish confidence trickster, Atwater, a travelling salesman who had accidentally run over and killed his father. Atwater provides an ambivalent comic focus, especially in a disturbing scene at London Zoo. As an archetypal modern man, he is compared to one of the captive apes, Humboldt's Gibbon, an image which combines a fearsome, predatory animalism with an implicit primitivism, reminding humanity of its Darwinian origins. Although, like Plant, Atwater remains undeveloped, he is a descendant of Corker in *Scoop* and a confidently sketched precursor to characters in the later fictions who embody the self-interested greed of the modern age, such as Hooper in *Brideshead* and Trimmer in *Sword of Honour*.

Clearly a technical experiment and drawing upon autobiographical material, *Work Suspended* remains one of Evelyn's most intriguing, if incomplete, literary ventures, tracing the destruction of a formerly ordered society by materialistic philistines. It also survives in two distinct forms since the more openly self-reflective version published in the 1942 limited edition was extensively revised for its reprinting in *Work Suspended and Other Stories* (UK edition, 1948/9; US, published as *Tactical Exercise*, 1954), recasting it as more of an allusive contemporary allegory. Hence, the first chapter, 'Death', simultaneously represents both the end of the unhappy period of Evelyn's life following his separation from She-Evelyn and, more broadly, the demise of England's traditional social and artistic standards. Similarly, the second, 'A Birth', draws upon his happier and more stable existence with Laura and the inexorable rise of the detested 'common man' within an egalitarian new society.[18]

Life for Alec also proved challenging during the 1930s. In mid-April 1930 he spent five days in France with Evelyn before heading off on a trip to the US, with each brother conscious that they were now choosing very different literary and personal roads. Despite a complicated personal life, he remained a diligently productive writer, publishing numerous long-forgotten works such as *Most Women* (1931a), short stories compiled as a companion to *Hot Countries*; *So Lover's Dream* (1931b), with a novelist hero, based upon one of his own many affairs; and *Leap Before You Look* (1932a), a novella about an impoverished young man postponing his marriage. He also wrote *No Quarter* (1932b), a history of piracy from the 1630s to the 1930s in novel form; *Thirteen Such Years* (1932c), sketches of England between 1918 and 1931; *Eight Short Stories* (1937) and three more novels, *Wheels Within Wheels* (1933), *Jill Somerset* (1936) and, as his thirty-first book, *Going Their Own Ways* (1938).

Alec's most important novel from the 1930s – containing plot and thematic elements later imitated by Evelyn – is his substantial Galsworthian saga, *The Balliols* (1934), tracing three generations of the same family. The novel's epigraph, Nietzsche's 'To build a sanctuary you must destroy a sanctuary', confirms its preoccupation with generational differences and social progress, especially the rise of the suffragette movement which figures prominently in its narrative. It commences in 1907 with Edward, a wine-merchant, planning to build in North End Road, Hampstead, a new house, Ilex, based on the Waugh family home at Underhill. The poignant death of his father marks the passing of an age and provides a precursor to the demise of Lord Marchmain in *Brideshead*.

> In the large four-poster bed in which he had been born, old Balliol lay looking with undimmed eyes through the half open window towards the curving hills which had been through so many years the first object on which his waking eyes had rested. He was dying, and he knew it. Each breath he took so shook his frame that the high canopy of the bed trembled. (51)

Edward has two sons, Hugh (whom he prefers and, like Alec, serves in World War I) and Francis (like Evelyn, overlooked by his parents). Their public school Fernhurst (echoing Sherborne), is recycled from *The Loom of Youth*; and its grand country residence, Tavenham, echoes Evelyn's fascination with idealized great houses. The novel takes as its central theme an awareness of the importance of the 'tradition and dignity of English life' (247), especially when engendered by the social and international conflicts of the first two decades of the twentieth century. It proposes how in 1916 both the war and, more deeply, the English national psyche had been starkly divided:

> the war may be divided into two halves; up to the Somme and after the Somme. It was a different war after the Somme; it was fought in a

different spirit by different men . . . The post-Somme armies went to the front in a different mood. Though the young ones most of them had been fretting till they had passed the age test, they had come not of their own free wills: there was an atmosphere of coercion.

In terms which might equally be applied to the transition in Guy Crouchback's understanding of the dispiriting progress of World War II in *Sword of Honour*, Alec concluded of the post-1916 wartime period: 'The crusade spirit had been exchanged for a spirit of distrust' (381). *The Balliols* warns that relentlessly modernizing 'progress' driven by an opportunistic new proletariat will inexorably lead to the destruction of traditional social values. Alec concludes this huge novel of 520 pages with the demolition of their family home, Ilex, to make way for an ugly block of flats – just as John Plant's family house in Evelyn's *Work Suspended* (1941/2) and Marchmain House in *Brideshead* (1945) eventually suffer the same fate.

As Evelyn's fame soared during the 1930s, so Alec's reputation steadily declined. Although he always generously acknowledged his younger brother's literary genius, Alec became more convinced of his own irredeemable mediocrity. His advantageous second marriage in 1932 to Joan Churnside embarrassed him since he feared that he would become a kept man living off her considerable wealth. Although their marriage supposedly lasted until her death in 1969 (even though he had obtained a secret, but legally dubious, divorce at Reno after being granted US citizenship), Alec was repeatedly unfaithful. At the outbreak of war he rejoined the Dorset regiment as a lieutenant in the Regular Army Reserve of Officers (RARO) and was evacuated from Boulogne in May 1940 with other members of the British Expeditionary Force (BEF). He was also enmeshed in an unrewarding affair with a much younger admiral's daughter, Joan Duff, prompting his wife's return in July to her native Australia with their children. His next work, an indifferent novel, *No Truce With Time* (1941), was drafted while working back home for the Petroleum Warfare Department. It was loyally praised by Arthur and its serial rights were purchased for $5,000 by the magazine *Redbook* and its film rights by MGM. But it attracted little critical attention and only served to consolidate Alec's fears that he was outmoded as a popular writer.[19]

Crete and *Put Out More Flags*

On 3 September 1939, when Chamberlain declared war, Evelyn advertised Piers Court in *The Times* as available to rent by a 'civilized tenant' for the duration. A tenancy was agreed with some teaching Dominican nuns and the Waughs moved back to Laura's family home, Pixton Hall, now also housing child evacuees and their helpers. Evelyn first made unsuccessful attempts to find employment at the Ministry of Information (run by

Duff Cooper) and the Foreign Office. He then decided to enlist as a soldier, both through a sense of national duty and because he feared that an office job would stultify his literary creativity, noting in his diary that a 'complete change of habit' would stimulate him as a writer. After numerous rebuffs, he gained in late-November 1939 an unexpected (for a short, plump, myopic thirty-six-year old) commission in the Royal Marines Infantry. This posting was gained largely through the support of no less a personage than Winston Churchill, First Lord of the Admiralty, who had been lobbying on his behalf after Evelyn had visited his private secretary, Brendan Bracken (the model for Rex Mottram in *Brideshead*). On 17 November Laura gave birth to their first son, Auberon Alexander, and Evelyn received his call-up papers, instructing him to report to the Royal Navy base at Chatham Barracks on 7 December 1939 to begin basic training.[20]

After moving around various training camps during the first half of 1940, Evelyn was promoted in May to the rank of captain (Churchill became Prime Minister on 10 May), although his naturally subversive instincts made him an unlikely officer. Notoriously, he once asked a visiting senior officer if it was true that no one beneath the rank of major was allowed to wear lipstick in the Romanian army and from 1944 onwards he insisted on always referring to Marshal Tito as a woman. During the summer, again with Bracken's support, Evelyn applied to join the newly formed 8 Commando, founded after Dunkirk for raiding parties into occupied France, under the command of Brigadier (later Lieutenant-Colonel) Robert Laycock.

In the meantime, his brigade was moved to Scapa Flow in the Orkneys, with Evelyn now acting as its intelligence officer, before departure for Freetown in Sierra Leone, where Graham Greene was also posted at New Year 1942. On 23 September 1940 his ship, the *Ettrick*, joined an Anglo-French naval force supporting General De Gaulle's unsuccessful Free French landing at an unexpectedly heavily defended Dakar in Senegal, four hundred miles north of Freetown. On 5 October the *Ettrick* sailed for Gibraltar where Evelyn met Father Gilbey who had assisted at his marriage to Laura. Laycock then offered him a posting as a lieutenant in the Commandos. Cheered by this news, he considered reviving his temporarily dormant writing career with a pleasurable excursion into a kind of 'modern Arcadia' (*Brideshead*). But 1940 ended on an unexpectedly tragic note when on 1 December Laura gave birth to another child, Mary, who lived only for twenty-four hours.[21]

In early February 1941 8 Commando, then stationed at Largs and drawn largely from the Guards and the aristocracy, left Scotland on the *Glenroy* for Egypt with Evelyn sharing a cabin with Henry Lord Stavordale (later Earl of Ilchester) and Churchill's riotous son, Randolph, who was then also MP for Preston (1940–45). They reached Suez on 8 March, where they resumed commando training, interspersed with brief periods of leave spent at Cairo, the Allies' headquarters in the Middle East. At first they had little to do since their planned participation in the capture of Rhodes had fallen through. But, finally, after a move to Alexandria on 19 April they undertook a botched raid on Bardia near Tobruk in Libya. Evelyn acted as a non-combatant timekeeper but later described the mission in heroic terms in a propaganda article, 'Commando Raid on Bardia' (*Life*, November 1941), the first such account to be published of a commando covert action.

More time-wasting followed until 22 May when orders arrived for 8 Commando to head for Crete, a British base since October 1940 but now under threat from the Axis powers after they had overrun Greece and Yugoslavia. A sustained aerial bombardment had already reduced the Allied forces to chaos and by the time the commandos arrived on 26 May the situation was untenable. Troops were being evacuated via the port of Sphakia, with the commandos acting as a rear-guard and Evelyn appointed as Laycock's liaison officer. It was never going to be possible to take all the Allied troops off the island and many of the officers and soldiers, including the commandos' own Lieutenant-Colonel Felix Colvin (found cowering under a table during a stuka raid) were suffering from shell-shock. Ignoring orders to stay until the completion of the Allied evacuation, Laycock led a section of his unit (including Evelyn) into a small motor boat and then a destroyer, arriving back at Alexandria on 1 June. This ignominious action, abandoning to capture most of the Royal Marines, two battalions of Australians and almost three-quarters of his commando colleagues, weighed heavily on Evelyn. No. 8 Commando was temporarily disbanded and he disconsolately returned to the Royal Marines. Although never free to describe exactly what had happened, this betrayal of his colleagues swept away his previous military idealism, leaving a lasting cynicism over the war. The chaos, shame and dishonour experienced on Crete haunted his later fictions (especially *Officers and Gentlemen*, with its self-serving Ivor Claire and the terrified Major 'Fido' Hound).[22]

Evelyn's troop-ship, the *Duchess of Richmond*, left Alexandria on 12 July and, sailing via Cape Town, Trinidad and Iceland to avoid U-boats, arrived back in Liverpool on 3 September 1941. After a fortnight's leave, he was posted to Hayling Island, near Portsmouth, with 12th Battalion Land Defence Force. He had been busy on the long sea-voyage home, drafting most of *Put Out More Flags*, evocatively capturing the shifts in the nation's spirits during the early phase of the war. It was completed by 26 September and, despite his despair over Crete, loyally dedicated to Laycock. Published in March 1942 and selling some 18,000 copies in hardback as a Book Society selection, the zany characters and lively observational comedy of the novel's first half are gradually displaced by a more sombre tone. It offers an elegiac lament for a lost world as its once bright young things – an aging 'race of ghosts' (7) and the 'wreckage of the roaring twenties' (36), including Peter Pastmaster, Margot Metroland, Basil Seal, the Trumpingtons and Ambrose Silk (a precursor for Anthony Blanche in *Brideshead*) – find themselves adrift in a defeatist and chaotic world.

The novel is set in the Phoney War, days of 'surmise and apprehension', during the weeks between Chamberlain's declaration of war and the

disastrous Norwegian campaign of spring 1940 which led to his replacement
by Churchill. The novel has four sections named after the seasons and its
first chapter, 'Autumn', opens with a luscious description of Malfrey, the
Edenic home of Basil Seal's sister, Barbara Sothill:

> There was something female and voluptuous in the beauty of Malfrey . . .
> it had been built more than two hundred years ago in days of victory and
> ostentation and lay, spread out, sumptuously at ease, splendid, defenceless
> and provocative; a Cleopatra among houses. (9)

But standing for English traditional values in this imperilled paradise, Malfrey
is insidiously threatened with external conquest and annihilation. The local
village, half a mile away down a graceful avenue of limes, evokes an image
of idyllic rural tranquillity, with its church, two inns, vicarage and cottages
clustered around a green shaded by three ancient chestnuts. Bewildered and
exhausted evacuees arrive from Birmingham, Barbara's husband Freddy is
already in uniform and Malfrey's domestics are departing to join the war
effort. Only Barbara's brother Basil, now thirty-six (the same age as Evelyn
when he joined the Marines), has no desire to fight, even though his sister
fondly imagines him as an heroic figure from the World War I like Siegfried
Sassoon, T. E. Lawrence or Rupert Brooke.

Similarly, in London the well-connected Lady Seal, who personally knows
the Chamberlain brothers and ardently despises Hitler and Ribbentrop,
sadly recalls the horrendous casualties of World War I. She is consoled by
her belief in Britain's traditional strengths being marshalled to oppose the
forces of evil. Her spirits are raised by the memory of past triumphs, 'Crécy,
Agincourt, Cadiz, Blenheim, Gibraltar, Inkerman, Ypres', viewing these great
English victories as evidence of 'divine rectitude' (19). She is also hopeful
that the war will prove the making of her black-sheep son, Basil, and she
instructs her old friend, Sir Joseph Mainwaring, to arrange a commission for
him. But, instead, the racketeer inside Basil is awakened and he regards the
war as an opportunist's paradise, telling Alastair Trumpington that he wants
to be like those calculating opportunists who in 1919 were admired for
'doing well' out of the first war. Unfortunately, his exploitative skills require
a peacefully vulnerable society in which to operate most effectively. For the
first time, Basil feels at a disadvantage in this chaotic new world which now
externally reflects his own innate sense of disorder.

Other characters are equally disconcerted by the social disruptions of
wartime England. Basil's friend, Ambrose Silk, 'a cosmopolitan, Jewish
pansy' (73), visits the bureaucratic Ministry of Information where his
former publisher, Geoffrey Bentley, ludicrously fixes him up with a post
in their religious department since atheism is not currently represented
there. Another disturbed lifestyle is that of Alastair Trumpington, one of
the privileged, self-indulgent figures from *Decline and Fall*. He joins up as
a private soldier, regarding military service as a penance or 'whatever it's

called that religious people' (106) are supposed to do. Similarly, Cedric Lyne (a precursor to Charles Ryder and Guy Crouchback), the aesthete husband of Basil's mistress, Angela, lays aside his arcane fascination with continental grottoes and enters the forces while his faithless wife begins her solitary slide into hopeless alcoholism.

The second chapter, 'Winter', marks the novel's stark transition into the harsh realities of war, symbolized by the closing up for the duration of parts of Malfrey. Basil returns there to keep his sister company and, reduced to the ignominy of writing for a living, begins drafting a spurious book on his plans to annex Liberia. Fortunately, she is the area billeting-officer for evacuees and Basil comes up a devious plan to extort money from their wealthier neighbours by threatening to billet on them the three terrifyingly awful Connolly children from the slums of Birmingham. First encountered in Malfrey Parish Hall with 'one leering, one lowering, and one drooling, as unprepossessing a family as could be found in the kingdom' (81), the Connollys are led by the precociously pubescent Doris, her brother Mickey and their imbecile sister Marlene. Basil makes a decent return on his racket until Freddy returns home and he has to sell on the Connollys to the billeting officer in the adjoining neighbourhood.

No less farcical is Ambrose Silk's role in the religious department of the Ministry of Information. His office is shared with a fanatical Roman Catholic layman earnestly exposing discrepancies between *Mein Kampf* and the encyclical *Quadragesimo Anno*, a Non-conformist minister and an Anglican clergyman. Ambrose's task is to demonstrate to Allied atheists that Nazism is essentially a corrupt form of agnosticism, tinged with religious superstition. He diligently counts how many times Hitler used the word 'God' in his speeches and drafts articles on the religious origins of Nazi anti-Semitism. He is also required to collect newspaper clippings about Storm Troopers attending a Requiem Mass in Salzburg for republication in the *Atheist Advertizer* and *Godless Sunday at Home*. As he labours over these deranged tasks, his mind seeks a transcendental flight from the chaotic turmoil of war into a fantasy world of biblical manuscript illumination:

> his thoughts began to soar lark-like into a tempera, fourteenth-century sky; into a heaven of flat, blank, blue and white clouds cross-hatched with gold leaf on their sunward edges; a vast altitude painted with shaving soap on a panel of lapis lazuli; he stood on a high, sugary pinnacle, on a new Tower of Babel; like a muezzin calling his message to a world of domes and clouds; beneath him, between him and the absurd little figures bobbing and bending on their striped praying mats, lay fathoms of clear air where doves sported with the butterflies. (113)

In the third chapter, 'Spring', Freddy returns to Malfrey and sets up camp for his unit in the Park with the officers' mess lucratively located in the Grinling Gibbons saloon. Back in London, Basil joins the Supplementary reserve at his mother's insistence and bluffs his way into the War Office where the ADDIS (Assistant Deputy Director Internal Security), Colonel Plum, turns out to be a former acquaintance from his sham-journalism days in Jibuti and Prague. Basil is recruited for intelligence work watching communists and given the rank of Second-Lieutenant in the 'Crosse and Blackwell' regiment, with the promise of a captaincy in the Marines if he catches a Fascist. Meanwhile, a madman who surreptitiously accompanies him into the building blows up the Deputy Assistant Chaplain General in Ambrose Silk's office. Cedric Lyne also re-joins his regiment and, like Evelyn, is made battalion intelligence officer, attends gas and aerial photography courses, and supervises a chaotic embarkation of his regiment onto the *Duchess of Cumberland*.

Ambrose Silk sets up a literary review, *Ivory Tower*, and writes the entire first issue under various pseudonyms, unwisely including an artistic account of his love-affair with a young German boy, Hans, at Munich in 1936. Basil steals a copy of its proofs from Ambrose's office and deviously persuades him to turn his story into what appears to be Nazi-propaganda for the Hitler Youth. He then presents it to Colonel Plum, reminding him of his promise to make him a captain in the Marines if he caught a Fascist, who in turn hands the 'evidence' over to Scotland Yard. Angry that Plum seems to be taking the credit for his 'discovery' and (as the ramifications of his trickery turn more serious) mildly concerned for Ambrose's safety, Basil visits his Bloomsbury Flat and provides his Jewish friend with the disguise of an Irish Jesuit, Father Flanagan, along with his passport which he had stolen from the Ministry of Information.

Ambrose is packed off to Euston Station on route to Ireland now, paradoxically, a Wandering Jew in the guise of a Wandering Jesuit. Basil offers to look after his flat, thereby providing himself with a convenient base for the seduction of Susie, an alluring lance-corporal in Plum's office. With Ambrose hidden in a quiet Irish village where his fastidious ways lead his landlord to suspect that he is a 'spoilt priest' (203), his former boss at the Ministry of Information, Mr Rumpole, is deemed to be the leader of his fascist cell. Recalling Paul Pennyfeather's undeserved incarceration in *Decline and Fall* and that novel's comic resolution through black farce, he is arrested and imprisoned at Brixton Gaol. Locked up in his cell, Rumpole discovers the pleasures of reading since he had always been the kind of publisher who hated all writers and their books. Contentedly working his way through the dire novels of one of his own authors, a Mrs Parker (alias Ruth Mountdragon), he finally attains true contentment. Meanwhile, comfortably ensconced in Ambrose's flat, Basil instructs Susie to unpick the monogrammed 'A's from his clothing and to substitute 'B's. In contrast and far away in Norway, Cedric Lyne is thriving on the thrill of danger, only to be killed instantly by a stray bullet as he carries a message to another company. When his widow, Angela, offers to marry Basil and, thereby, make him very wealthy, he hesitates, offering an apt snippet of self-knowledge by admitted that he only cares for the entertaining side of obtaining money rather than actually possessing it.

In the novel's brief epilogue, 'Summer', the foolish optimism of Sir Joseph Mainwaring satirizes the deluded sense of pacifist hope which still prevailed in some circles. Undeterred by Dunkirk and the fall of France, he is hopeful that Italy will soon sign a peace treaty with England and insists that the war is now entering a new and 'more glorious phase' (213). Alastair's battalion finds itself immersed in frenetic preparations for active engagement but ends up merely stationed in a former holiday camp for coastal defence work. Seeking excitement and a genuine commitment to the war effort, he volunteers, like Evelyn, for a newly formed commando unit which Peter Pastmaster is setting up. Basil also joins this elite gang of desperadoes, like Evelyn, as its liaison officer and in the hope of killing some Germans. *Put Out More Flags* concludes with Mainwaring's jingoistic delight in a 'new spirit abroad' – qualified by the ominous authorial comment: 'And, poor booby, he was bang right' (222).

Although this new novel offered a productive blending of Evelyn's well-honed satiric skills with a more explicit commentary on the anarchy engendered by war, it remains a problematic work to define generically. It adopts an omniscient narrator, enabling the reader to eavesdrop on private thoughts, and utilizes long interior monologues (as developed in the still unpublished *Work Suspended*), including for the first time those of a woman, Angela. But it also experiments with an impressionistic, 'point of view' style of delivery, even though the novel lacks any unifying sense of a central hero figure as its action (and its reflections of Evelyn's own experiences) constantly shift around Basil, Ambrose, Cedric and Angela. Nor does it offer any unifying moral or spiritual perspectives as it seemingly attacks 'everything' but defends 'nothing'.[23]

Disillusionment, drafting *Brideshead* and Croatia

The Waugh family met together for the last time on 4 October 1941 just before Alec's posting to Syria as an intelligence officer working for General Spears and liaising with MI5. Arthur was by then in poor health and Alec remained despondent over his wife's return to Australia since he had not seen his children for eighteen months. His increasingly unsatisfactory affair with Joan Duff led to him moving out of a comfortable flat (where Joan also lived) above the offices of A. D. Peters, into a depressing *pied-à-terre* near Great Portland Street Station. While in Syria, he penned a desultory memoir, *His Second War* (1944), which his publisher, Cassell, at first declined because of paper shortages. Terrified that his literary career would collapse if this work did not reach print, Alec persuaded them to reverse their decision – but hostile reviews soon made him regret its publication.[24]

Meanwhile, at Hayling Island Evelyn was also unhappy with his mundane military posting and was overjoyed when on 28 October, his thirty-eighth birthday, he was granted a transfer to 5 Royal Marines at Hawick. Once there, he continued to have run-ins with his new commanding officer but at least enjoyed in January 1942 his company commander's course at Edinburgh when he discovered that it was held in a mansion, Bonaly Tower, modelled on Walter Scott's house at Abbotsford by Evelyn's great-great-grandfather, Lord Cockburn. His prominence as a novelist, revitalized by *Put Out More Flags*, also elicited an invitation to appear on the BBC's 'Any Questions?' panel programme.

In May 1942 Colonel Laycock offered him a posting at Special Service Brigade headquarters, requiring him temporarily to join the elite Royal Horse Guards (the Blues) so that he could then be transferred to No. 8 Commando at Ardrossan, near Glasgow. In June he was sent on a five-week air photographic training course at Matlock, Derbyshire, which enabled him to spend some time with Laura who on 10 June had given birth to their fourth child, Margaret. In September Laycock's HQ was moved to Sherborne, Dorset, where Laura was also able to stay with him and which facilitated frequent visits to London. But the next two years proved a period of constant frustrations and boredom, despite the war turning the way of the Allies after El Alamein in November 1942. Evelyn had no part to play in these stirring events and his reattachment to the Commandos brought not exciting action but the tedium of administrative work, mainly in London. His awkward personality irritated both his fellow officers and the ranks and by March 1943 even the loyal Laycock advised him that he was generally unpopular.

Nevertheless, Evelyn was still named as Laycock's liaison officer in the following April but, when in late-June his brigade left camp for North Africa in the advance party (HUSKY) for the invasion of Italy (via Sicily), he was left behind. Arthur, aged seventy-six, died on 26 June and Laycock insisted (probably with relief) that Evelyn should take compassionate leave. Lord Lovat, the deputy brigade commander, despised his sybaritic lifestyle and added to his humiliations by ordering him to Achnacarry, Scotland, for basic training with new recruits to RM Commando. An outraged appeal to Lovat's superior, General Haydon, merely resulted in Evelyn's sacking from the Special Service Brigade and even a personal approach to Lord Louis Mountbatten (Chief of Combined Operations) did not lead to any new army openings. He was posted back to the Royal Horse Guards and sent on to the Household Cavalry Training Unit at Windsor. In his diary, Evelyn recorded that he now disliked the army and needed no more 'experiences in life' to become once again a serious and productive writer: 'I simply want to do my work as an artist'. As Martin Stannard notes, here we finally see the 'cenobitic aesthete, the ungentle priest-craftsman, cured of chivalry and waiting for the moment to write his great, reflective work'.[25]

Yet again, Laycock came to his aid when David Stirling, the founder of the Special Air Service (SAS) Regiment, was captured in North Africa.

His brother, Bill, was attempting to reform his disbanded unit into a small brigade under the overall command of Laycock. Evelyn was invited to join Stirling's battalion, with the special brief of compiling a convincing written case for an enlarged SAS regiment. As part of his SAS induction, he attended in November 1943 a Special Operations Executive (SOE) parachute training course. Although he found parachuting exhilarating, he cracked his fibula on his second jump and had to spend the next weeks in plaster recuperating.

By late-1943 he was planning *Brideshead Revisited* (then 'The Household of Faith') and in January 1944 he successfully requested three months leave without pay to draft the novel. The war was now approaching a key period, with Allied forces landing at Anzio on 22 January and plans for the Normandy landing well advanced. Evelyn hoped for a more active role later that year. He retired to a favoured writing location, Easton Court Hotel at Chagford, Devon, and made excellent progress, convinced that his creative imagination and literary skills were finally amounting to something of significance in a heavily autobiographical first-person narrative. But in late-February he was called back to Windsor to become ADC to Major-General Ivor Thomas. Fortunately, Thomas rejected him outright but another general, Miles Graham, was found who did not object to his reputation and immediately granted him a further six weeks' leave. He was summoned back again to Windsor in early April but found that there was little for him to do and so appealed directly to Laycock for some additional time to finish the novel before returning to Chagford. Once again recalled to Windsor, he was given the stark choice of servicing as a welfare officer in a transit camp in India or as an assistant hospital registrar. Fortunately, Laycock then arranged for him to be readmitted to No. 2 SAS and Bill Stirling obligingly granted him yet another six weeks' leave. Evelyn's fifth child, Harriet, was born on 13 May 1944 and Stirling's successor, Colonel Brian Franks, granted him yet further leave. The novel was completed on 8 June, with a final decision made to revise Charles Fenwick's name to Charles Ryder and that of Bridget to Cordelia. One copy was sent to Chapman and Hall on 20 June 1944 and another to Father D'Arcy for him to verify the various aspects of Catholicism incorporated into the novel. Father Knox had previously checked his description of the Marchmain's private chapel and Lady Marchmain's Requiem Mass.[26]

No longer wanted by the SAS at their base at Ardchullery, Evelyn was delighted to be invited by Randolph Churchill to join his mission to Croatia, commanded by Brigadier Fitzroy Maclean, to act as a liaison between the British and the Yugoslavian resistance. Randolph also briefed him on the clashes in the local area between the Roman Catholic and Orthodox communities. After the Germans and Italians had overwhelmed the country in 1941, the British had been covertly supporting the resistance movement which was then split between two groupings: the Chetnicks (led by Marshal Mihailović who supported their titular King Peter II, then serving as an RAF officer in England) and the Partisans under Marshal Tito. It seemed to

Maclean that the Partisans were the more successful grouping, even though
Tito was a communist and seemed more sympathetic to Russia than to
Britain and America.

Evelyn and Randolph Churchill, who together made a brave but often
anarchic pairing, flew out to Gibraltar on 4 July 1944 and then crossed to
Algiers where they stayed with the Coopers, since Duff was then British
representative to General de Gaulle's Committee of National Liberation.
Soon, they headed off to Bari, rear HQ of the British Military Mission
(Macmis), and from there to the British garrison on the island of Vis.
Despite Evelyn's running joke that Tito was a woman (sustained even in
the Marshal's presence), he and Randolph continued to participate in the
operation. They returned to Bari to catch their Dakota transporter flight
into Croatia on the evening of 16 July. As they approached their destination
in total darkness, the plane crashed with two of the nineteen on board killed
and Evelyn severely burnt on his hands, legs and head. He was evacuated
to Algiers and then in August left for Rome where he stayed in a flat on the
Via Gregoriana.

At the end of August Evelyn left Rome with Randolph and they drove
to Naples from where they caught a flight to Corsica. From here they were
finally able to fly to their original intended destination in Yugoslavia on
the outskirts of Topusko (Begoy in *Unconditional Surrender*), a small spa
town which served as Tito's Croatian headquarters and a crucial point in
the Balkans escape route for Allied prisoners of war. Their duties as liaison
officers, with Evelyn as Randolph's second-in-command, were far from
demanding. Consequently, he suffered intensely from both boredom and
the boorish presence of Randolph. The situation was not improved by the
arrival on 13 October of Major Freddy Birkenhead for whom Randolph
had fagged at Eton. They eventually laid a wager with Randolph that he
couldn't read the entire Bible in a fortnight but even this ploy didn't silence
him, leading instead to his expostulation as he ploughed through the Old
Testament: 'My God, what a shit God is'.[27]

The proofs of Brideshead arrived by parachute drop on 20 November
and were checked during the following week before being returned to
his publishers via Downing Street. For Christmas Evelyn ordered fifty
paper-covered copies of the novel to distribute as presents to family and
Catholic friends. On 6 December he travelled to Bari from where he moved
on to Dubrovnik (Ragusa) on 19 December, the base of a new Combined
Operations brigade (Floydforce). He was again to act as a liaison officer
between the English forces and the Partisans. Evelyn held little sympathy
for Tito and his communist-leaning Partisans (who were now in league with
the Russians) and was more concerned over the reported persecution of
Roman Catholics in Croatia. While Tito disingenuously professed to support
religious toleration, contributors to *The Tablet* were more sceptical. In mid-
1944 the British delegation to the Vatican received leaked reports of Partisan
atrocities among the non-communist Slovenians, including the murder of

twenty-seven priests and the desecration of seventy churches. These reports were bravely publicized in *The Tablet* (15 July 1944) in an attempt to disseminate Catholic concerns over the Partisans' anti-clericalism.

With permission from Fitroy Maclean, Evelyn conducted interviews with the local bishop and parish priests. He even flew to Rome in February 1945 for an audience with Pope Pius XII to discuss the Croatian situation. Although he failed to unearth clear evidence of church and clerical suppression comparable to that seen earlier in Mexico, he completed in March a controversial 7,500-word report, 'Church and State in Liberated Croatia' (1944). It argued that the Catholic Church would be under grave danger in a communist state and warned of their systematic plan to exterminate Christianity. He quietly ignored suspicions that some members of the Franciscan and Dominican orders had been active in anti-communist terrorist organizations and concluded that Britain was tacitly supporting the suppression of freedom of faith in a region with some five million Catholics. Evelyn returned to London on 15 March and found that the pragmatic political priority was to foster continuing good relations with Tito. His report was ruthlessly repressed under the Official Secrets Act to which he was bound as a serving officer. Although he wrote two angry letters to *The Times* denouncing Tito and also spoke against his regime at Oxford, Cambridge and London universities there was little else he could do. Despondently, he concluded that his personal contribution to both the war effort and Catholics in Yugoslavia had ultimately been of little significance.[28]

4

The acclaimed author: 1945–50

'Et in Arcadia ego'

The earliest reference to the literary conception of *Brideshead Revisited: the Sacred and Profane Memories of Captain Charles Ryder* (1945), dates from November 1940 when Evelyn told Laura that he might soon begin a book purely for his own pleasure about a 'kind of modern Arcadia'.[1] This dense and spiritually complex work was to become his eighth and first explicitly Catholic novel. The first of its three books is titled, 'Et in Arcadia Ego' ('I too in Arcadia'), a phrase derived from a pastoral painting by Nicolas Poussin (1594–1665). Arcadia had been imagined from the time of Virgil's *Eclogues* as a Greek rural paradise in which carefree innocence and contentment prevails. But Poussin's darker interpretation presents an Arcadian group of three shepherds and one female figure discovering a tomb bearing the carved motto, '*Et in Arcadia ego*', referring to both its dead incumbent and the now-realized presence of Death among them. Poussin painted two versions of this picture, the best known in 1655 ('*Les bergers d'Arcadie*', Louvre) and an earlier, more explicit version in 1627. In this first exposition, a skull is visible above the tomb, recalling a 1622 painting (Galleria Nazionale d'Arte Antica, Rome) by Il Guercino, in which two shepherds gaze upon a large skull placed in the forefront of the picture on a stone pedestal bearing the identical motto. This image is echoed by Ryder's morbid purchase from the Oxford Medical School of a human skull, on the forehead of which he inscribes '*Et in Arcadia ego*' (43).

Evelyn had visited the Louvre at Christmas 1925 and viewed its Poussins (including his other masterpiece, '*Dance to the Music of Time*'); and the earlier version of Poussin's '*Les bergers d'Arcadie*' was at Chatsworth, the seat of the Duke and Duchess of Devonshire, which he had visited in late-1932 with Diana Cooper.[2] The potent imagery of one or both of these versions may have lingered in his mind as an encapsulation of the four insistent dualities – innocence and experience, love and loss, life and death, sin and redemption – which haunt the narratives of *Brideshead*. Its composition sets up an ironic contrast between the hitherto joyously contented life of the figures discovering the tomb and the ominous shadow of mortality and death which henceforth hangs over them through this *memento mori*. Their growing understanding of its meaning leads them (and Charles Ryder) from an enviable state of childlike innocence to the mature, tragic world of transience and loss.[3] Significantly, Evelyn began drafting the novel soon after the death of his own father, Arthur, and the phrase, '*Et in Arcadia ego*', clearly had a profound meaning for him:

> the novel is both panegyric and valediction, inspired by a yearning for a lost arcadia; inspired also by Evelyn's romantic veneration for the aristocracy, for the past, and for English Catholicism, a Catholicism that had survived centuries of persecution, sheltered and nurtured by the great recusant families.[4]

The novel's valedictory panegyric for a more secure but now lost English society implicitly reiterates his preoccupation from the mid-1940s with the essential meaninglessness of daily life without religious belief.

Waugh envisaged the central purpose of *Brideshead* as an exploration of the workings of 'divine grace' (7), narrated through Ryder's fascination with the aristocratic but dysfunctional Flytes. He explained on the UK dust-jacket that his purpose in the novel had been to trace the processes of 'divine purpose' in a 'pagan world' within a Catholic English family who had become 'half paganised themselves' between 1923 and 1939. Its narrative also echoes key elements of Evelyn's earlier life. Ryder's intense relationship with Sebastian hints at Evelyn's youthful passion for the fascinating but drunken Alastair Graham (whose name sometimes replaces Sebastian's in the manuscript). Similarly, shifting (like Evelyn) during his twenties from homosexual to heterosexual love, Ryder's later marriage to the shallow and unfaithful Celia Mulcaster echoes elements of Evelyn's unhappy first marriage to She-Evelyn. Ultimately, his devotional love for the Catholic Julia Flyte facilitates Ryder's own conversion, just as Evelyn's spiritual journey had drawn him into the Catholic Church of Laura Herbert's family. It finally leads him into an understanding of the simple profundity that to love another person is the 'root of all wisdom' (46). Martin Stannard explains:

> *Brideshead* was to be a lament in the waste land but it was also to be a statement of faith. The end of Ryder's story is its beginning: the Epilogue confirms that he has become a Catholic and the whole focus of his sceptical, controlling voice is shifted from the secular to the theological, eating its tail, demanding a re-reading in the light of this revelation. By this simple fictional device, Waugh created a double focus in the narrative ... it concerned the double focus of Catholic life in which the supernatural was the real and the material world an illusion.[5]

The narrative of *Brideshead* is tinged by a melancholy tone of loss and disillusionment, especially in relation to Ryder's (and, implicitly, Evelyn's) army service. The Prologue begins in 1942 with 'C' Company and Ryder (like Evelyn, aged thirty-nine) about to leave the desolate Pollock Camp near Glasgow (recalling Evelyn's dismal time there) for Brideshead. Ryder acknowledges that his love for the army has now withered and died. Modern man is represented within his regiment by an unsympathetic colonel and Hooper, a cheerfully casual subaltern who epitomizes for Ryder the hopeless future of English youth. Ironically, the camp is located next to a lunatic asylum and its deranged inmates are viewed as the 'undisputed heirs-in-law' (10) of social progress. The thought insistently plagues Ryder's mind that something inside him has sickened and 'quietly died' (11). But as his convoy approaches the winding valley of the Bride, a tributary of the Avon, he again recognizes its familiar landscapes with its great house nestling among lime trees. He quietly comments to the uninterested Hooper that he had been there before as the scene is set for book one, 'Et in Arcadia Ego'.

While *Brideshead* brilliantly recreates the lost world of 1920s Oxford, Evelyn's autobiographical reminiscences tend to be eclectic and composite rather than focused on individuals. Although Sebastian recalls Alastair Graham, memories of another purposeless Oxford friend, Hugh Lygon, also contribute to the fictional Sebastian. Some minor characters may equate primarily to a single individual, such as the unctuous Mr Samgrass of All Souls who echoes a renowned Oxford don, Maurice Bowra. But the depraved aesthete, Anthony Blanche, is an inventive amalgam of two-thirds Brian Howard and one-third Harold Acton (who, like Blanche, recited *The Waste Land* from a balcony at Christ Church). Blanche had reputedly known Proust, Gide, Cocteau, Diaghilev and Firbank and is also the first to recognize Ryder's true artistry, extolling his ability to draw like the young Ingres.

The novel's dominant concern remains its all-pervading fascination with Catholicism and its practices. Newly arrived at Oxford, Ryder's pompous cousin, Jasper, warns him of Anglo-Catholics, whom he dismisses as sodomites with low-class accents. When he first visits Brideshead, Ryder is taken to meet the Flytes' long-retired Nanny Hawkins whom he finds asleep, seated at an open window with rosary beads in her hands and a picture of the Sacred Heart over the mantelpiece. The house chapel (based on the Victorian gothic chapel at Madresfield), a wedding present from Lord Marchmain to his ultra-devout bride, is decorated in the arts-and-crafts style of the late nineteenth century and remains garishly fascinating, with its prettified saints in armour and angels in printed smocks.

As with the chapel at Brideshead, the novel challenges the reader to identify in religious matters what is true and what is merely superficial or false. At Oxford one Sunday morning Ryder wonders at the confusing diversity of English churchgoing, noting how students and tradespeople alike carry with them the liturgies for divergent sects as they hurry to various local places of worship. Sebastian's elder brother, Bridey, is an observant Catholic who once wanted to become a Jesuit priest but, as Blanche notes, he is merely a 'learned bigot, a ceremonious barbarian' (54). Similarly, Lady Marchmain is a well-meaning individual whose zealous piety prevents her from divorcing her husband. But the spark of Christian kindness seems lacking in her icy and inflexible adherence to her religious faith. The thought of returning to her after his experiences during World War I became intolerable for Lord Marchmain. Instead, as the ever-astute Blanche notes, he readily handed over Brideshead and Marchmain House so that he could be free of her withering spiritual influence and live in Venice with, Cara, with whom he is comfortable rather than in love.

The difficulty of distinguishing between illusion and reality constantly permeates Ryder's relationships with the Flytes. While he finds their social set urbane and charming, Sebastian warns him that they can also be 'ravening beasts' (77), echoing the Geneva Bible's ominous gloss of Psalm 76:4 (comparing the 'kingdom full of extortion and rapine to the mountains that are full of ravening beasts'). Infatuated with Sebastian, he at first finds it difficult to differentiate him from his sister Julia, confused by an illusion of both 'familiarity and strangeness' (74). As with the quasi-incestuous relationship between Basil Seal and his sister Barbara in *Put Out More Flags*, Evelyn creates a disturbingly intimate bond between Sebastian and Julia, blending them together for Ryder in androgynous duality. This confusion is only finally resolved when his homosexual love for Sebastian is displaced by his intense awareness of Julia's sexual allure.

Along with the maturing of Ryder's sexual tastes, the fabric of Brideshead itself plays a major role in his development as an artist which, in turn, becomes a key factor in his spiritual journey. The choice of his narrator's name possessed a special significance for Evelyn since at the corner of Ryder Street and Duke Street in St James's was one of his favourite art dealers, Neumann's, a symbolic 'convergence between the aristocrat and the artist'.[6] Ryder himself regards it as an aesthetic education to visit Brideshead, wandering freely from the Soanesque library to the Chinese drawing-room and then on to the Pompeian parlour and the great hall decorated with centuries-old tapestries. The terrace, supported on massive stone ramparts, is the house's 'final consummation' (78), with its grand perspective across the estate dominated by a huge Italianate fountain brought from Naples in the early nineteenth century.[7]

Ryder's first artistic challenge at Brideshead is, at Sebastian's request, to sketch this fountain, with its sculptured rockery, fantastic animals and Egyptian obelisk. He produces a technically accomplished drawing in the style of Piranesi but knows that he is still merely a copyist. The architectural ambiance of Brideshead, a 'life-giving spring' (80), subtly converts his tastes to the visual sensuality of the baroque, stimulating in him a more profound level of aesthetic awareness. He tries his hand at an oil painting on one of the rococo panels in a small derelict office near the colonnade and produces a lush romantic landscape of an ivy-clad ruin, backed by a waterfall and framed with white clouds and blue skies. But, it merely remains a pretty pastoral without human forms – a Poussin-like landscape without a *memento mori* significance. He then attempts a second and more expansive pastoral, a *fête champêtre* or pastoral party with male and female figures. Yet again, his creativity languishes because Ryder does not as yet possess either the artistic depth or personal experience to render it truly meaningful.

Ryder's spiritual education begins in earnest after these impotent artistic endeavours when he encounters the first priest he has ever met, a monk from the local monastery, who says Mass in Brideshead chapel each Sunday. He is fascinated by the contrasts between his conventional schoolboy Anglicanism and the mysteriously profound devotions of the Flyte family. Sebastian's childish faith remains an enigma to him but he is reminded on a daily basis how his friend's familial Catholicism remains central to his sense of identity. He laments to a bemused Ryder that it is difficult to be a Catholic and quotes the Augustinian prayer: 'O God, make me good, but not yet', before admitting that he even once prayed childishly to St Anthony of Padua (the patron saint of lost items) when he had mislaid his teddy-bear, Aloysius.

When the local bishop wishes to close the chapel at Brideshead, Sebastian, Bridey and Cordelia are passionately united in their opposition to his plans. Ryder is warily drawn into a discussion of the chapel's artistic merits (which he thinks are minimal) but his hesitancy merely emphasizes his spiritual distance from the Flytes. Cordelia offers to say a decade of the rosary for him since she also regularly prays for other difficult cases such as Lloyd George and the Kaiser. Her childlike Christianity, like Sebastian's, provides a source of gentle comedy in the novel. She has a pet pig called Francis Xavier who receives her novena and she sponsors six black African children who have all been christened Cordelia in return for five shillings sent to a mission run by nuns.

Ryder's artistic, spiritual and sexual education continues when Sebastian invites him to Venice to meet his father. This plot-line was borrowed from the exile of the father of Evelyn's Lygon friends, Lord Beauchamp, who lived abroad following the exposure of his homosexuality.[8] Lord Marchmain's Palladian *palazzo* dazzles Ryder with its frescos from the school of Tintoretto and he is enraptured by the spectacular pageant on the Grand Canal below their window. His first encounter with Lord Marchmain is cast as a portrait of a patrician Renaissance cleric with a noble face: 'weary', 'sardonic' and 'voluptuous' (95). He recommends that they should limit their sight-seeing to churches to avoid the sun and, when he enquires about Ryder's artistic interests, casually exposes his ignorance that there were three Berninis.

As these Venetian days pass sweetly, Ryder remains an innocent abroad, 'drowning in honey, stingless' (97), like a simple Poussin shepherd before discovering the tomb. And yet his education relentlessly progresses. One afternoon Cara explains to him that his passionate friendship with Sebastian is a form of love indulged in by children before they understand its meaning, which does no harm if not unduly prolonged since it is merely a form of personal maturation. In England, she muses, this kind of childish intimacy seems to happen when youths are 'almost men' (98) and she notes sadly that

Lord Marchmain had experienced just this kind of adolescent passion for his wife. Cara wisely observes that Lady Marchmain is a good woman who has been loved in the 'wrong way' (99). She concludes her instruction of Ryder by observing that Sebastian is still dangerously in love with his own childhood and is running the risk of becoming an irredeemable drunk, just as his father might have become without Cara.

As Ryder begins his second year at Oxford his artistic and spiritual worlds remain undeveloped and unrewarding. Anthony Blanche (his only true guide to artistic merit) has left the university to live in Munich with a policeman and Ryder loses touch with their other friends, bonding him and Sebastian together in solitary intimacy. He joins the Ruskin School of Art where he learns to draw antique casts from the Ashmolean Museum and tries his hand at life-drawing but all of his sketches and pastiches prove 'worthless' (103). Inexorably, the Flytes absorb him further into their still puzzling world. Lady Marchmain confides in him while she works with Mr Samgrass on a panegyric biography of her brother Ned and two other younger brothers who had all died heroically during World War I. He also meets Julia's boyfriend, the opportunist Canadian Rex Mottram (based on Churchill's private secretary, Brendan Bracken), and 'Boy' Mulcaster whose sister, Celia, he later marries. At Brideshead, Catholicism seems all-pervading with Mass and Rosary said both morning and evening and Lady Marchmain overt in her desire to convert of Ryder. She engages him in earnest theological debate, suggesting that Divine Grace has the power to sanctify all aspects of human life, even her great wealth. When Ryder tactfully raises the aphorism of the camel and the eye of a needle she argues that the rich can still enter heaven and proposes that the gospel is simply a compendium of 'unexpected things', illustrating the poetic or 'Alice-in-Wonderland side' (122–3) of religious belief. In the face of such sophistical arguments, Ryder appreciates all the more how Sebastian both needs and yet feels threatened by Catholicism as he grows ever more wary of both his family and his religion.

Ryder finally realizes that, while he uses alcohol merely to enhance pleasure, Sebastian is 'sick at heart' (124) and seeks through his reckless drunkenness to escape his own conscience and family. Lady Marchmain confirms that her husband had previously behaved in an identical manner before fleeing to Venice. It dawns on Ryder, browsing through Samgrass's book on Lady Marchmain's three war-hero brothers, that a key problem for both Lord Marchmain and Sebastian lies in their inability to live up to such illustrious examples of English Catholic manhood. Ned's photograph in Grenadier uniform reveals him as an impressive 'man of the woods and caves, a hunter' (133) and her family's distinguished history seems typical of England's Catholic elite, who lived nobly sequestered lives and yet responded heroically in their country's time of need. Like Campion and his fellow Jesuits, Ned willingly sacrificed his life during World War I with the same 'high-spirited, serious, chivalrous, other-worldly air'. But, unlike the

Elizabethan Jesuit martyrs who initiated an unbroken succession of heroic Catholic priests, Ned was sacrificed like 'vermin' (134) by his callous country merely to create a brave new world for the likes of Hooper and nondescript travelling salesmen. The twentieth century's ruination of the long tradition of Catholic recusancy has created a void at the heart of both the Marchmain family and English society which cannot now be repaired by anything other than the intervention of Divine Grace.

While Lady Marchmain is staying with nuns at Oxford, Sebastian's behaviour degenerates further. She is especially troubled that he seems isolated from all other Catholic undergraduates and now hardly ever attends Mass. Unsuccessful attempts are made to make him reside at the University Chaplaincy with Monsignor Bell, followed by his departure from Oxford with his mother after being rusticated for a term. This first book of the novel, 'Et in Arcadia Ego' draws to its sombre conclusion with Ryder returning home to London. He discusses with his father whether he should also leave university to focus upon his intended career as a painter. Ever emotionally distant, Mr Ryder merely hopes that he will opt to study at art-school somewhere abroad.

Doubt and divine grace

Book two of *Brideshead* begins during the Christmas following Sebastian's departure from Oxford. He has been travelling abroad in the Near East with Mr Samgrass and Ryder (now studying art at Paris) is invited to stay with the Flytes. He continues his series of pastoral paintings in the garden-room but the three completed medallions give him little satisfaction due to the maturing of his artistry over the eighteen months since the project began. Ryder eventually leaves Brideshead in disgrace when Lady Marchmain discovers that he has given Sebastian some money which, predictably, he spends on alcohol. He feels that he is leaving behind him the alluring secular trinity of youth, adolescence and romance but also senses that he has escaped from a seductively debilitating world of transitory illusion. He gladly returns to his art studies in Paris but there seems no escape from the Flytes since Rex Mottram soon turns up in his room, having lost Sebastian on the way to a drying-out clinic in Zürich. Over dinner he informs Ryder that the Flytes are in financial difficulties and that Lady Marchmain is seriously ill but refuses proper medical advice because her 'crack-brain religion' (168) neglects the body. He also triumphantly announces his intention of marrying Julia and confirms that he is happy for her to bring up their children as Catholics, even though all spirituality seems nonsense to him.

Perversely determined to marry Rex, Julia jokes that she will be saving him from mortal sin. Despite his continuing affair with another woman, she refuses the advice of a Jesuit at Farm Street to give him up and even rejects his offer to hear her confession, attempting henceforth to close her mind against her own religion. Lady Marchmain is now grieving for Julia, Sebastian, her husband and her own sickness, with her heart pierced with the 'swords of her dolours, a living heart' (182) matching plaster statues of the Sacred Heart. Crassly impressed by the splendour of a royal wedding at Madrid, Rex determines to become a Catholic so that he can stage a similarly lavish event. His instruction by Father Mowbray at Farm Street provides a momentary glimmer of comedy as the compliant Rex seeks to agree with the priest on all points without demonstrating an inkling of natural piety. His instructor sadly concludes that Rex doesn't match any form of paganism known to missionaries. Ultimately, Bridey learns that Rex is divorced from a wife whom he married in Canada in 1915 and so the wedding has to be a muted affair under Protestant rites at the Savoy Chapel. Years later, Julia admits to Ryder that Father Mowbray had accurately defined Rex when he said that he wasn't a 'complete' person. She had hoped that he would prove a kind of 'primitive savage' but he turned out to be exactly what Evelyn hated most, a 'modern and up-to-date' man who could only have been produced by this 'ghastly age'.

Ryder returns to London from Paris during the 1926 General Strike, believing that it bodes badly for the survival of a civilized England. Like Campion and his fellow Elizabethan missionaries, he crosses the channel in a 'high-spirited, male party' (193), expecting to participate in an exhilarating social revolution. Instead, he finds that nothing much is happening and ends up at a party where he meets Blanche and 'Boy' Mulcaster. He learns of Sebastian's continuing alcoholism and his new friend Kurt, a syphilitic German ex-legionnaire, with whom he now resides in French Morocco. The strike soon fizzles out and, unexpectedly, Ryder is summoned to Marchmain House where Julia informs him that her mother is terminally ill and wishes to see Sebastian before she dies. Ryder duly travels to Fez in Morocco and is advised by Kurt that Sebastian has been taken by the Franciscans to their infirmary, where he finds him in a cubicle, gazing upon an image of the Seven Dolours, an implicit reference to his mother's sufferings. Sebastian is too ill to travel and on Ryder's last day at Fez, news arrives of Lady Marchmain's death. With the family's finances under growing pressure, her requiem becomes the last Mass said in the chapel at *Brideshead* before it is deconsecrated.

Back in London, Bridey asks Ryder as his first professional commission to paint four pictures of Marchmain House, soon to be demolished to make way for a modernist block of flats. Cordelia happily watches him paint and their conversations seek to define the spiritual problem which haunts the second book of *Brideshead*, namely, why Lady Marchmain's worthy Catholicism seems so problematic to her family. Ryder is puzzled by Cordelia's speculation that people hated Lady Marchmain when they really hated God because, although she was saintly, 'she wasn't a saint'. This disturbing discussion closes the second book of the novel as, more optimistically, Ryder realizes that painting Marchmain house has invigorated his artistic confidence: 'I had had my finger in the great, succulent pie of creation' (213). As the Flytes' world relentlessly crumbles, so Ryder's artistry comes to life, almost as though he now finally understands, through their demise, the message behind Poussin's 'Les bergers d'Arcadie'. As with Evelyn's own commitment to both his writings and Catholicism, Ryder has had to work long and hard to discover his true vocation as an artist and can only then begin to apprehend the allure of Catholicism.

At the end of this second section, Cordelia refers to one of G. K. Chesterton's Father Brown stories, 'The Queer Feat', in which the priest-detective describes how he caught a thief with a metaphorical fishing line and hook. He allows him to wander freely but then, suddenly and unexpectedly, hauls him back with a 'twitch upon the thread' (212), before hearing his confession and letting him go. This phrase, recalling Jesus's invitation to Simon Andrew beside the Sea of Galilee (Mark: 1.16–20), provides the title of the final book of Brideshead, covering the period 1936–39. It describes the intervening decade in Ryder's life, during which he becomes an architectural painter, especially of grand and ancient buildings. Poignantly, he is often commissioned to paint great English houses just before they are demolished, thereby becoming (like Evelyn) the commemorator of a lost age of aristocratic family living. He compiles three expensive folios, Ryder's Country Seats, Ryder's English Homes and Ryder's Village and Provincial Architecture, but deep down he knows that he is still just an accomplished copyist rather than a true artist. Above all, what he strives for but fails to attain is a sense of (divine) inspiration in his artistry, indicative of a belief that it was not 'all done by hand' (216).

Now unhappily married to Celia, the sister of 'Boy' Mulcaster, Ryder leaves his wife and son, John, to travel for two years through Mexico and South America, hoping that such a radical change of environment will reinvigorate his creativity and lead to a fourth successful publication, Ryder's Latin America. Celia crosses to New York to travel back with Ryder and claims that he now also has a daughter, Caroline, although he believes that the child is illegitimate. During the voyage from New York, he discovers that Julia Mottram is also on board and a passionate affair rapidly develops between them. He admits to her that his love for Sebastian had been the archetype of all of his subsequent relationships – a view which Julia unquestioningly comprehends. She had become pregnant with Rex's child but it was born dead, prompting her to view her recent tribulations as Divine punishment for marrying Rex. Despite such Christian scruples, she and Ryder then voraciously consummate their sexual affair.

Ryder duly stages a London exhibition of his paintings and is finally acclaimed by those critics who had previously dismissed his skills as an artist. Celia has also lined up various architectural painting commissions for Ryder but they only prompt him to realize that English urbanization is just 'another jungle closing in' (221). He is haunted by the opening words of the Lamentations of Jeremiah from the Vulgate Bible on the destruction of Jerusalem, '*Quomodo sedet sola civitas [plena populo]*' ('How the city sits solitary [that was full of people]'), previously quoted by Cordelia in the drawing-room of Marchmain House, and which he had also heard sung by a half-caste choir in Guatemala – a truly global lament for humanity. At the London exhibition, Ryder is obliged to face up to some hard truths. He realizes that his wife is aware of his affair with Julia and meets again Anthony Blanche who rightly dismisses his South-American art as 't-t-terrible t-t-tripe' (257).

Ryder travels back with Julia to Brideshead and while there constantly paints her portrait. His artistic potential is finally fulfilled by this shift from inanimate architecture and the wildernesses of South America to the aesthetic centrality of the human form and emotions. In banal contrast, Bridey is also living at Brideshead and preoccupied with his matchbox collection, an all-consuming hobby which symbolizes how this dimly unimaginative heir to Brideshead is dead to the cultural and spiritual significance of his aristocratic inheritance. This pursuit, incidentally, prompted Evelyn to accept in 1948 an invitation to judge the annual essay writing competition of the British Matchbox, Label and Booklet Society.[9] It also transpires that Bridey is engaged to Mrs Beryl Muspratt, a luminary of the Catholic Players' Guild and the widow of an Admiral whom Bridey knew through their shared passion for matchboxes. Julia's amusement at this news turns to fury when she realizes that Bridey will not bring his fiancée to Brideshead to meet them because of her sensitivities as a woman of strict Catholic standards to the irregular relationship between her and Ryder which he views as '*Living in sin*' (273).

Seeking to ease her angst, Ryder reads aloud Ruskin's response to a favourite morality painting of the Victorian period, 'The Awakened [Awakening] Conscience' by Holman Hunt (who had married, successively, two of Evelyn's great-aunts). The picture depicts a woman sitting on the lap of her adulterous lover, rising up as the folly and sinfulness of her situation suddenly dawns upon her. Julia responds that she must indeed seek some moral order in her life, insisting that this is why she wishes to marry Ryder and have his child. Celia's divorce settlement is drawn up, granting her custody of the two children and Ryder makes over to her and her new lover, Robin (probably Caroline's father), the Old Rectory which his father had given them as a wedding present. For purely political reasons, Rex is less enthusiastic to grant Julia a divorce while Bridey and Mrs Muspratt patronizingly ponder Julia's intended divorce as a lapsed Catholic, only to marry another divorcee.

In November 1938 Cordelia returns home to Brideshead, just as Julia and Rex are leaving so that Bridey, with his new wife and her children, can take up residence. After first entering a convent, Cordelia had gone to Spain as a medical worker and is now returning to England, realizing that her skills may soon be required closer to home. She also brings news of Sebastian who is living with missionaries in a monastery near Carthage at Tunis (the land of St Augustine) and notes that he is now supposedly 'very religious'. This news triggers a key realization in Ryder's own mind: 'He was with me daily in Julia; or rather it was Julia I had known in him, in those distant Arcadian days' (288). Sebastian had been turned down as a missionary lay-brother but was loved by the monks for his 'Holiness' (291) and, as Cordelia notes that no one can be holy without 'suffering' (294). The possibility of redemption, she implies, has grown ever stronger for Sebastian as his body steadily weakens and he seems to be living out his final holy days as an ascetic saint.

The concluding chapter of the novel recounts the return home of Lord Marchmain to die at Brideshead. Too weak from heart failure to manage stairs, he takes up residence in the Chinese drawing-room into which the grandiose Queen's Bed is placed for his living lying-in-state. This room confirms the empty splendour of his worldly inheritance and Lord Marchmain grimly quips to Ryder that he should record the scene as a narrative painting titled the 'Death Bed' (303). After dinner that evening, served in the Chinese room with Lord Marchmain propped up in bed, he asks Cordelia to stay with him to 'watch for an hour in this Gethsemane' (304). Filled with loathing for Mrs Muspratt, Lord Marchmain considers making over Brideshead to Julia and Ryder, an idea which seems immensely attractive to Ryder's artistic spirit. His decline becomes terminal by Easter 1939 and Bridey insists that his father must have a priest. Ryder thinks it would be 'tomfoolery' and a sham if a priest claims him as a 'death-bed penitent' (309), given Lord Marchmain's decades long hostility towards the Catholic Church. But Julia and Cordelia are unsure and the question hovers uneasily over them all. One morning after Mass Cordelia unexpectedly brings back with her the parish priest, Father Mackay, a genial Glasgow-Irishman but Lord Marchmain angrily refuses to see him.

In June Ryder's divorce comes through and Celia immediately marries Robin, with Julia's divorce expected in September. Ryder is summoned to the War Office and put on the reserve list for the 'emergency'. The family continues to discuss the spiritual significance of the Last Rites, while Ryder still struggles to comprehend their spiritual meaning. As the end approaches, Lord Marchmain takes refuge in memories of his distinguished ancestry and his mind wanders through the old church, filled with the tombs of his illustrious Catholic and Protestant ancestors. His forebears had turned Protestant at the Reformation and much of his unease stems from the fact that it was Lady Marchmain's family which had provided the genuine recusant line at Brideshead. He had only half-heartedly converted to Catholicism for his marriage and laments that the chapel, built for Lady Marchmain with stones from the old house, was the last part of Brideshead to be built and also the first to become redundant. Finally, in mid-July his condition worsens and Julia immediately goes for Father Mackay, despite Ryder's disapproval.

Evelyn based elements of the last days of Lord Marchmain on his recent experience with his Oxford friend, Hubert Duggan, the step-son of Lord Curzon and godfather of Evelyn's daughter, Margaret. The ferocious alcoholism of his late brother Alfred had also provided a model for Sebastian's decline. By September 1943 Hubert, a lapsed Catholic, was dying from tuberculosis and was being nursed by his mother (an Anglican) and his sister Marcella (actively hostile to Catholicism). Hubert wished to return to the Catholic Church but had been living in sin with a recently deceased lover, Phyllis de Janzé, and he felt that this renewed allegiance would betray his love for her. Marcella did not want Hubert to receive the last rites and her mother was hesitantly uncertain. Evelyn had already contacted Father Dempsey, a London Forces' chaplain, who promised to visit Hubert. When his health suddenly declined Evelyn rushed round to Farm Street and brought back with him its rector, Father Devas, who duly administered absolution and, in the face of Marcella's protests, the last rites – after which Hubert crossed himself.[10]

In the climactic scene of *Brideshead*, Father Mackay is recalled and reassures Ryder that through God's Grace Lord Marchmain may well be glad to see him and that his lapsed Catholicism is no obstacle to a final repentance since Christ came on earth to call not the righteous but 'sinners to repentance' (320). Julia takes command of the situation and invites Father Mackay into the Chinese drawing-room. The priest blesses him and gently asks if he is able to offer any sign to indicate that he is truly repentant for his sins. As he begins the absolution, '*ego te absolve in nomine Patris*', Ryder is so moved by the scene that he finds himself kneeling and offering a semi-sceptical prayer of the Stoics: 'O God, if there is a God, forgive him his sins, if there is such a thing as sin'. At this point Lord Marchmain opens his eyes and sighs, as Ryder's prayer is adjusted to one of simple and heartfelt pleading: 'God forgive him his sins' (322). Father Mackay completes the anointing and Lord Marchmain silently makes the Sign of the Cross. In the face of this miraculous moment, Ryder's own conversion is almost complete as he recalls the tearing of the veil of the temple in Jerusalem at Jesus' death, a key image from the Easter service, marking the arrival of the Divine in human affairs. Outside the room, the priest describes Lord Marchmain's blessing of himself as a 'beautiful thing' and explains that, even if the devil resists until the very last moment, the 'Grace of God' (323) will ultimately prove all powerful. Lord Marchmain dies peacefully at five the same evening. Abruptly, but not unexpectedly, Julia and Ryder then agree that they must part forever since she now realizes that living with Ryder would mean giving up God and she can no longer exclude herself from 'his mercy'. He also comprehends that by genuinely loving her and all that she truly values he must now, paradoxically, freely lose her since he can never be a 'rival good to God's' (324).

In the novel's brief 'Epilogue', the narrative returns to Ryder's arrival at Brideshead in 1942 as a soldier when he is put in command of a fatigue party clearing up the requisitioned house from the chaos left by its previous military occupants. The chapel has been reopened and proves popular with the troops. The Quartering Commandant reports that Brideshead now belongs to Lady Julia Flyte, since she no longer uses her married name of Mottram and has gone abroad on war service. He also remarks on Ryder's pastoral paintings in the pavilion, describing them as the 'prettiest in the place' (327). The dry fountain, once the initiation of Ryder's artistic education at Brideshead, is covered with wire and littered with cigarette ends and half-eaten sandwiches. Ryder goes up to see Nanny Hawkins who informs him that both Julia and Cordelia are probably in the biblical land of Palestine where Bridey's yeomanry is also fighting. He also visits the *art-nouveau* chapel and says a prayer, in an 'ancient, newly-learned form of words'. In temporary despair, he deems Brideshead a fallen Jerusalem as depicted in the Lamentations of Jeremiah. He recalls the generations through which the great house had been built and enriched, only for the sudden 'frost' of the present to arrive, leaving the estate desolate and its heritage reduced to nothing; *Quomodo sedet sola civitas*. Vanities of vanities, all is vanity' (330–1).

But a Catholic reader may also appreciate how his despair is gently turned towards hope at this point since Jeremiah's lament is traditionally sung at matins on Maundy Thursday at the opening of a liturgy, celebrating at Easter the miraculous transmuting of death into life. Ryder finally realizes that his self-reflective autobiography has also traced in the novel a providential plan, leading him both to Catholicism and fulfilment as an artist. The reopening of the re-consecrated chapel, the newest and aesthetically least impressive part of the house, reasserts the potency of Divine Grace over the secular splendours of Brideshead and its grand post-Reformation history. At the same time, true beauty is seen as vital nourishment for the soul and the novel carefully maps Ryder's artistic progress from optimistic innocence to pragmatic experience. He steadily journeys through an ascending hierarchy of various manifestations of art, just as he also moves from one kind of love to the next, as though climbing a providential neo-platonic ladder, 'from Sebastian through Julia to God'.[11]

Brideshead Revisited was critically acclaimed and became an immediate success, with the first edition selling out overnight. Wartime restrictions on paper, however, curtailed a second edition as well as the potentially lucrative reprinting of his other novels, thereby losing its author considerable financial returns. Fortunately, in June 1945 it was chosen by the American Book-of-the-Month Club (and the Book Society in England), thereby enabling Evelyn to fix his income at £5,000 per annum (double his previous salary) for the next five years. He wryly noted in November 1946 that an American publisher had offered him £50 for fifty words which was exactly the fee he had received for writing his biography of Rossetti two decades earlier.[12]

Disengagement and *Scott King*

The result of the post-war general election (5 July 1945) came as a profound shock to Evelyn. It swept Churchill and the conservatives from power, replacing them with a Labour government, led by Clement Atlee and committed to the establishment of a socialist society. Evelyn regarded their prioritizing of the proletariat and high taxation for the wealthy as the beginning of a new Dark Age for England and also viewed the rest of Western-Europe as in a state of godless, terminal decline. He continued to sit on the board of Chapman and Hall but it had been acquired by Methuen and was focusing more on technical books, leading to his resignation with considerable acrimony in September. No longer able to view himself as part of contemporary society, he 'began slowly to disengage himself from the modern world'.[13] At the heart of the problem, he felt, was a decline in the hierarchical values of English society. In a September 1946 essay with Swiftian overtones and intended as an attack on the Labour government, 'What to Do with the Upper Classes: a Modest Proposal', he concluded that the transformation of England from being one of the most attractive countries in the world to one of the ugliest was traceable in no small measure to the decline of the aristocracy.[14]

After six years away from home, Evelyn returned on 10 September 1945 to Piers Court as soon as it was vacated by its resident nuns. He spent his forty-second birthday on 28 October reviewing Cyril Connolly's collection of *pensées*, *The Unquiet Grave*, and preparing for a single-volume collection of his travel writings. He was also drafting the opening to an aborted novel set in 1919 and based on his Lancing diaries, 'Charles Ryder's Schooldays', intended as a prequel to *Brideshead* (published posthumously). It echoed his schoolboy relationship with Frank Crease and explained how the young Ryder's mother had died in Bosnia as a volunteer during World War I. From the surviving draft, it seems that this novel would have focused on two major concerns of *Sword of Honour*, the demise of chivalry and Yugoslavian political history. After the success of *Brideshead*, there was an understandable slowing down of Evelyn's fictional productivity during 1946, with only a macabre new short story, 'Tactical Exercise' (1947; US title, 'The Wish'), being completed. Set during post-war rationing, it tells of a Liberal war veteran called John Verney (whose angry irrationality reflects Evelyn's), and his wife Elizabeth. They are both involved in Intelligence work and, as their marriage disintegrates, are planning to murder each other. In December 1946 Duckworth also published its selective compilation (omitting *Robbery Under Law*) of his travelogues, *When the Going Was Good*, with a stringent preface lamenting a lost golden age of Western-European travel.[15]

Evelyn was invited in March 1946 to attend the Nuremberg war trials as an observer and he hoped that the experience might lead to a book. But, disappointed by endless legalistic wrangling and the nondescript appearance of the Nazis (Ribbentrop looked like a seedy teacher), he stayed there for only two days in April and then headed off to stay with the Coopers at Paris where Duff was British Ambassador.[16] In mid-June he accompanied Douglas Woodruff, the editor of the *Tablet*, to Madrid for a conference in honour of a sixteenth-century Dominican jurist, Francisco de Vittoria, the founder of International Law. This experience was grim, with endless delays, oppressive heat, tedious events and major problems with transportation home. But it at least prompted a satiric short novella, *Scott-King's Modern Europe* (1947; US title, 'A Sojourn in Neutralia'), in which an ascetic public school master deplores modern decadence and instead buries himself in classical literature.[17] He greatly admires the work of a neglected seventeenth-century poet, Bellorius, whose *magnum opus* is a 15,000 hexameter poem in Latin about an imaginary society in the New World where a harmonious community lives in primitive simplicity, without tyranny or the modern corruptions.

Scott-King eagerly attends a conference to mark the tercentenary of the poet's death in Neutralia, echoing both Franco's Spain and Tito's Yugoslavia as a typical totalitarian state: 'governed by a single party, acclaiming a dominant Marshal, supporting a vast ill-paid bureaucracy whose work is tempered and humanized by corruption' (376). He views the trip as a kind of pilgrimage while the other delegates regard the conference merely as an enjoyable jaunt. Neutralia's government manipulates the event to cultivate international favour and when a monument is unveiled, supposedly to Bellorius, it really represents the Marshal. Undaunted, Scott-King presses on with his carefully prepared Latin speech, concluding that by honouring Bellorius the rulers of Neutralia are 'lighting a candle that day which by the Grace of God should never be put out' (415). This ironic phrase echoes Hugh Latimer's stoical words to Nicholas Ridley when they were being burnt at the stake in 1555 under Queen Mary. But to Evelyn, both men were Protestant traitors to Catholic truth and the reference cynically 'signals the illusoriness of hopes of progress by political means'.[18]

Eventually, Scott-King has to be smuggled out of Neutralia disguised as an Ursuline nun. He ends up in a Jewish Illicit Immigrants' camp in Palestine before an arduous trip back to the safety of his school. He vows henceforth to bury himself away in the exclusive study of the classics since 'it would be very wicked indeed' to train boys for the 'modern world' (429). George Orwell remarked in a shrewd review that Evelyn seemed now to regard the modern world as 'so unmistakably crazy, so certain to smash itself to pieces in the near future, that to attempt to understand it or come to terms with it is simply a purposeless self-corruption'.[19] But Scott-King at least remains a scholarly and honest man who represents intellectual decency and the need to stand up for the vestiges of Christian civilization.

Combining post-war family life with writing at Piers Court was also becoming increasingly problematic for Evelyn. Soon after his arrival back from Spain, Laura gave birth to another son, James, but he stayed away from home for as long as possible, residing in an expensive suite of rooms at the Hyde Park Hotel. As the Labour government's high taxation policies and the growth of the Welfare State thrived, he considered emigration and put Piers Court on the market. He made two half-hearted attempts to buy properties in Ireland, one in Wicklow and the other near Dublin, although Laura remained deeply opposed to any move which would have isolated from her family's home at Pixton. More realistically, Evelyn also considered converting his aunts' home at Midsomer Norton into a writer's retreat where he could recreate the congenial setting of a wealthy Victorian bachelor's residence.[20]

Evelyn's unhappiness with English life after 1945 was compounded by his intensely logical and hierarchical form of Catholicism. While its intensity did not necessarily bring him emotional solace, it at least validated his writer's role in life and provided a potential route to personal salvation. He genuinely regarded his career as an author as a Christian vocation and with missionary zeal viewed his pen as a means of asserting Divine authority over a world which had descended into the hands of barbarian hordes. In a revealing article for *Life* magazine, 'Fan-Fare' (8 April 1946), he explained how the blended integrity of his art and religious belief in his post-*Brideshead* writings would provide the foundations of his literary creativity. He berated modern novelists such as James Joyce for minimizing God's authority over the humanity and insisted that his future books would unapologetically concentrate mankind's relationship with God.[21]

Dutifully maintaining his religious observances, Evelyn also frequently made charitable bequests to the clergy, wrote without fees for the *Month* and the *Tablet* and, although uncongenial to him, accepted speaking appointments for Catholic institutions. Royalties from his publications were often channeled to approved causes, with those for *Scott-King* going to the Jesuits and translation rights of other books made over to the Catholic primate of the country concerned. He abandoned plans for living abroad and, instead, turned more inwards towards home life with his young family. At the same time, Catholicism offered him a reassuring sense of belonging to a wider, global family and community of faith. It was as though the duality of family and the Church were now his only bastions against the post-war worldly chaos outside the gates of Piers Court which, famously, bore the warning: 'No admittance on Business'.[22]

The Loved One and Graham Greene

Evelyn made a brief trip to California in late-January 1947 to discuss with MGM plans to film *Brideshead* and then undertook in mid-August a commission from the *Daily Telegraph* to tour Sweden, Norway and Denmark. He enjoyed Stockholm and Copenhagen but was troubled by the lack in Scandinavian society of any overt spiritual context to its daily life.[23] Although, predictably, his discussions with MGM proved abortive, he enjoyed visiting the Jesuits at Loyola University and was fascinated by both the 300-acre cemetery at Forest Lawn Memorial Park, Glendale, and a local pets' cemetery. He recognized that their garish sentimentality, saccharine landscapes and utter avoidance of the reality of death supplied rich material for a comic novel. He duly met Forest Lawn's founder, Dr Hubert Eaton, obtained a copy of its *Art Guide of Forest Lawn*, and charmed its chief embalmer, Mr Howells, who presented him with a signed copy of Roy Slocum's *Embalming Techniques* which he annotated.[24] Evelyn was delighted by the habitual American euphemism for a corpse as 'The Loved One', prompting the title of his ebullient black satire on the Californian funeral business, *The Loved One: An Anglo-American Tragedy* (1948). He and Laura returned to England in March 1947 and, after an Easter retreat at the Benedictine Downside Abbey, he drafted a two-part feature on Hollywood for the *Daily Telegraph* and an article on 'Death in Hollywood' for *Life* (with all fees donated to the Jesuits). Following the success of *Brideshead*, in 1946 his biography of Campion was also reprinted in the US (with proceeds again going to the Jesuits).

   The Loved One, intended as a 'novelette', was begun on 21 May and a first draft was finished by early July. Evelyn compiled another two complete drafts before submitting it in mid-September to his agent, Peters, who strongly advised against a US publication because of its potential for libel suits. Nevertheless, it appeared first in Cyril Connolly's magazine, *Horizon* (February 1948), followed by UK and US hardback editions, dedicated to Nancy Mitford. She was delighted by its dark satire, even though its cynical protagonist, Dennis Barlow, was based on Basil Seal who, in turn, echoed Nancy's estranged and unreliable husband, Peter Rodd. Its satire of modern society's exploitation of religious consolations without a requirement to believe in them was widely appreciated in America, with only a few (largely British) dissident voices. Nancy had in 1946 given Evelyn a complete set of the novels of Henry James and was enjoying working his way through them. *The Loved One* rewrites Scott-King's plight into an American context by adopting a Jamesian perspective. Its anti-hero, Dennis Barlow, is even made to remark at one point that he had become a protagonist in a Jamesian dilemma, exploring the tragic implication of a clash between American innocence and European experience.[25]

   The wicked satire of *The Loved One* delights in the follies of its ridiculous but engaging characters. Dennis Barlow, a self-interested English expatriate and former war poet had hoped to become a highly paid film script writer. Instead, he is reduced to working in a tacky pet cemetery, The Happier Hunting Ground, and passing off poetic classics as his own compositions. Dennis and the English expats who reside in Bel Air as employees of the Megalopolitan Studios draw together the two great false churches of California – the film and funeral industries. In the much grander human necropolis of Whispering Glades, founded by Wilbur Kenworthy (alias 'The Dreamer'), its chief embalmer, Mr Joyboy, is ably assisted by his devoted female acolyte, Aimée Thanatogenos (whose name combines '*Thanatos*', the Greek god of non-violent death, and '*genos*', a kinship group). Dennis meets Aimée when he arranges the funeral of Sir Francis Hinsley, who had hung himself after being made redundant by his longtime employers, Megalopolitan Pictures. Mr Joyboy, Aimée and Dennis create a preposterous love-triangle in a California where secular values have not merely replaced religious ones but seem overtly to parody their significance. Whispering Glades and The Happier Hunting Ground are essentially identical in terms of their relentless denial of the reality and spiritual significance of mortality.

Both cemeteries are set within tasteless parodies of the Garden of Eden or even of Heaven itself, with 'The Dreamer' as God and Joyboy as St Peter. The insensitivities of the male characters equate them to a group of pastoral shepherds in a satirically perverted '*Et in Arcadia ego*' painting – rustics who are too spiritually stunted to appreciate the significance of the countless graves which fill their everyday landscapes. Only the naively aspiring Aimée, the 'sole Eve in a bustling hygienic Eden' (46), seeks something more profound. But even she remains tragically grounded in the secular world, placing her hopes largely in the unprepossessing form of Mr Joyboy whom she finds 'kinda holy' (76). Ending in tragedy, Aimée commits suicide in a grim parody of classical Greek tragedy and Dennis covers up the potential scandal of her death by cremating her remains in the pet cemetery incinerator. In this tawdry world – unlike Poussin's shepherds or the undergraduate Charles Ryder with his skull – Dennis holds no veneration for the bones of the dead as a *memento mori*. Instead, he grinds up her skull and pelvis and then illicitly disperses her ashes. His final thoughts, as Fortune's 'favourite', recall the language of pagan epic even though, paradoxically, a judgemental God still seems ominously present. 'Others', he thinks 'had floundered here and perished' with their bones metaphorically lying all around. But he was departing 'not only unravished but enriched' and was now bearing 'the artist's load, a great shapeless chunk of experience; bearing it home to his ancient and comfortless shore; to work on it hard and long, for God knew how long. (127). This final statement confirms how *The Loved One* implicitly validates Christian values by noting their absence and negation in a vapidly secular Californian society. It is packed with pretentious references to Hindu love songs, Egypt of the pharaohs, French existentialism, Guru Brahmin and the Grand Sanhedrin, exemplifying the characteristic need of lapsed Christian societies to take comfort in other spiritual alternatives. Even Dennis's cynical opportunism leads him to consider the hopefully remunerative career of a non-sectarian clergyman. What seems pointedly missing from these self-deceptive lives is any sense of support and solace brought by the timeless presence Christian values.

Given his damning views on Californian life, it seems surprising that Evelyn also found genuine cause for religious optimism during his American travels. He regarded some facets of its spiritual culture as offering hope for the future of Christian faith. He was especially impressed by Thomas Merton (Frater Louis), a Catholic convert and monk who was member of the abbey of Our Lady of Gethsemani, Kentucky. He had joined in 1941 the Order of Cistercians of the Strict Observance (Trappists), the most ascetic Roman Catholic monastic order. At the instruction of his abbot, he had written a voluminous autobiography, *The Seven-Storey Mountain*, which was radically edited down by Evelyn for publication in England as *Elected Silence* (1949). He was sympathetic towards the monk's view that the role of the writer was essentially that of a skilled artisan and the two men remained on friendly terms, with Evelyn continuing to offer literary advice and receiving, in return, spiritual guidance. He also hoped in his forward to *Elected Silence* that America would soon experience a major monastic revival since for centuries prior to the Reformation these cloistered worlds had been at the very heart of Western-European civilization.[26]

In an austere 6,000-word article, 'The American Epoch in the Catholic Church', based on return trips to American between November 1948 and March 1949, Evelyn examined the conflicts there between Christian teaching and secular hierarchies. He advocated the advantages of a modern society committed unambiguously to Divine authority and insisted that the Incarnation had, above all, restored order to the world.[27] In England he regarded old aristocratic recusant families as the vital, if dispossessed, backbone of Catholicism but, in contrast, he discovered in America that the most devout and humble Catholics were often found among the poor and immigrants. He especially praised the devotions of black Catholics and admired at a Jesuit Church at New Orleans on Ash Wednesday how a huge multi-racial congregation humbly processed up to the altar rails to receive together the cross of ashes on their foreheads. Although never egalitarian by temperament, Evelyn's American experiences repeatedly reminded him that all men and women were equal in the eyes of God and that only through shared religious devotions could social and racial integration be ultimately achieved.

During this visit Evelyn also met various members of American Catholic high society, including the playwright and journalist Clare Booth Luce, a devout Catholic convert and wife of Henry Luce, the wealthy proprietor of *Life, Time* and *Fortune*; Dorothy Day, a Labour Movement supporter and co-founder of the *Catholic Worker*; and Anne Freemantle (formerly Huth-Jackson), another Catholic convert who possessed the dubious distinction of being the only woman to receive a marriage proposal from Evelyn's hated Oxford tutor, Cruttwell. He also briefly met up with his brother Alec and was introduced to W. H. Auden and the French Catholic philosopher, Jacques Maritain. He travelled to the Jesuit Loyola College at Baltimore where he was given an honorary doctorate and also renewed his friendship with Thomas Merton. He returned to America in late-January 1949 to deliver a series of lectures to enthusiastic audiences on 'Three Vital Writers': Chesterton, Knox and Greene. He also had two awkward encounters with the Russian composer Igor Stravinsky and again made his way to Kentucky to meet with Merton. With his article, 'The American Epoch in the Catholic Church', now widely acclaimed, Evelyn returned yet again in October 1950 to be lionized by the Luces and the friends in the US Catholic community. He continued to pursue diligent research into numerous small Catholic communities and colleges and remained deeply impressed by the extent and diversity of the Catholic faith in America.[28]

At this period Evelyn's personal relationship with Graham Greene was flourishing. They had known one another since 1937, when Greene invited him to contribute to his short-lived journal, *Night and Day*, and they viewed each other's work with admiring respect. Greene had been profoundly moved by *Edmund Campion* and regarded Evelyn as the consummate literary stylist of their generation. Both were Catholic converts whose literary interests often focused on the eternal struggle between Good and Evil, although they were very different kinds of Catholics:

> Greene was broadly 'Left' and cared little for country-house priests like Knox. There was no allegiance to a 'European tradition' in Greene's writings, nothing supporting the Church Militant. His Church was not a precise organization with absolute rectitude on its side but a tangle of paradox and heretical temptation . . . As a writer he felt the need, even within his Faith, to live on the borderline, owing no loyalty which would demand the faithful lie.[29]

Greene had separated in 1947 from his devoutly Catholic wife, Vivien, and was deep in an adulterous affair with Catherine Walston, the glamorous American wife of a tacitly compliant Anglo-Jewish husband. Although Evelyn sternly disapproved of relationships which threatened the sanctity of marriage, he seems to have made an exception in Greene's case. As he got to know Catherine and was clearly charmed by her, he indulgently recalled how a devout pope had reputedly run through Rome wearing a paper hat to counter any risk of developing spiritual pride. Catherine Walston, he proposed, was his friend's 'paper hat'.[30]

The publication of Greene's *The Heart of the Matter* (1948) drew the two writers much closer together. Evelyn requested to review the novel for the *Tablet*, despite the hostility of its co-owner, Tom Burns, who condemned Greene as a 'sort of smart-Alec of Jansenism' in his treatment of adultery and suicide. In contrast, Evelyn's review, 'Felix Culpa', describes Greene as an inspired story-teller and commends his courage in depicting challenging spiritual issues through Scobie's self-torturing lapses of faith. He treats Greene as a rigorous theologian who is neither a Jansenist nor perversely addicted to paradox. Instead, Evelyn argues, he expresses a profoundly honest vision of original sin, noting that in Greene's novels Adam's children are not simple savages who need only a divine spark to cleanse them but rather are 'aboriginally corrupt'. Although they disagreed over whether Scobie finally received Divine Grace or could be regarded as a saint, Greene was immensely grateful for this literary support and profusely thanked Evelyn, noting that there was no other living writer from whom he would rather receive either praise or criticism.[31]

During the latter half of 1948 Evelyn also became involved in Father D'Arcy's plans to invigorate the Jesuit periodical, the *Month*, with a new editor, Father Caraman, who was to become a close friend and the celebrant of his last Mass (Easter Day, 1966). The intention was to re-launch the journal as a Catholic *Horizon*-like review of the arts, literature, philosophy and theology. Evelyn offered for the first issue some extracts from his new work-in-progress novel, *Helena*, and Greene contributed a review of *The Loved One*. Most significantly, Evelyn's short story, 'Compassion', examining the plight of Jewish refugees in Yugoslavia during the war (and of central importance to the *Sword of Honour* trilogy) also appeared in the *Month*'s August 1949 issue.[32]

5

A dysfunctional author trapped in a dystopian society: 1950–5

Helena

Evelyn intended that 'The Three Quests of the Empress Dowager', later *Helena* (1950), should be his great study of vocation and he tenaciously regarded it as his best book. Having defined his purpose as a Catholic writer in *Brideshead*, his later novels, including *The Loved One*, *Helena* and *Sword of Honour*, all focused in different ways on the unique challenges posed by God for their respective protagonists. He had first conceived the project during his 1935 visit to Jerusalem and in May 1945 began serious work on this imaginary life of St Helena, the Christian convert mother of Constantine and the discoverer of the True Cross. His purpose was to trace her spiritual growth from pagan, pre-Raphaelite-like girlhood at Colchester to pious old age at Rome and Jerusalem, thereby demonstrating to his readership the literal historical truth of the foundation of the Christian Church. The character of Helena embodied for Evelyn his key doctrinal belief that God had put humans on earth to fulfil divinely ordained roles. He also projected himself into the novel's Christian convert, Lactantius, who plays a crucial role in bringing Helena to the true faith. He is the 'greatest living prose stylist' (78) of Constantine's period and an author who, like Evelyn, 'delighted in writing, in the joinery and embellishment of his sentences, in the consciousness of high rare virtue when every word had been used in its purest and most precise sense' (79). Crucially, he is also the individual who first interests Helena in historical evidence for Christian religion.

Although Evelyn carefully researched the historical and Jewish background of the period, little factual information was available about her life which could be reconstructed only through legend and surmise. He felt free to claim her as British (a daughter of Coel, the Trinovantes chieftain) and set much of her story in Dalmatia, familiar from his wartime service. But his labours failed to bring her character and spirituality to life, not least because he decided to base her partly on his friend, Penelope Betjeman (to whom the novel was dedicated) and that of her husband, Constantius

Chlorus, with his 'small, cold soul' (54) on Fitzroy Maclean. Most bizarrely, he self-consciously deploys anachronisms as a stylistic device supposedly to render the text relevant to modern readers and to transcend historical temporality. Hence, the young Helena speaks the sparky language of a 1920s 'bright young thing', describing a party as a 'beano' (14) and delights in slangy phrases: 'What a lark!', 'Oh, what sucks!'(20) and 'What a blow-out!' (22). Elsewhere, a black West-Indies jazz-singing witch pops up with a song about Napoleon's exile on St Helena; Constantine parades an arts-and-crafts military banner; and some salacious sexual horse-riding fantasies are gratuitously inserted.

Such devices have been viewed as a 'vital technical experiment, neither modernist nor realist, but postmodernist, metafictional', and as an ambitious means of challenging the conventions of narrative realism.[1] But for most readers, *Helena* remains a strangely lifeless amalgam of Evelyn's religious, historical and literary convictions, uneasily blended together in a disjointed narrative. The opening sections of the novel were published in the *Tablet* (22 December 1945) and the first three chapters were largely completed by late-January 1946. Still nervous over the literary value of this highly prized project, Evelyn received genuine encouragement from the praise of Ronald Knox who felt that these preliminary chapters manifested a powerful spiritual theme. But work progressed so slowly that it took until late-December 1949 for the second section of the novel to be drafted, with the concluding part completed in the following March, enabling publication in October 1950.

The central thesis of *Helena* is that Christianity offers a peaceful haven or Eternal City, safely enclosed from the barbarous world beyond its rigorously defended orbit. Constantius explains how he similarly views the great Roman wall in Swabia, a prime example of the efficacy of Empire:

> a single great girdle round the civilized world; inside, peace, decency, the law, the altars of the Gods, industry, the arts, order; outside, wild beasts and savages, forest and swamp, bloody mumbo-jumbo, men like wolf-packs; and along the wall the armed might of the Empire, sleepless, holding the line. (39)

This image chimed in with Evelyn's belief that Faith had not only to be espoused but also rigorously defended from the forces of evil. But one day, as Helena explains to her defensively minded husband, the force of Good may be so strong that true believers residing within the wall will triumphantly break out and overwhelm the savagery outside. Evelyn was keen for Christopher Sykes to organize a radio dramatization of the novel, broadcast by BBC Radio 3 (15 December 1951), with Flora Robson as Helena and John Gielgud as Constantine. He also delivered an introductory commentary on the previous evening, which was published in the January 1951 issue of the *Month* and as the first item in his *The Holy Places* (1952). In a letter to John Betjeman (9 November 1950), Evelyn delineated *Helena*'s central theme that all believers must attain sanctity after their own fashion before being admitted to heaven. Helena, he noted, was no contemplative or ascetic martyr but instead had readily accepted God's purpose for her, just as he now envisaged his own literary career as a divinely ordained spiritual and aesthetic role in life.[2]

The *Month* published a substantial retrospective review of Evelyn's writings by Frederick Stopp, 'Grace in Reins' (August 1953), which productively compared the spiritual impulse of *Brideshead* to that of *Helena*, focusing on their shared concern to incorporate the supernatural into the reality of personal faith. Both works examined the intersection of nature and grace, privilege and suffering and the natural and supernatural in the lives of characters who are ultimately imbued with a sense of divine purpose. Stopp's critique of *Helena* still remains the most judicious guide to Evelyn's creative purpose in attempting such a spiritually challenging novel:

> by choosing as the central character one about whose life almost nothing else is known but this one supreme, final and yet constitutive act, the author has a clear field in which to build up the total rounded picture of a life and a social and historical setting whose every line of development converges on to that point. Legendary in its beginning and its end, historical in its middle course, the book is a striking representation in artistic form of that living and inherited historicity which is known as the tradition of the Church.[3]

Financial crisis, Rome and *The Holy Places*

Despite Stopp's perceptive analysis and some supportive comments from Greene, other reviewers were more negative, identifying the same elitism cloaked in piety as had been suspected in *Brideshead*. This critical reception accentuated Evelyn's personal sense of being a writer increasingly alienated from the moral values of society. More mundanely, his chaotic personal tax affairs were also being scrutinized by the Inland Revenue and, despite his considerable post-*Brideshead* earnings, he remained permanently anxious about money but unable to rein in his lavish spending. At the beginning of 1950 he also discovered that Laura had unknowingly run up an overdraft of £6,420. Images of the Marshalsea haunted Evelyn's mind and he gloomily wrote to Nancy Mitford on 5 December 1949, claiming incipient signs of lunacy and, only half-facetiously, deeming himself ever closer to madness.[4]

However, in late-1949 Penguin Books, which had published most of his early novels, planned to reprint his complete fictional canon, although at first he did not appreciate the financial potential of cheap paperback fiction. Fortunately, Peters rapidly spotted the value of such a deal and also recommended that Evelyn should sign over the profits into a trust for the benefit of his children, henceforth known as his 'Save the Children Fund'. In a scheme worthy of Basil Seal, all of his UK literary earnings and royalties were paid into this trust. In return, he was able to fund personal purchases from it, including paintings, silver, interior decorations and even his own manuscripts, claiming that these items had been acquired by the Trust as sound investments for his children.[5]

In March 1950, with Laura heavily pregnant, Evelyn planned to spend Easter of the Holy Year at Rome. He first enjoyed a congenial visit to Paris, meeting Nancy Mitford and her friends, before taking up residence at the British Embassy at Rome. He then moved on to the Herberts' villa at Portofino for the annual St George's Day festival, before renewing his contacts with Harold Acton, the Sitwells and Max Beerbohm at Florence, Verona and Rapallo. Despite these varied pleasures, he was still mentally debilitated by his awareness that the war had radically changed the face of Western Europe forever. Returning to England in late-May, he found Laura close to her confinement at Pixton and absorbed himself in the correction of the proofs of *Helena*, before making a brief trip to Amsterdam. Always distant from the process of childbirth, he took up his seasonal residence at the Hyde Park Hotel and merely scanned *The Times* each morning for any notice of the birth of Septimus on 9 July. It was a week before he paid a brief visit to Pixton to see his last-born child and he then returned to London as rapidly as possible. Despite his frenetic social life there, attending the Devonshire's fancy-dress ball and enjoying bibulous lunches with Tom Burns and Graham Greene, he remained painfully trapped in an increasingly depressive frame of mind.[6]

In January 1951 Evelyn undertook a tour of the Holy Land with Christopher Sykes, financed by a commission for some articles from *Life*, since the Luces had been greatly impressed by *Helena*. They travelled via Paris and Rome and, while at the Vatican, he explored the possibility of installing a private chapel at Piers Court (comparable to Brideshead's) and lobbied for Ronald Knox to be named as Cardinal in recognition of his recent translation of the Bible. They then passed through Damascus, Beirut, Tel Aviv and Jerusalem. He was deeply moved by an all-night vigil at the Church of the Holy Sepulchre, Jerusalem, before moving on to Ankara and Istanbul. They arrived back in England in late-February and his essay on their travels, 'The Defence of Holy Places', was published in both *Life* and the *Month*. It was then reprinted in a limited edition by the Queen Anne Press as *The Holy Places* (1952), including a brief preface, 'Work Abandoned', and two essays, 'St. Helena: Empress' (the text of his radio talk) and 'The Holy Places', with illustrations by Reynolds Stone. Evelyn's view of the Holy Land was deeply pessimistic. The independence of Israel and the end of the British Mandate in May 1948 had brought renewed conflicts between the Jews and the dispossessed Arabs. While the holy sites at Jerusalem crumbled, Pope Pius XII issued ineffectual encyclicals urging their protection. Evelyn was convinced that the United Nations' peace-keeping measures would prove fruitless and, already suspicious of Zionism, his sympathy for the Palestinian Arabs soon diminished as he viewed the resentment, ambitions and atrocities of both sides as an affront to what he regarded as the world's most sacred city.[7]

Men at Arms

Despite the creative momentum provided by this itinerary, once back home Evelyn's literary energy, even for religious projects, seemed to be wavering. He eagerly accepted, but then soon rejected, commissions to write the lives of St Thomas More and St Ignatius Loyola. In retrospect this hesitancy seems regrettable since both projects offered an opportunity for him to recapture the productive combination of scholarly research and inspiring Catholic hagiography which had made his *Edmund Campion* so successful. These substantial projects would have offered a route back into mainstream Catholic literature and away from the intensely experimental style of his study of St Helena.[8]

Greene's *The End of the Affair* was published in August 1951 and Evelyn was loyally supportive when rumours circulated that his friend had lost his faith. In his review of the novel he praised its representation of direct supernatural intervention and the Church's implicit potency. Of course, he was well aware that the novel's genesis lay in Greene's adulterous affair with Catherine Walston but exceptions could be made for his closest friends. In October he also stood unsuccessfully for the Rectorship of Edinburgh University, a failure which left him angry and bruised. This sense of vulnerability was compounded by a hostile review of *Helena* from Father Gerald Meath, comparing it to Dorothy L. Sayer's *The Emperor Constantine* which communicated sanctity through the power of the Holy Spirit rather than, Meath implied, merely through Helena's social status. New Year 1952 proved even worse when Evelyn was finally obliged to pay to the Inland Revenue substantial amounts of super-tax arrears on his film earnings since 1944.[9]

Nor was life much better for his brother Alec who was now permanently based in America. He had continued to produce ever more mediocre books (his nephew, Auberon Waugh, quipped that he penned many books but each was worse than the last), including *The Sunlit Caribbean* (1948a), *These Would I Choose* (1948b), *Unclouded Summer* (1948c), *The Sugar Islands: A Caribbean travelogue* (1949), *The Lipton Story* (1950), *Where the Clocks Chime Twice* (1951), and *Guy Renton* (1952).[10] The two brothers had only met briefly in New York during these years but, despite various family difficulties, Alec remained a loyal admirer of his sibling's remarkable talents as a man of 'genius'. On 11 July 1951, he proudly wrote to their mother of Evelyn's great contribution to English letters and 'how much honour he has brought to the name of Waugh'.[11]

Such a positive view of his own talents was far from Evelyn's mind at this period. Plagued by a dampening sense of creative uncertainty, sporadic ill-health and a belief that he was an aging writer well past his best, he dismissively remarked to Greene that he was drafting a new novel about army life, steeped in recollections of military dialogue.[12] This was the beginning of *Men at Arms* (published, September 1952), the first book of the *Sword of Honour* trilogy. Initially motivated by his admiration for Ford Madox Ford's *The Good Soldier* (1915) and his trilogy, *Parade's End* (1924–28), it refashioned many of Evelyn's own wartime experiences into fictional form. *Sword of Honour* was later described by Cyril Connolly as 'unquestionably the finest novels to have come out of the war'.[13] Certainly, it stands comparison with Anthony Powell's twelve-volume, *A Dance to the Music of Time* (which, like *Brideshead*, has a Poussin painting at its conceptual heart), the first volume of which, *A Question of Upbringing*, was published in 1951.

In some respects, Evelyn's literary experiments in *Helena* had usefully prepared the ground for his war triology. Martin Stannard explains:

> Waugh's creation of an ancient world in a theological vacuum . . . is directly paralleled to that of post-war Europe. *Helena* can be read as an entirely 'contemporary' work offering a complex analogy with modern times. In many respects it is Waugh's (displaced) spiritual autobiography, a dry-run for the *Sword of Honour* trilogy.[14]

Work began on *Men at Arms* (then titled 'Honour') in June 1951 during a visit to France and was completed by December, with the published edition dedicated to his future biographer, Christopher Sykes. Making extensive use of his own war diaries, Evelyn intended the novel to be a study of the concepts of chivalry, covering the same period as *Put Out More Flags* (from 1939 to Dunkirk). Its dutiful Catholic protagonist, Guy Crouchback, is stunted by his 'few dry grains of faith' (33) and lack of emotional engagement with the world. Middle-aged, divorced and mired in spiritual sloth, he is a kindred spirit to the older Charles Ryder (but without the artistic impulse). The slow regeneration of his faith becomes the major motif of the trilogy.

> Into that wasteland where his soul languished he need not, could not, enter. He had no words to describe it . . . There was nothing to describe, merely a void . . . It was as though . . . he had suffered a tiny stroke of paralysis; all his spiritual capacities were just perceptibly impaired. (14)

Crouchback's aged father, Guy Senior, is depicted as the benevolent remnant of a once distinguished recusant family who epitomizes the true decencies of life. The novel opens by recalling how his parents travelled to Rome on their honeymoon and were granted a private audience with Pope Pius IX (d.1878) who blessed their 'union of two English families which had suffered for their Faith . . . Forbears of both their names had died on the scaffold' (9). During the war, their son has leased to a convent school (like Evelyn's Piers Court) his country house, Broome, where his ancestors had resided since the reign of Henry I. He now rents rooms at nearby Matchet in a nondescript seaside boarding-house run by old family servants, meekly accepting with saintly humility his fallen social status. Guy Junior is at the family villa in Italy at the outbreak of war and is pathetically grateful for the conflict because it seems to give him back a role in English society: 'Whatever the outcome there was a place for him in that battle' (12). He visits his local Italian church to pray at the tomb of Roger of Waybroke, an English knight from the Second Crusade who has been adopted by the locals as 'il Santo Inglese'. Evoking the honour of Sir Roger's ancient chivalry, Guy prays for his personal protection and for 'our endangered kingdom' (13). Back in England, he joins the Royal Corps of Halberdiers, even though during the 1914–18 war his elder brother, Gervase, had gone straight from Downside into the Irish Guards and had been killed on his first day in France. In his memory, Guy receives from his father Gervase's medal of Our Lady of Lourdes which he regards as his talisman during military engagements. Tragically, Guy's other brother, Ivo, had been mentally disturbed and eventually starved himself to death, a loss which their aged father stoically bears.

Guy's father had wangled a position for him in the Halberdiers and he experiences a rare sense of euphoria in these new and refreshing soldierly contacts which give him a kind of 'happy adolescence' (47) and a 'honeymoon' (78) feeling. In due course, however, the drab barracks of their Training Depot at Kut-al-Imara House, Southsand-on-sea, starkly reflect Evelyn's own gradual disillusionment with day-to-day army life. Guy's earnest naivety is contrasted to the bureaucracy and mindless chaos of the military authorities. The turning point comes with a disastrous campaign at Dakar when their attack, 'Operation Truslove', is unexpectedly cancelled, prompting only a sense of embarrassed relief among the men. Guy is then surreptitiously ordered by his commanding officer, Brigadier Ritchie-Hook, to lead a patrol ashore to check out whether a beach landing point would have been accessible or was wired and impracticable. It turns out to be the latter and, as they evacuate under heavy fire, Guy realizes that Ritchie-Hook has secretly joined his reconnaissance party. Although wounded in the leg, Ritchie-Hook triumphantly returns with a gruesome memento, the severed head of an African soldier from the French colonial infantry. Guy is disillusioned by this experience and takes solace in reading Greene's *The Heart of the Matter*. Indeed, he feels that he would like to confess to Greene's Father Rank (who hears Scobie's confession) his 'increasing sloth' and 'lingering resentment' (232) as his military idealism steadily crumbles.

After this fleeting confessional moment, Evelyn's preoccupation with the regeneration of Guy's Catholic faith becomes more explicit, although it remains unresolved until the trilogy's final volume. Guy is viewed as a man

whose soul languishes in a spiritual wasteland, following the breakup eight
years earlier of his marriage to the promiscuous, agnostic Virginia (echoing
Brenda Last), due to her affair with their friend, Tommy Backhouse. In a
disturbing scene, Guy attempts to make love to her after they happen to
meet in a London Hotel. She is humiliated and enraged, describing him
as a 'wet, smug, obscene, pompous, sexless, lunatic pig' (133), when she
realizes that his attempted seduction has only occurred because she is the
one women with whom his Catholic faith will allow sexual congress.

At the centre of the military action in *Men at Arms* lie two memorable
characters whose comic energy confirms the vigour of Evelyn's creative
imagination as he was drafting this war trilogy. The devious alcoholic,
Apthorpe, recalls Atwater from *Work Suspended* and is directly compared
to that archetype of comic misbehaviour, 'Mr Toad' (237). He also becomes
Guy's *doppelgänger* and the novel's three sections, 'Apthorpe Gloriosus',
'Apthorpe Furibundus' and 'Apthorpe Immolatus' (the triumph, lunacy
and slaying of Apthorpe), are named after him. Like Evelyn, both Guy and
Apthorpe are thirty-six in 1939 and join the Halberdiers on the same day.
Often childlike and recalling the student Ryder's intimacy with Sebastian,
they seem like a pair of immature 'twins' (97), even though they are both
called 'Uncle' by younger soldiers. Eventually, Apthorpe is revealed as a
fraud and ends up half-mad in a military hospital. Guy brings him a bottle
of whisky which Apthorpe greedily consumes and dies. To hush up this
scandal, Guy is posted out of the Halberdiers and his return with Ritchie-
Hook to England marks an important stage in his gradual movement from
idealism towards disillusioned maturity.

In stark contrast to Apthorpe's venal figure is the ferocious Brigadier
Ritchie-Hook, the Halberdier *'enfant terrible'* (66) of the First War. He is a
blood-thirsty, eye-patched warrior of piratical heroism, based upon Evelyn's
Marines commander, Brigadier Albert Clarence St Clair-Morford. He is also
addicted to practical jokes and insouciantly refers to lethal armed combat as
the 'art of biffing' (140) and views warfare as a glorious 'booby trap' (72).
Apthorpe possesses an ancient 'Bush Thunder-box' (98), an arcane field-
latrine which the brigadier covets. Their comedic impact is drawn together
by this ludicrous piece of military kit, embodying a bygone age of Victorian
soldierly endeavour. Apthorpe and Ritchie-Hook (like Grimes in *Decline
and Fall*) ultimately belong to Evelyn's pantheon of comic immortals –
characters who transcend their ridiculous realities through sheer anarchic
vitality.

Greene regarded *Men at Arms* as possibly Evelyn's best book and,
although grateful for such encouragement, he noted that he had just
completed his forty-ninth year and was now at the 'grand climacteric' which
would determine the direction of the rest of his creative life.[15] Just as *Scott-
King* and *Helena* focused upon the danger of politics and state-craft, so *Men
at Arms* instigates a new concern in his fictions with the insidious threat
of public causes.[16] This powerful first novel in his war trilogy marked the

ascendancy of a creative polarity which was to guide the remainder of his writings. Although laced with reassuringly comic touches, it also offers a sober and challenging reflection upon the personal vicissitudes and global destructions of war. It defines Evelyn as an authoritative commentator on the follies and aggressions of humankind but also as one who should not merely be defined through his religious affiliations.

In November 1952 Anthony Eden invited General Tito to visit London since his independent Yugoslavia was now crucial to Britain's Cold War dealings with Eastern Europe. In what was to be his last intervention in public affairs, Evelyn drafted, an angry article, 'Our Guest of Dishonour', denouncing his despicable talent for deceiving the British. He claimed that Tito had only fostered Allied support so that he could deal with the internal conflicts between the Serbian royalists and Croatian nationalists. He suspected that the British had been tricked into supporting Tito so that he could convert his once Christian nation into a godless, communist state. He also sent letters from Piers Court denouncing Tito to the *New Statesman*, the *Spectator*, *The Times* and the *Sunday Times* and delivered a well-attended lecture in March for the Catholic Truth Society at Glasgow (coinciding with the award of the James Tait Black prize to *Men at Arms*). His earnest Catholicism also impacted on other potentially lucrative writing opportunities. He turned down an offer from the Beaverbrook Press to cover the Coronation (2 June 1953) because, as the author of *Edmund Campion*, he found distasteful the celebratory euphoria for a new 'Elizabethan' age. Like Guy Crouchback, Evelyn recognized no British monarch after James II and he refused to be drawn into celebrating the accession of a new Protestant monarch.[17]

Love Among the Ruins and *The Ordeal of Gilbert Pinfold*

In contrast to this confident, worldly persona, Evelyn's writings also increasingly focused upon a neurotic sense of mental and physical disintegration. Such problems were exacerbated by his chronic insomnia and habitually excessive use of alcohol and medicinal drugs, especially chloral and bromide. Family life was also more fraught with constant money worries and his energetic children less easy to ignore as they grew older. A disturbing sense of social and psychological alienation came to the fore in his experimental novella, *Love Among the Ruins* (published, 1 June 1953, the day before the Coronation), a fantasy-satire tracing the exploits of a previously incarcerated arsonist who finds himself let loose into a dystopian quasi-egalitarian Britain.[18] Its title – previously utilized in novels by Warwick Deeping (1904) and Angela Thirkell (1948) – echoes Browning's poem, 'Love Among the Ruins', in which a disconsolate shepherd views a desolate city, ruined because its inhabitants failed to recognize that only 'Love is best'. He had begun in early 1951 to draft a long story about the euthanasia trade, 'A Pilgrim's Progress', and had tinkered with it over the next two years. It encapsulates many of his current pet-hates, including politicians, the Welfare State, egalitarianism, plastic, abstract art, psychoanalysis, utilitarian architecture and post-war urban development.

Miles Plastic, an archetypal 'Modern Man' expensively educated by the State, is employed by the Department for Euthanasia which provides an essential service for its godless and proletarian society.

> Euthanasia had not been part of the original 1945 Health Service; it was a Tory measure designed to attract votes from the aged and the mortally sick. Under the Bevan-Eden Coalition the service came into general use and won instant popularity. (479–80)

The aged and terminally ill regard it as an essential service and teachers are even pressing for it to be applied to difficult children. Christian festivals are historicized as merely folklore and religion has been usurped by psychology, with all children psycho-analysed on a monthly basis. The novella is subtitled *A Romance of the Near Future* since Miles loves the artistic Clara, a young ballet dancer. She has grown a golden beard after a botched sterilization operation and when she becomes pregnant by Miles she impassively has the child aborted. She then has her beard surgically removed, at 'Santa-Claus-tide' (490), but Miles is disgusted by the sight of the synthetic salmon-pink lower-face mask covering her scars. Eventually, Miles abandons Clara and returns to his only true source of solace – arson. It enables him to purge the dehumanized monotony of the new, godless Welfare State by burning down his former rehabilitation hospital, Mountjoy Castle. Incorporating so many of his pet-hates, this novella becomes Evelyn's grim pastiche of dystopian science fiction. Even art itself is diminished and maimed in this dysfunctional world, as symbolized by his cutting up of old Canova-style engravings for the illustrations, onto which he then inked essential details such as Clara's beard. Similarly, the frontispiece depicts Miles and Clara as Cupid and Psyche but in this emotionally sterile world, Cupid has lost his wings.

While Evelyn's literary persona as a worldly wise novelist and social commentator was being steadily obliterated by that of a self-disgusted and mentally disorientated satirist, Catholicism provided his only remaining source of sanity and personal solace. At the end of 1952 he undertook a personal pilgrimage to the Portuguese dependency of Goa to witness the final exposition of the relics of the co-founder of the Society of Jesus, St Francis Xavier (1506–52), whose bones had remained miraculously uncorrupted until the eighteenth century. The resulting article, 'Goa: the Home of a Saint' (commissioned by *Picture Post* but withdrawn when they sought to edit it down), proved exceptionally difficult to place. This was mainly due to Evelyn's irascible personal dealings with editors of journals which had previously published his work and his article eventually only appeared (without fees) in the December 1953 issues of the *Month* and *Esquire*. The once lionized novelist was now reduced to hawking his wares around what he viewed as a base and unsympathetic press. 'Having entered manhood as Lupin-Hamlet', Martin Stannard comments, 'Waugh saw himself in his early fifties becoming Pooter-Lear'.[19] The time was ripe for the total collapse of this disturbed and disillusioned author.

By autumn 1953 Evelyn was enduring various physical and mental discomforts, including rheumatism, arthritis, sciatica, insomnia, deafness, headaches, loss of memory and internal 'voices'. Two insidiously probing interviews (the second recorded twice because he was so unhappy with the first version) for the BBC's *Personal Call* and *Frankly Speaking* radio programmes also proved psychologically draining. For his fiftieth birthday in October, John Betjeman gave him a William Burges wash-stand which he examined with delight in London before having it transported to Piers Court. But when it arrived, Evelyn became convinced that a bronze spigot extruding from its tap was missing, even though it soon became clear that he had entirely imagined this artefact. What he feared most was a steady decent into a pathetically dependent form of schizoid madness, just the kind of decline recalled in Sir Hall Caine's *Recollections of Rossetti* of the painter's final drug-induced hallucinations. Evelyn's own artistic and personal life had echoed Rossetti's in so many ways and he well knew that the painter had become seriously deranged at fifty – exactly the age he had now reached.[20]

Instead of sensibly consulting a reputable doctor, Evelyn decided upon a restorative period of sun and travel, sailing from Liverpool on 29 January 1954 for a brief trip to Ceylon, via Port Said and Aden. During the voyage his behaviour became dangerously irrational as he was haunted by aural hallucinations and threatening fantasies, many of which seem to emanate from his pathological dislike of his recent BBC interviewer, Stephen Black. Following the captain's advice, Evelyn was disembarked at Port Said (where She-Evelyn had been hospitalized during their disastrous honeymoon in 1929), from where he travelled to Ceylon and then rapidly back to London. Fortunately Father Caraman (Father Westmacott in *Pinfold*) dined with Evelyn and Laura that evening and wisely dismissed his suspicions that he might be diabolically possessed. Instead, he called the Catholic physician and psychoanalyst, E. B. Strauss, who swiftly diagnosed a case of severe bromide poisoning. Evelyn was relieved to find that once his bromide intake was stopped and his use of chloral replaced by paraldehyde, his terrifying symptoms ceased entirely. Moreover, these experiences now provided materials for a new novel – a genuine source of joy to a writer who had been convinced that his powers of literary creativity had been irrevocably waning.[21]

The Ordeal of Gilbert Pinfold (1957) offers a lacerating exposure of Evelyn's psychiatric collapse and is replete with multi-layered personal echoes. The name Pinfold was borrowed from the recusant family who once owned Piers Court, which itself supplied the model for Pinfold's residence, Lychpole (a name in turn borrowed from the village where Frank Crease had lived during Evelyn's Lancing days). As the title of its first chapter suggests, it offers a dark 'Portrait of the Artist in Middle Age'. Its protagonist is a devout Catholic novelist who shares most of Evelyn's emphatically negative tastes:

> He abhorred plastics, Picasso, sunbathing, and jazz – everything in fact that had happened in his own lifetime. The tiny kindling of charity which came to him through his religion sufficed only to temper his disgust and change it to boredom. (14)

Suffering from insomnia, Pinfold indulges in medicinal solutions and, like Evelyn, is traumatized by a hostile radio interviewer. He even receives a gift of an ornate wash-stand from which he thinks that a pipe is missing. When he goes on a sea-voyage the situation darkens. Evelyn's vessel, the *Staffordshire*, is renamed the *Caliban*, and is populated by malevolent sprites and devils. They are led by his radio interrogator, now known as 'Angel', and reveal the horrifying fantasies which had plagued Evelyn's imagination on the voyage out to Ceylon. 'Voices' overheard by Pinfold seem constantly to be plotting his demise. Eventually, Mrs Pinfold and his medical practitioner simply change his medication and the world of sanity is once more restored as the delighted Pinfold set to work to write up his experiences as 'A Conversation Piece'.

When *Pinfold* was published by Chapman and Hall on 19 July 1957, it was received with a bewildered mixture of acclaim for breaking new fictional ground and fascination over Evelyn's courageous self-exposure. Philip Toynbee wrote of *Pinfold* in the *Observer*: 'These are the self-revelations of a remarkably honest and brave man who has also allowed us to see that he is a likeable one'. Others saw Pinfold's habitual offering to the world 'a front of pomposity mitigated by indiscretion' as Evelyn's half-hearted apology for his renowned irascibility and boorishness. Pinfold's catacomb mentality, his habit of digging 'ever deeper into the rock' (13), accurately described Evelyn's own sequestered life in rural Gloucestershire. Writing *Pinfold*, then, had proved a crucial psychological purgation and literary restorative, enabling Evelyn to move on from a peculiarly challenging and unhappy period to complete the major achievement of his later years, *Sword of Honour*.[22]

Officers and Gentlemen

After his return from Ceylon and significant health improvements due to sensible medicinal changes, Evelyn contributed a moving foreword to a translation from the Latin of the life of a Jesuit missionary, *William*

Weston: The Autobiography of an Elizabethan (1955) by Philip Caraman who had previously published the life of another Jesuit martyr, John Gerard (including a preface by Graham Greene). While he viewed Gerard as a heroic adventurer, Weston seemed more like the recently deceased French Catholic author and polemicist, George Bernanos (d.1948):

> With Gerard we were reading Buchan. Here it is Bernanos; one the unambiguous man of action; the other the mystic beset with the mystic's devils, drawn to the desperate; contemporaries of the same Society, pursuing the same ends and the same dangers, but distinct from one another by all the breadth of catholicity. (viii)

He was also able to complete by December 1954 the second volume of his semi-autobiographical war trilogy, *Officers and Gentlemen* (1955). But his anticipated pleasure at finishing this major work was curtailed by the death on 6 December of his mother aged eighty-four. Seeking escape, he gladly accepted an invitation from Ann Fleming, then the wife of James Bond's creator, to visit in January their home, 'Goldeneye', at Jamaica. Predictably, Evelyn found Ann's delight in the rich landscapes and birdlife of the island exceptionally tedious but his relentless boredom was productively channelled into the early drafting of *Pinfold*.

Officers and Gentlemen, eloquently expressing his characteristic preoccupations with family dishonour, personal betrayal and moral failure, had been long in gestation. In March 1953 Evelyn had assured his agent Peters that he had begun it promisingly under the title 'Happy Warriors'. But progress was slow over the coming months, leading to a determined effort to complete it in October 1953. Yet again, his energy levels seemed to let him down and by December he had accumulated only 25,000 words before grinding to a complete halt, probably at the section published as 'Book One', 'Happy Warriors'. This narrative marked Guy's entry into the Commandos and traces his complicity in the tragic chaos of the British militia on Crete and, ultimately, the cultural collapse of post-war Europe. It can be readily imagined just how difficult Evelyn found it to draft this material.[23]

Evelyn's own war diaries provided the basic framework for *Officers and Gentlemen*. The shame of their memories is echoed when Guy, in a 'symbolic act' (240) of attempted self-purgation, casts into the incinerator his pocket-book containing notes on his military experiences. In this second novel Guy joins the upper-class Commandos after the failed Dakar expedition, undergoes training in Scotland and then embarks for the disastrous Crete engagement, the focal point of his disillusionment with war. After his arrival there, with a ramshackle evacuation of Allied troops already underway, he finds that his 'Hookforce' commandos and the Second Halberdiers are the only units still 'capable of fighting' (180). The novel concludes with his ignominious escape from Crete, his gradual physical and mental recovery and his disillusioned reversion back to the Halberdiers.

The novel's moral momentum is generated by an intriguing range of characters, thrown together in a calculatedly fragmentary plot which reflects the jarring dislocations of wartime. Almost as a morality tale, *Officers and Gentlemen* reveals how self-interest, disloyalty, cowardice and basic military disorganization leads inexorably to a casual indifference for the value of human life and the failure of crucial strategic operations. Guy himself represents a progressively less innocent version of the traditional picaresque naïve narrator. At the opening of the novel he still resembles a Poussin shepherd who has not as yet fully engaged with mortality. The sight of bombed London ablaze merely reminds him of 'Holy Saturday at Downside', and how beside the 'glowing brazier' the priest stood 'with his hyssop, paradoxically blessing fire with water' (9). Returning to the Southsand of *Men at Arms*, he is cheered by the bland optimism of his friend, Mr Goodall, who is 'elated by the belief that a great rising was imminent throughout Christian Europe; led by the priests and squires, with blessed banners, and the relics of the saints . . . this Pilgrimage of Grace' (40–1).

In a poignant echo of *Brideshead*, Guy has to report to Flat 211 of Marchmain House on St James's. He is invited to train with X Commando on the Isle of Mugg, under the command of Tommy Backhouse, the former husband of Virginia his former wife – an awkward personal association, suggesting that even the sacrament of marriage no longer seems to mean much during wartime. Another Catholic sacrament, confession, seems fatally comprised when Guy is briefly at Alexandria, an 'ancient asparagus bed of theological absurdity' (122). Before his mission to Crete, Guy dutifully goes to confession as part of his Easter duties but, after confessing, he is suspiciously quizzed by a priest who turns out to be an Alsatian spy.

The total collapse of traditional religious and military values is evident when Guy finds on Crete a dead British soldier whose dog-tag reveals him to be a Catholic. Guy dutifully utters the traditional prayer for the dead and, following army procedure, leaves the green tag on the body and takes the red one for later identification. During his arduous evacuation from Crete in an open boat, he clings onto the red ID badge, hallucinating that it is Gervase's holy medal and praying to 'Saint Roger of Waybroke' (228). Eventually, he puts it in an envelope and asks Mrs Stitch to post it to British Headquarters. She readily agrees but, as soon as Guy is out of sight, discards the envelope in a bin since she thinks that it really contains Guy's written statement about the ignominious behaviour of one of her officer friends, Ivor Claire. Guy feels that he has returned, sullied and disheartened by his experiences on Crete, to an irredeemably fallen world. He has also finally learnt that modern warfare can never be regarded as a quasi-mythic or holy war but rather that his 'country was led blundering into dishonour' (240) – a phrase repeated in the 'Synopsis' of *Unconditional Surrender*.

The two characters from *Men at Arms* who supply Guy with a clear moral and military compass, his father and Brigadier Ritchie-Hook, are largely absent from *Officers and Gentleman*. At the opening of the novel

Mr Crouchback contributes to the war effort by teaching at Our Lady of Victory's Preparatory School but the boys constantly side-track him into nostalgic accounts of the capture of his Jesuit missionary ancestor, the Blessed Gervase Crouchback. Later he testily grumbles about endless wartime restrictions, remarking that the government might even 'try and stop us praying for people next' (28). But he still remains for all those who encounter him a 'heavenly old man' (33) and a 'symbol of their security' (35). Guy, however, sees little of his father during *Officers and Gentlemen* and an episode in which he appeared at the end of the novel was removed from later drafts.

Similarly, Ritchie-Hook lends his name to the 'Hookforce' operation on Crete, with Guy appointed as its intelligence officer. As a figure of battlefield heroism, his absence from his natural sphere is ironically emphasized when he pops up in the unexpected location of Mrs Julia Stitch's yacht, *Cleopatra*. The imperturbable aged Greek soldier, General Militiades, is a kindred spirit who shares his name with the renowned Athenian general at the Battle of Marathon. Other mythological figures, such as Achilles, Jason, Hector, Hercules, mysteriously populate this twentieth-century military landscape. But Ritchie-Hook remains only a ghostly presence in the novel and at one point Mrs Stitch casually asks: 'Isn't he dead?' (241). As though in preparation for his glorious return in *Unconditional Surrender*, Colonel Tickeridge notes that he has recently been spotted 'biffing' in western Abyssinia and is rumoured to be heading for Cairo.

The novel's other central characters epitomize the morally fallen and self-serving world in which Guy now finds himself. The recently promoted leader of 'Hookforce', Tommy Backhouse (based on Evelyn's commander, Robert Laycock), is pointedly removed from the fictional action (unlike Laycock who had led his unit to safety during the Crete evacuation) by accidentally damaging his leg on board the troop-ship heading to Suda (Souda) Bay. Hence, Backhouse is tactfully absent when as a 'human sacrifice' (198) Hookforce's men are ordered to cover the withdrawal but instead ignominiously save themselves. Major 'Fido' Hound (recalling Evelyn's own shell-shocked Major Colvin), is a coward who is only in the army because he failed the Civil Service examination. He is exposed as a pompous and unimaginative 'lost soul' (177), only able to function according to the rulebook. Eventually, he cracks up in an 'Arcadian vale' and, like a helpless Poussin shepherd, is silently robbed by a 'phantasmagoric' (200) Cretan peasant who strips him of his military equipment and the last vestiges of his self-respect. The sinister soldier-servant, Corporal-Major Ludovic comes to his aid before coldly murdering him on the way back to camp.

Ivor Claire, 'the fine flower of them all', seems the ultimate embodiment of an aristocratic chivalric officer and in Guy's eyes stands for a 'quintessential England' (114). He and Guy share a melancholy humour, 'each in his way saw life *sub specie aeternitatis*' (87). But Ivor's Dunkirk Military Cross had been spuriously won by shooting three territorials who were threatening to swamp his escaping boat. Blatantly ignoring orders to protect the rear-guard during the Crete evacuation, he abandons his own men and cynically remarks that it should be 'quite honourable' (221) for officers to prioritize their own welfare in hopeless situations. Mrs Stitch, like an amoral but all-powerful goddess of the privileged classes, assists Claire in avoiding a court-martial 'for desertion in the face of the enemy' (236), ensuring that he is able to spend the rest of the war safely hidden away in India where his cousin is Viceroy. The machinations of Julia and Ivor illustrate how the Protestant ascendancy no longer acts as the time-tested backbone of England (like the recusant aristocracy) but has become a self-serving elite who cares nothing for the rest of British society.

Officers and Gentlemen suggests how the decline of the English aristocracy has also facilitated the rise of the social-climbing modern man, as embodied in Trimmer (formerly Gustave, a hairdresser on the *Aquitania*), the rapidly promoted Captain/Major/Colonel McTavish. In reality, a deserter from the Argylls, Trimmer is an example of the new proletariat whose natural guile ensures his survival during the chaotic 'Operation Popgun' raid into occupied France. He becomes a grubby nemesis to Guy, casually seducing his former wife, Virginia, and receiving the medal which Guy should have won at Dakar. Through the connivance of his two fraudulent accomplices, General 'Brides-in-the-Bath' Whale and his worldly publicist Ian Kilbannock, Trimmer is finally resurrected by the Ministry of Information as the valiant 'Demon Barber' (212), a national military hero.

In a late addition to the drafting of the novel, Evelyn added the alluring Corporal-Major Ludovic who at first seems a kindred spirit to Guy. As they flee from Crete they climb onto the same boat and Ludovic, 'godless at the helm' (228), dispassionately watches over the delirious Guy. With the other evacuee, a deranged sapper sergeant, mysteriously disappearing overboard, Ludovic eventually carries Guy ashore at Sid Barani and ensures his safe return to Egypt, thereby earning a recommendation for a commission from Tommy Backhouse. Like Guy and Evelyn, Ludovic keeps a meticulous diary and is 'intrigued by theological speculation' (224). But like Guy's brother, Ivo, he also seems oddly attracted to suicide and, thereby, becomes an essential if disturbing fraternal counterpoint to Guy. While his strength seems to rise as Guy weakens in *Officers and Gentlemen*, this process is reversed in *Unconditional Surrender* where he is finally exposed as a deranged interloper.

6

The last years: 1955–66

Piers Court to Combe Florey
and *Ronald Knox*

Evelyn had often considered moving from Piers Court during the early1950s and when his privacy was invaded on 21 June 1955 by a *Daily Express* journalist, Nancy Spain, matters came to a head. She arrived uninvited on his doorstep, with Lord Noel-Buxton, a former Minister of Agriculture and Fisheries, hoping for an interview. They were angrily turned away, leading to a disrespectful account of the incident three days later in Spain's newspaper column and a wry response from Evelyn, 'Awake my Soul! It is a Lord', in the *Spectator* (8 July). He later gained revenge by suing her for libel in the following year. A few days after this unpleasant intrusion, he put Piers Court on the market and a year later completed its sale. Even these domestic affairs caused him further tribulations when the *Daily Mail* ran a headline, 'The Waughs Move On', sneering at Waugh's wealth of books, paintings and statues and claiming that he was searching for a personal Brideshead. The Waughs finally left Piers Court on 1 November 1956 and after a short stay at Pixton moved in January 1957 into their new home, an attractive eighteenth-century manor house in the village of Combe Florey, near Pixton. He hoped to convert its sixteenth-century gatehouse into a private chapel but the Bishop of Clifton declined permission. At the end of this month he finally managed to finish *Pinfold* which was sent off for publication in July.[1]

The battle with Nancy Spain coincided with the resurrection of Alec's literary fortunes. In June 1954 he had begun a new novel which seemed promising and was also happy in a developing relationship with the Mormon writer, Virginia Sorensen, who became his third wife in 1969. She had enjoyed considerable success with her novel, *A Little Lower Than Angels* (1942), and was then writing *Miracles on Maple Hill* (1956), dealing with post-traumatic wartime stress. Alec returned to England in December 1954 for his mother's funeral and collaborated with Evelyn in May 1955 over the Waugh coat-of-arms. His new novel, *Island in the Sun* (1955), dealing with inter-racial romance and made into a film (1957) with James Mason,

Joan Fontaine and Harry Belafonte, proved a runaway success. Alec had struck the 'jack-pot' and the novel made more through its early sales than the total for all of his previous books. With his new-found wealth, he set up a home in Tangier where he spent much of the rest of his life. His novel was published in America just before *Officers and Gentlemen* and for the first time the two brothers were both internationally acclaimed as writers.[2]

To celebrate his triumph in February 1957 over Nancy Spain, Evelyn had hoped to take Laura to the sunshine and luxury hotels of Monte Carlo. Instead, they stayed at Torquay for a week with Ronald Knox, now terminally ill with liver cancer, where Evelyn diligently worked on final revisions to *Pinfold*. After Laura's return home, Evelyn took Knox to Sidmouth for a second grim week and then brought him back to Combe Florey for another fortnight. Only in May were the Waughs able to take their private holiday in Monte Carlo. Knox eventually died on 24 August. Evelyn had already written a long essay on Knox for *Horizon* (May, 1948) and had edited his selected sermons (1950). Knox returned the compliment by dedicating to him his *Enthusiasm* (1950), covering two thousand years of religious affairs. Evelyn had agreed to act as his literary executor and authorized biographer, by far his most ambitious non-fiction project. He corresponded about Knox's life with his confessor, Dom Hubert van Zeller, the Woodruffs and the Prime Minister, Harold Macmillan (who in 1910 had been tutored in the classics by Knox). He also travelled to Rhodesia in February 1958 to interview Daphne Acton who had been instructed by Knox and converted to Catholicism after her marriage into the Catholic family of her husband, John, third Lord Acton (whose sister had married Douglas Woodruff).

Evelyn returned home in March but on 9 June he received news that his eldest son, Auberon, had been seriously wounded in an accident with a jammed Browning machine-gun during his National Service with the Royal Horse Guards in Cyprus. Laura immediately flew out to be with him while Evelyn asked his Catholic friends and the Poor Clares to pray for his son's recovery, visiting him in hospital at London when he was flown home for to recuperate. At Christmas he and his daughter Meg stayed at the Hyde Park Hotel to be to see Auberon more regularly. In November 1959 Auberon was involved in another serious accident, suffering a fractured skull in a car crash, but, as his father noted wryly in mid-December, it had no discernible effect on his behaviour.[3]

After two years work *The Life of the Right Reverend Ronald Knox* was published by Chapman and Hall in October 1959, following serialization in the *Tablet*. It presented Knox as a 'cherished and privileged survivor of a golden age' (134) and was respectfully received by Catholic reviewers. But Knox's preference for being a private chaplain in 'patrician country-houses' to prominent Catholics, such as the Lovats at Beaufort Castle, the Actons at Aldenham and the Asquiths at Mells, associated his life in the public imagination with the privileged world of *Brideshead*. Evelyn had studiously avoided potential accusations of hagiography and tended merely to assert rather than illustrate his subject's spiritual attainments. But Knox and his now largely forgotten translation of the Bible which Evelyn claimed 'brought the Vulgate to life for his own generation' (134), was delineated more as a loyally remembered friend than as a seminal source of spiritual and intellectual inspiration for the majority of English Catholics.

Like his biographies of Rossetti and Campion, Evelyn's account of Knox's life revealed much about his own failings, conversion and aspirations and also seemed to echo the disconsolate tone of *Men at Arms* and *Officers and Gentlemen*. Evelyn paid special attention to the gradual processes of Knox's conversion to the Catholic faith. Born into a well-established family of English churchmen (his father later became Bishop of Manchester), Knox had first developed Anglo-Catholic tastes at Eton, inspired by R. H. Benson's *The Light Invisible* (1903) on the near-reality of the spiritual world. These theological interests grew during a brilliant undergraduate career at Oxford, culminating in his election to a fellowship at Trinity. He was also profoundly moved just after his Finals in June 1910 when he saw the 'Passion Play' at Oberammergau, where he bought his first rosary. He handles delicately how Knox was tutor to the young Harold Macmillan ('C' in the biography) but obliged to leave this congenial post because of his high church leanings. As a student he delighted in his visits to the Caldey community, established in 1906 by Anglican Benedictines, and was intrigued by news in 1913 of their 'defection to Rome' (231). He regularly prayed in Latin and followed high church practices forbidden at Trinity at St Stephen's House and St Thomas's Convent.

During World War I Knox taught at Shrewsbury School to free up men for the front and Evelyn writes movingly of the steady diminution of his circle of Eton and Oxford friends during the ensuing conflicts. Matters culminated in a chance meeting with the Jesuit priest, Father Cyril Martindale (himself a convert), who shrewdly advised Knox that his unease with the Church of England was not enough reason to assume that the Church of Rome was his true spiritual home. The final stages of his conversion and attainment of 'inner peace' are recounted in detail in a 'dry, logical essay' (267), *The Essentials of Spiritual Unity* (1918) and in a more engaging account addressed to his friends, *A Spiritual Aeneid* (1918). He was received into the Catholic Church on 22 September 1917 and confirmed by Cardinal Bourne on 6 October, followed by residence at Brompton Oratory during his studies for the priesthood.

Evelyn avoids attempting to dissect Knox's personal spirituality once he became a Catholic, although he notes how much he had depended (like himself) upon Father D'Arcy who regularly supplied both of them with wise spiritual counsel. Like Evelyn, Knox also manifested many of the personal sensitivities of the convert and felt alienated from the modern world, preferring the enclosed lifestyles of Catholic country houses. Knox was just the kind of priest Evelyn might have become if his own circumstances had turned out differently during the 1920s. Rather than defining Knox's personal theology,

Evelyn casts him as a kindred spirit to Gervase Crouchback, a dignified reminder of a better but now lost world of humility and personal integrity. In his later years, he argues, Knox was unappreciated by the Catholic hierarchy (especially Cardinal Bourne, patron of the despised Ernest Oldmeadow) and he depicts him as an ignored intellectual, bereft of appropriate official recognition – just as he often viewed himself during the late-1950s and, later, in his autobiography, *A Little Learning* (1964).

A Tourist in Africa

In autumn 1958, F. J. Stopp's pioneering study, *Evelyn Waugh: Portrait of an Artist*, was published, confirming Evelyn's reputation as a major literary figure. Worn out by completing his *Knox* biography, he now hoped for some all-expenses-paid time in the sun and asked his agent, Peters, to set up a magazine deal to revisit India to research possible publications on Indian Christianity. Instead, Peters negotiated with Union Castle a promotional trip to Africa, in return for a favourable travel book about his experiences. Before the arrival of the *Knox* proofs, Evelyn left London on 28 January 1959, travelling first to Genoa by train where he joined up with Diana 'Mrs Stitch' Cooper. They visited together the Campo Santo cemetery, which afforded an aesthetically pleasing contrast to the garish memorials of Forest Lawn, California. He then sailed on the *Rhodesia Castle* to Mombasa, repeating his voyage of 1930–1 when, as a disillusioned young man, he had travelled to Abyssinia. After several weeks touring through Central and East Africa, he returned in early April via Cape Town on Union Castle's flagship liner, the *Pendennis Castle*. Evelyn found an account of his experiences (also required to provide positive publicity for Union Castle) exceptionally difficult to draft. He based some of its narratives on his earlier journey to Rhodesia to interview Daphne Acton for his *Knox* and padded out his prose with information derived from guide-books. *A Tourist in Africa* was published in September 1960 to mixed reviews. As Cyril Connolly noted, Evelyn's narrative pose: 'of an elderly, infirm and irritable old buffer, quite out of touch with the times' was little 'suited to enthusiasm, a prerequisite of travel writing'.[4]

Even a visit to a remote Jesuit mission, where Western-European and African religious cultures harmoniously coexisted, is frustratingly truncated. Also, *A Tourist* – researched in 1959 and published in 1960 – should have offered valuable commentary on a crucial moment in world affairs. These were key years in the rapid decolonization of Africa by both Britain and France, leading to a series of flimsily constructed new 'constitutions' and, inevitably, subsequent decades of coups and counter-coups. But, instead, Evelyn chose largely to side-step the intractable complexities of modern African politics. Ultimately, *A Tourist* seems to offer little more than a valedictory rewriting of his earlier *Remote People* and to hold up Africa in 1960 as merely a 'cracked mirror' to his 'mythology of Victorian England'.[5]

Evelyn's personal relationship with his children was often fraught at this period, especially with Auberon who left Oxford after failing his examinations but then enjoyed some early literary success and an expensive bachelor life in London. He was also anxious over his daughter Teresa's relationship with a presentable (but Protestant) American scholar, John D'Arms. But his personal pride in his home, lifestyle and family was much in evidence when in April 1959 he invited Mark Gerson to compile a photographic record of life at Combe Florey, published in both *Good Housekeeping* and the *Tatler*. It is possible that these images were compiled because Evelyn was tacitly anticipating some wholesome publicity for his literary career. He hoped to be awarded a knighthood in the forthcoming list of the Birthday Honours but when in May 1959 the expected letter arrived, it merely offered a CBE. Enraged, Evelyn crumpled up this invitation and angrily turned down the honour as beneath his dignity. He soon regretted this decision since it effectively marked the end of a lifetime of meticulous social climbing.[6]

During summer 1959 Evelyn was planning to write, as a companion to his *Rossetti*, a biography of Holman Hunt. However, the demands of more lucrative commissions side-lined this scheme which could have proved beneficial to his spirits since his passion for Victorian art had remained a constant source of pleasure. Instead, *Brideshead* was out of print by 1959 and a new edition was planned. He seized this opportunity to make numerous emendations (especially excising passages considered sentimental) and also rewrote the awkward love-making scene on the ship between Ryder and Julia. In an explanatory 'Preface' he explained how the novel had been drafted during a time of hardship and rationing and now seemed 'infused' with 'gluttony', not only for food and drink but also for historical splendour and overly ornate language – an excess which he now found distasteful.[7] The revised edition appeared in July 1960 and remains the toned-down version of the novel read by most modern readers.

Money was still perilously short and Laura even gave up her beloved herd of cows because they were no longer deductible against income tax. Evelyn agreed to write for the *Daily Mail* (28 December 1959) and article, 'I See Nothing But Boredom . . . Everywhere', offering his predictions for the new decade. He professed indifference towards escalating worries over a nuclear holocaust and predicted another world war within ten years. He also lamented the loss of the aristocracy and the total breakdown of the class system which he viewed as having once been at the heart of the British character's rich diversity. This article was followed up by a revealing interview with Kenneth Allsopp, 'The Living Arts 1960 . . . Waugh Looks Forward to Poverty' (26 April 1960), for the same newspaper. Seeking to sustain this potentially lucrative line of income, Peters hastily set up another deal with the *Daily Mail* for four articles, involving Evelyn and Laura travelling during January and February 1960 to Venice, Monte Carlo and Greece, with Meg joining him for the final stage to Athens.[8]

Still stressed over financial affairs, Evelyn readily accepted £250 for a radio adaptation of *Pinfold* (broadcast, 7 June 1960) which was well received and usefully boosted his public profile. Keen for more positive publicity, he agreed to appear on the BBC's inquisitorial interview series, *Face to Face* (broadcast, 26 June 1960), hosted by the former Labour MP, John Freeman. Evelyn prepared meticulously for this interview, even asking Tom Driberg whether he knew anything damaging about Freeman which he might utilize if questioning became too hostile. Freeman specialized in probing his interviewees for difficult memories and was then notorious for having recently reduced Gilbert Harding to tears. Happily, Evelyn's interview proved a resounding triumph, concluding with Freeman asking him why he had agreed to appear on the programme and receiving the succinct reply: 'Poverty'.[9]

Unconditional Surrender

At the height of the Cold War Evelyn began in spring 1960 the third volume of his war trilogy, 'Conventional Weapons', with a prescient awareness that it would probably be his last major work of fiction. Completed in April 1961, it was published in the autumn by Chapman and Hall as *Unconditional Surrender* (US title, *The End of the Battle*). This elegiac novel conveys Guy's terminal disillusionment with the concept of heroic war and his sense of personal betrayal. It also implicitly echoes Evelyn's own sense of despair over the post-war state of Western-European society. 'With that book he drew a line beneath his career as a novelist, and his detachment from the future was complete'.[10]

The novel opens with a synopsis of the first two volumes in the trilogy, describing the Crouchbacks as an old, west-country Catholic family from gentry stock, related to many other notable recusant English families. It explains the sad history of Guy's marriage to Virginia and how he had once viewed the war as a means of revitalizing an interest in his fellow men. The Prologue, 'Locust Years' (years of adversity, cited by Churchill in 1936 to refer to Britain's failure to respond to Germany's rearmament), finds Guy back with the Halberdiers and enviously hearing of Ritchie-Hook 'biffing' his way across North Africa. But after two dreary years of training camps, he is deemed too old to join his battalion overseas on active service. Guy is on leave, staying with his father at Matchet, when news of Italy's surrender reaches them. They discuss the role of the Catholic Church during the war, with Guy deriding the optimism once generated by the Lateran Treaty (1929) between Pope Pius XI and Mussolini. Under its terms Catholicism was established as the official religion of Italy but the Pope was required to observe perpetual neutrality in political affairs. Guy's father angrily rejects his son's cynicism over the treaty, reminding him in a letter of just how many souls may have been 'reconciled and have died at peace' (17) because of it and insisting that suffering and injustice are unavoidable aspects of the human condition.

The first book of *Unconditional Surrender* begins on 29 October 1943, Guy's fortieth birthday, with the display of the 'Sword of Stalingrad' at Westminster Abbey. The original Sword of Honour had been commissioned by King George VI in February 1943 and, after being displayed at Westminster Abbey (29–31 October), was presented to Stalin by Churchill at the Tehran Conference (November 1943). In the novel, the upright sword is piously displayed between two candles on a table made to resemble an altar. It offers a debased comparison to the sword of Sir Roger de Waybroke on which Guy had 'dedicated himself' (19) four years earlier. The idea for the sword had been inspired by the bogus heroism of Trimmer who had wielded a rarely used commando dagger in a propaganda raid. The sword symbolizes a secular union of a Christian England with communist Russia and confirms in Guy's dispirited mind that the war will prove a spiritual disaster even if the Allies claim military victory.[11]

As an Italian speaker, Guy is recruited to assist with the liberation of Italy but receives a telegram from his sister, Angela Box-Bender, announcing the peaceful death of his father. The funeral is attended by representative members of renowned English Catholic families, including the Treshams, Bigods, Englefields, Arundells and Dacres. As the service progresses, Guy remembers his father's simple piety and humility, acknowledging him as the 'best man, the only entirely good man' (65) whom he had known. He becomes a kind of patron saint for Guy, when he prays *to* rather than *for* him, leading to his recognition that his devotions have been tainted by deadening influence of spiritual apathy. Praying is for Guy merely like signing the visitors' book at an embassy or dutifully reporting for unknown military duties. He can only sustain himself through a vague expectation that somehow he will eventually be called upon to fulfil a Divine summons. As he watches over the melancholy dispersal of the contents of Broome there are hints that through the death of his father Guy will begin to find a way of re-kindling the dying embers of his former faith and, thereby, finally confirm his personal role in the world.

Guy's spiritual malaise and empty prayers closely reflect Evelyn's own depression at this period. At the heart of *Unconditional Surrender* lies an exploration of how through prayerful humility, a believer may shake off spiritual sloth and embrace God's predetermined vocation. Ultimately, Guy must make a slow and painful journey towards contrition and compassion as the only viable route to revitalizing his moribund spirituality, long withered by personal and wartime misfortunes. As in *Brideshead*, readers of *Unconditional Surrender* are invited to sustain an awareness of two contrasting levels of reality. On one side is the fallen human world of wartime indifference and deception and, on the other, the divinely ordered world of God – a distinction hinted at by the trilogy's persistent use of the liturgical calendar (especially Christmas and Easter) to mark key events. Both novels have as a central moment the death of a father and its spiritual aftermath. But in *Unconditional Surrender* God's providential signs are not found in moments of high drama, such as Lord Marchmain's deathbed Sign of the Cross, but rather through more mundane aspects of ordinary life.

Guy's uncle Peregrine, his father's younger brother, is a supposedly devout Catholic and a Knight of the Order of St John of Jerusalem. But his outward conformity masks an inner spiritual emptiness. He despises Catholic converts and regards secular Marxism with equal distaste, remarking that he would prefer a Japanese invasion of Europe because they at least have a king and a religion. Much to Virginia's amusement, he admits that he has only ever been to bed twice with a woman, the same one twenty-five years apart. He even seems pruriently interested in a casual sexual liaison with her until he is shocked by her plan to remarry Guy after becoming pregnant with Trimmer's child. Ultimately, Peregrine is a dried-out old hypocrite and hints at what Guy himself may become if his ennui with life continues.

When Virginia cannot locate an abortionist she tentatively raises with Peregrine, in despair, the idea of her becoming a Catholic and also bluntly admits to Guy that she is pregnant by Trimmer. Her friend, Kerstie Kilbannock, is shocked at what she sees as Guy's easy entrapment, even though it was her husband, Ian, who had first suggested this solution to Virginia. Surprisingly, Guy welcomes this chance to remedy a life in which previously he has never done a 'single, positively unselfish action' (150). When Kerstie remonstrates and asks what difference it would make if there were one or more less child in the world without a father, Guy turns once again to the wise words of his father's letter: '*If only one soul was saved, that is full compensation for any amount of "loss of face"*' (151).

Written words are of profound significance in *Unconditional Surrender*. In one of its most challenging aspects, a dialogic tension is set up between the misleading powers of writers and the true potency of simple human kindness, charity and humility. At the heart of this debate lie the duplicities of officially sanctioned literary disseminations and the self-deceptive *pensées* of individual writers. Under the first category, fun is poked at the grand aspirations of Cyril Connolly's *Horizon* through the guise of the Everard Spruce and his vacuous magazine, *Survival*, which is guaranteed rare paper supplies by the Ministry of Information. Its title is ironic in that its editor, Spruce, is depicted as a man who despairs of the future and is convinced that humanity is hurtling towards chaos. He has also recently published Ludovic's sparse and precious '*Pensées*' (32). During the 1930s Ludovic had been a protégé of the influential diplomat and general fixer, Sir Ralph Brompton, who was renowned for his predilection for effeminate young 'pansies' (96). But, like other aspects of his character, Ludovic's sexuality remains ambiguous and, instead, his energies are now exclusively focused on his literary ambitions. Forever writing down notes on his ideas, Ludovic finds that the less he concerns himself with society and conversation, the more the fluency of printed and written words fill his mind. Perhaps echoing Evelyn's own fears over using the solitude of writing as a means of withdrawing psychologically from everyday human society, he is described as an addict of the most powerful 'intoxicant, the English language' (39).[12]

In *Officers and Gentlemen* Ludovic had assumed the role of a kindred spirit to Guy, acting as his secular guardian angel during the arduous voyage from Crete. But, as Guy's spiritual awareness revives in *Unconditional Surrender* through the posthumous influence of his saintly father so the potency of the malevolent Ludovic, now a major in the Intelligence Corps, steadily diminishes. In *Pinfold*, Evelyn had traced the frightening psychological disintegration of a fundamentally decent writer who had temporarily destroyed his sanity through medicinal abuse. But in Ludovic he tracks the more disturbing mental collapse of a calculating sociopath who fears that his murderous past is catching up with him. Evelyn may have seen in this godless but highly literate character a diabolical parody of his own identity as a writer – Ludovic is a nightmare vision of what Evelyn could have become without religious faith and Laura. Consequently, Ludovic views Guy (who echoes so many of Evelyn's own wartime experiences) with unmitigated horror and unceremoniously flees when they meet up again at one of Spruce's dire literary parties. He is afraid that Guy will expose his murders of Major Hound and the sapper who disappeared overboard during the sea-voyage from Crete. When he then finds that he is commanding Guy's parachute training at No. 4 Special Training Centre, Ludovic's sanity entirely collapses. He orders his own name to be removed from all official documents and hides away upstairs, much to the consternation of his junior officer and the chief training instructor who assume that he is suffering from persecution mania.

As Ludovic, self-imprisoned in his bedroom, sinks further into his private hell at the camp, Guy makes his first parachute jump and seems, spiritually, to ascend in the opposite direction. He experiences a transcendental moment of ecstatic rapture, something as close to a 'foretaste of paradise' as his 'earthbound soul' (102) can ever hope to attain. Unluckily, he damages his knee on landing and is spirited away to a nearby hospital. Ludovic, now unambiguously Guy's 'angel of death' (104), hopes that he has been killed in a 'Roman candle' accident (when a jumper plummets to his death, shrouded in his unopened parachute) and happily comes downstairs again to dine with his trainees, who promptly dub him 'Major Dracula'. When he realizes that Guy is still alive, he contradicts the instructor's negative recommendations about Guy's age and agility and recommends him for immediate transfer to combat action. In a final, bizarre twist, Ludovic then acquires 'for *love*' (107) a pet Pekinese puppy and christens it Fido, in depraved memory of the first (known) victim of his homicidal tendencies, Major 'Fido' Hound.

The action of Book Three shifts from England to Bari as Guy, having remarried Virginia, joins up with British forces in the Adriatic. Back home, Virginia is living with Peregrine and completing her Catholic instruction as Trimmer's child develops within her. In a strange parallel of gestation,

Ludovic's embryonic *Pensées* also grow into a novelist's urge as he is possessed with unwavering fluency and his literary inspiration finally takes flight. As new life grows within Virginia and Ludovic, in disturbing contrast, a visiting English musician at Bari, Sir Almeric Griffiths, bluntly tells Guy that he sees in him a 'death wish' (170). Two days later Guy is ordered to fly to Croatia and beforehand goes to confession in the local church, confirming that he wishes to die. The priest dismisses this disclosure as a mere scruples rather than sinfulness and, after granting Absolution, craftily enquires whether Guy can spare any cigarettes. At the same moment, Virginia is making her first confession at Westminster Cathedral. As she feels 'Little Trimmer' stirring inside her, she is delighted to find that five minutes honest confession can sweep away all her previous misdemeanours.

In Croatia, all religions are under siege from the communist partisans, who lounge around at the back of Catholic masses, listening for subversive sermons. Elsewhere, a mosque is burned and an Orthodox church is blown up and its cemetery desecrated. Guy and the rest of the Allied forces become unwilling participants in the subversion of a once proudly Christian nation. His camp at Begoy then receives an influx of over one hundred Jewish refugees, survivors from an Italian concentration camp. Their spokeswoman, a Hungarian called Mme Kanyi, communicates with Guy in Italian and explains that many Jews have been massacred by the Ustachi. She and her husband, an engineer, had been captured in 1939 when on their way to Australia but they all now wish to travel to Italy where many of the group have relatives. The appearance of the Kanyis enabled Evelyn to incorporate into the ending of *Unconditional Surrender* his short story, 'Compassion', written twelve years earlier about the frustrations and guilt of a Major Gordon who tries to help some Jewish refugees caught in a Displaced Persons camp run by Partisans. He had been planning since at least 1954 to utilize Gordon's dilemma as a means of concluding his war trilogy and many elements of 'Compassion', a key concept in Guy's spiritual journey, reappear in conclusion of *Unconditional Surrender*.[13]

Guy receives a garbled radio signal informing him that Virginia has given birth to a son on 4 June, symbolically, also the day of the Allies' entry to Rome. The infant is christened Gervase and the un-maternal Virginia has it sent away to be looked after by an old family nanny. Simultaneously, Ludovic also gives 'birth', with the completion of his novel, twice as long as *Ulysses*. His lavish melodrama draws on his experiences with Sir Ralph Brompton during the 1930s and seems a parodic reworking of *Brideshead*, although with God entirely removed from the narrative. His heroine, Lady Marmaduke is a passionate woman who, like Lord Marchmain, is destined to die in a luxuriant decline. Finally, Ludovic endows the first page of his typescript with its lugubrious title, *The Death Wish* – a mocking reminder of Guy's earlier death wish before he left Bari for Croatia.

In Croatia, a world of 'hate' and 'waste', Guy remains determined to assist Mme Kanyi and the Jewish refugees as his personal opportunity for doing a 'single small act' which might 'redeem' (192) these fallen times. But he then receives two letters, one written six weeks earlier by Virginia, full of references to 'it' (baby Gervase); and the other sent two weeks later by his sister, Angela, informing him that Virginia and Peregrine were killed when a doodle-bomb destroyed their flat but that she has Gervase. Guy, strangely unmoved, simply attends Mass where the holy bell reminds him of his duty to his dead wife. He goes back to the presbytery to explain in Latin to the priest: 'Uxor mea mortua est' (197) and offers a Mass for her soul. But this brief contact is observed by partisans as a suspicious liaison and the priest is brought in for interrogation. Back home, Angela talks to her childhood friend, Eloise Plessington, about Virginia and takes consolation that her death occurred at a moment in her life when she might be reasonably sure of attaining heaven – 'eventually' (201). Eloise offers to look after her god-son, Gervase while Guy is still abroad, partly to lure her tomboy twenty-five-year old daughter, Domenica, away from her land-girl activities.

Throughout *Unconditional Surrender*, sporadic references are made to Ben Ritchie-Hook, variously, 'biffing' through North Africa. Guy laments his absence from Italy after his promotion to major-general and regrets the general lack of 'biffing' in Bari. But he then hears that Ritchie-Hook has had a monumental row with General Montgomery and is at a loose end. Keen to attract US support and generate some useful propaganda, the Partisans plan (with British connivance) a bogus raid not on Germans but on a small party of fellow Yugoslavs holed up in a small fort, formerly part of Christendom's defences against the Turk. Ian Kilbannock, now a press-officer, is scheduled to fly from Bari to Croatia with a small party drawn together to witness this sham engagement. At dinner, he is astonished to see in attendance a veritable ghost from the past, the stiff and aged figure of Ritchie-Hook, who also turns up uninvited at the airfield. After flying through the night, their plane crashes and bursts into flames with various fatalities. Ian is concussed but, predictably, Ritchie-Hook seems revitalized by this lethal incident.

Guy is one of the rescuers and, through him, Ritchie-Hook meets the fierce young Montenegrin who is leading the raid, clearly a kindred spirit since he also lacks an eye and part of a hand. Ritchie-Hook regards this sham action as his last chance of participating in active service. As he leads the charge on the fort he is shot but limps slowly on before being killed by a second bullet. His batman, Dawkins, admits that his master had a death wish, once hearing him say that he wished the enemy would shoot better since he didn't want to return home. Spiritually, Ritchie-Hook is seen to have shouldered the burden the death wish formerly carried by Guy. So dies the only true warrior of the *Sword of Honour* trilogy and, simultaneously, the spirit of heroic chivalry which Guy had venerated at the tomb of Sir Roger de Waybroke. The Germans discover his body and, admiring his courage, issuing warning orders to be vigilant for mythically heroic one-eyed men.

Guy still hopes to assist the Jewish refugees and on his forty-first birthday receives information that four Dakotas are being sent to pick them up. In archly biblical imagery, he is described as playing a historic and an ancient role by bringing hope of 'exodus' to the Jews. He is compared to Moses leading his people out of captivity and even his 'cuckold's horns' (226) seem to shine like the patriarch descending from Mount Sinai. Disappointments follow as the airfield becomes fogbound and on several occasions the Jews have to return to the town, although some supplies and new clothing are dropped for them. Meanwhile, Belgrade falls to the Russians and partisans and in celebration a *Te Deum* is sung in the church, followed by an anti-fascist choir. Suddenly, the Jews disappear, supposedly moved to a new camp to avoid enmity with the locals over their new provisions. Guy meets Mme Kanyi who has stayed behind with her husband since his skills with the electrical supply are still required. She laments that no place now seems 'free from evil' and at that moment Guy realizes that he has finally reached the end of his personal 'crusade' (232) to which he had pledged himself at Sir Roger's tomb. As he leaves Begoy, Guy sends magazines and food to Mme Kanyi, a fatal act of generosity since it seems to confirm partisan suspicions that she was Guy's mistress and spy. Back in Italy, he learns that the Kanyis were then arrested, tried by a Peoples' Court and executed.

An Epilogue to *Unconditional Surrender* draws together the plot-lines and moral messages of *Sword of Honour* by focusing on the Festival of Britain in 1951, designed to celebrate the beginning of a happier decade. Tommy Backhouse is retired from the army as a much-decorated major-general with a pretty new wife; Ivor Claire earned a DSO during six months in Burma with the Chindits; Trimmer has disappeared and Guy's brother-in-law, Arthur Box-Bender, has lost his parliamentary seat in the 1945 General Election. Guy has sold Castello Crouchback to Ludovic, now wealthy after the unmerited success of *The Death Wish* and living as a Harold Acton-like aesthete in Italy. Guy has married Domenica Plessington, by whom he has two of his own children, and they live happily in the agent's house at Broome. Box-Bender remarks in the novel's final words that everything seems to have turned out 'very conveniently' (240) for Guy. Although Trimmer's Gervase will displace his own children and inherit Broome, by adopting him Guy has completed his journey away from indifference, guilt and spiritual inertia towards the revitalizing of his soul through acceptance of his true role in life.

Evelyn was unhappy with the assumption that the trilogy had achieved a 'happy' ending and at one stage planned to revise the Epilogue to emphasize the disinheritance of the Crouchback line by Trimmer's child. But this would have blurred the profound, if stark, spiritual message of *Unconditional Surrender*. Bernard Bergonzi observed: 'To anyone brought up as a Catholic Mr Waugh's image of Catholicism is, to say the least, peculiar; and the same thing may well be true of his picture of the gentry. But this is beside the point; it is enough that Mr Waugh has found the myth creatively valuable'.[14] It may even be proposed that without God, Evelyn saw himself as little more than a Ludovic.

Basil Seal Rides Again

After completing *Unconditional Surrender*, Evelyn felt that he was unlikely to write another novel for several years. His creative lassitude was overwhelming and he was equally depressed by the literary outputs of his closest friends. He thought little of either Anthony Powell's *Casanova's Chinese Restaurant* (1960), the fifth volume in his Poussin-inspired *Dance to the Music of Time*, or Nancy Mitford's latest comic novel, *Don't Tell Alfred* (1960), her semi-autobiographical story of an Oxford don and his wife who find themselves in the British Embassy at Paris. Most seriously, Greene sent to him at Christmas a copy of his 'A Visit to Morin' (*London Magazine*, 1957; reprinted, 1960) about a once-acclaimed French writer who is paradoxically caught between his loss of belief in rational explanations for the existence of God and a half-hopeful faith in the truth of the Church. When he read Greene's next novel, *A Burnt Out Case* (1961), set in a leper colony and developing themes raised by 'Morin', Evelyn held genuine fears for his friend's apostasy. During summer 1961 he also sought to defend his literary hero, P. G. Wodehouse, after Duff Cooper's Ministry of Information had deemed as treasonable his broadcasts from Germany during the war. In a BBC radio talk to celebrate his eightieth birthday, 'An Act of Homage and Reparation to P. G. Wodehouse' (15 July 1961; printed, *Sunday Times*, 16 July), he enviously noted how Wodehouse's characters still occupied the Edenic world so longed for in his own fictions, in which there had been no 'aboriginal calamity' and the forbidden fruit had never been tasted. The landscapes of Blandings Castle, it seemed, were still in the original garden from which the rest of humanity seemed irreparably exiled.[15]

In late-November 1961 Evelyn left for British Guiana, accompanied by his daughter Meg, on a trip financed by the *Daily Mail*. The country was soon to gain independence and his brief was to write about the changes there since his previous visit in 1933, described in *Ninety-Two Days* (1934). At Georgetown he met with the premier and leader of the Marxist People's Progressive Party, Cheddi Jagan, and also interviewed members of the Marxist opposition People's National Congress (black nationalists who advocated racial segregation). On a more personal level, he was delighted to visit the old Jesuit missionary, Father Mather, whom he had much admired on his first trip. Generally, however, he was bored and fatigued by these experiences. His lack of engagement was also evident to the *Daily Mail*, which had hoped for a series of amusing articles on cruising and colonial social life, and only one of the originally five commissioned articles was published as 'Here They Are, the English Lotus-Eaters' (20 March 1962). Eventually, another article on the political situation in Guiana was withdrawn and, instead, appeared as 'Eldorado Revisited' in the *Sunday Times*.[16]

In a literary commission of direct relevance to his own mental condition, Evelyn penned another essay for the *Sunday Times* (January 1962) on 'Sloth', one of Ludovic's favourite *pensées* in *Unconditional Surrender*:

'*The penalty of sloth is longevity*' (91). He cast sloth as the unavoidable last deadly sin of the elderly and infirm (as he now saw himself) and the occasion for man to think primarily of his soul.[17] His stress levels escalated when Meg announced that she wished to marry a young Catholic Irishman, Giles FitzHerbert. Evelyn suffered extreme parental anguish at the thought of losing her to another man and sublimated his anxieties into a last work of fictional comic writing, *Basil Seal Rides Again, or the Rake's Progress*. This strangely incestuous story buries a wish-fulfilment fantasy about preventing Meg's marriage within a satiric lament for the amoral state of early1960s society. Basil is in his late fifties but prematurely aged through a life of self-indulgence, currently financed by his wealthy wife, Angela Lyne. Various characters from his past pop up, such as Ambrose Silk and Margo Metroland, but his only true love is his beautiful daughter, Barbara ('Babs'), a relationship echoing his incestuous intimacy with his sister Barbara in *Put Out More Flags*. He is distraught when he discovers Babs one evening with a raffish young man, Charles Albright, whom she intends to marry. He wonders what his daughter sees in him until Sonia Trumpington bluntly explains that Charles reminds Babs of himself. He is prompted by this outburst to recall a brief affair with Charles's mother and is grimly satisfied when able to advise Babs that her intended is probably her brother. This oddly inconclusive tale was first published in the *Sunday Telegraph* and in *Esquire* in America. In 1963 Chapman and Hall published it in a limited-edition of 750 copies, with a dedication to Ann Fleming, and a further 1,000 copies for distribution in the US by Little, Brown.[18]

1963 began badly with one of the severest winters on record. To escape these arctic conditions, Evelyn travelled to Menton for a week's holiday with Laura. She then headed off to Naples to meet up with Teresa and John D'Arms and to allow him some solitary time for writing in a comfortable hotel. But this time alone proved so depressing that on his return to England he booked into a health farm and managed to lose a stone in weight. His friendship with Father Caraman, who was himself distressed by various professional conflicts (including criticism of his employment of both Meg and Harriet at Farm Street), proved a rare source of consolation and mutual support at this period.[19]

A *Little Learning* and the Second Vatican Council

At Menton, Evelyn tried to begin a trilogy of memoirs since Peters had secured from the *Sunday Times* a £15,000 offer for the serial rights, with Chapman and Hall and in the US Little, Brown also keen to publish the book versions. Peters calculated that this project would earn about £5,000 a year for six years. Evelyn began sorting his personal papers and making contact with all those whom he would be mentioning in the first volume, concerning his ancestry, childhood, education and school-mastering. Most responded positively, even Dick Young, the model for the paedophile Captain Grimes in *Decline and Fall*. But as drafting began, Evelyn found it increasingly difficult to engage with his own early years and too many of his potential subjects were still alive, rendering him and his publishers vulnerable to libel laws.

The only volume eventually completed, *A Little Learning* (September 1964), its title borrowed from Alexander Pope ('. . . is a dangerous thing'), confirms these difficulties in that it is elegantly written but also strangely detached, almost clinical, for an autobiography. Nor is the opening promising of a vibrant portrait of the artist as a young man: 'Only when one has lost all curiosity about the future', he laments, 'has one reached the age to write an autobiography' (1). He writes well about his ancestors but largely from the perspective of a family genealogist rather than as a novelist intrigued by the origins of his own literary creativity. Evelyn paints a decently apologetic portrait of his father who was so often dismissed as a literary guide during his early career. This section was also redrafted for a 'Father and Son' series in the *Sunday Telegraph* (2 December 1962). But his ever-supportive mother receives little more than a perfunctory paragraph and, at best, his view of family life is thoughtfully analytical rather than intimate or revealing. Similarly, he fondly recalls the influence of Roxburgh and Crease at Oxford but is understated about his still-living Oxford contemporaries. The volume ends with his supposed suicide attempt by drowning while at Arnold House and concludes with a sad and hopeless figure swimming back to the shore and walking towards the 'sharp hill that led to all the years ahead' (230).[20]

The concluding psychological and spiritual trial in Evelyn's life was provided by Pope John XXIII's Second Vatican Council (11 October 1962–8 December 1965). When the elderly Pope John was elected in 1958 it was expected that he would prove a traditional and largely inactive pontiff but instead he became the major twentieth-century reformer of the Catholic Church. His predecessor, Pope Pius XII, had upheld a severe level of ultramontanism (absolute papal authority). He had introduced some revisions to the Holy Week liturgy, which had not impressed Evelyn, but his minor reforms were as nothing compared to those instigated by Pope John XXIII's Council. The traditional Latin of the Mass was replaced by the vernacular, with more communal responses introduced to emphasize the celebration's participatory nature; the priest's role was demystified with him now facing the congregation; and there was a distinct shift in the Church towards ecumenism. Evelyn offered a powerful summary of his religious beliefs in 'The Same Again Please' (*Spectator*, 23 November 1962), lamenting especially the loss of the centuries-old Latin Mass for which the Elizabethan martyrs had sacrificed their lives. He even sought official advice from the *Clergy Review*, asking what was the least required in formal devotions so as to ensure that he did not inadvertently sin. He found the new liturgy an affront to Faith, Hope and Charity, even though he was determined not to become an apostate. In early March 1964 Evelyn travelled to Rome for Easter, now realizing that the Council's revisions were irreversible. He later wrote an angry, despairing article, 'Understanding the Conservatives' (*Commonweal*, 7 August 1964), defining '*Romanitas*' as the highest form of civilization and venting his personal alienation from the new regimes of the Catholic Church.[21]

Financial problems also continued to pile up at this period, culminating in a crisis over his 'Save the Children Fund' which, it now appeared, had been ambiguously drafted and was taxable, prompting the Inland Revenue to pursue him for fifteen years of back taxes. Eventually, Peters managed to negotiate payments for only six years which was just manageable in terms of his current liquidity.[22] Always helpful, Peters secured £3,000 for the serial rights of *Basil Seal* and various film rights were agreed for *Decline and Fall*, *A Handful of Dust* and *The Loved One*. Evelyn also appeared on the BBC *Monitor* programme, interviewed by Elizabeth Jane Howard (later Mrs Kingsley Amis). In 1965 Chapman and Hall republished his three war novels as the *Sword of Honour* trilogy with a new preface presented them as a literary obituary for the historical English Catholic Church.[23]

He struggled both with finding a new plot for a novel and with drafting the second volume of his memoirs, 'A Little Hope', which would have had to deal with still painful memories of his divorce from She-Evelyn. Other prospective commissions did materialize, for both a history of the papacy and the crusades. But his literary productivity had virtually ground to a halt and the subject matter of his few outputs did little to raise his spirits. An old friend, Alfred Duggan, died soon after his Easter visit to Rome and he delivered in July an elegiac BBC radio broadcast, 'Alfred Duggan: An Appreciation' (2 July 1964), emphasizing the role of supernatural grace in his later life. Even a short break in Spain during autumn 1964 with Laura, who was herself exhausted and depressed, did nothing to revitalize his intellectual curiosity and literary creativity.[24]

As his health declined and depression mounted, Evelyn realized that his literary career was probably over. For Easter 1966 he asked Ronald Knox's advisor, Dom Hubert van Zeller, to celebrate a Latin Mass at Combe Florey but his abbot refused permission since he felt that he should be with his Downside community at Easter. Coincidentally, Evelyn's last published work was an admiring review of van Zeller's autobiography (*Downside Review*, April 1966). He was intrigued by his view of possible death in 1916 as a welcome emancipation for someone who at that point in his life did not wish to live – Evelyn now felt the same. Instead, he turned to Father Caraman who duly celebrated a Latin Mass on Easter Sunday at the local Catholic Church in Wiveliscombe. Evelyn's calm and contentment as he left the church seemed apparent to all. His sudden death has already been recounted in the Preface.[25]

7

Posthumous reputation and the literary Waughs

Lasting achievement

During the five decades following his death, Evelyn Waugh has been cited, along with Graham Greene, as one of the most significant English novelists and prose stylists of the mid-twentieth century. Greene described him in a letter to *The Times* (15 April 1966) shortly after his death as 'the greatest novelist of my generation'. Most of his major works remain in print and his reputation as a rebarbative social satirist and Catholic commentator seems assured. The 1973 serializing in *The Observer* of his diaries (sold to the University of Texas without the family first reading them) was followed in 1976 by Michael Davie's edition. Public fascination with the compiler of these often intolerant and outrageous private commentaries prompted a renewed focus on the acerbic wit of his fictional writings. Mark Amory's 1980 selection of his letters generated yet more interest in his lively mixture of informal and calculated self-presentation through his correspondence. Donat Gallagher's 1983 edition of selected essays, articles and reviews also proved retrospectively informative in relation to his views on social, religious and political issues of the day.

In Britain, and later America, the 1981 adaptation of *Brideshead Revisited* by John Mortimer for Granada Television proved an immensely successful means of introducing new readers to Waugh's fictions, an interest reactivated by Julian Jarrold's 2008 film of the novel. Similarly, his continuing popularity has been fostered through major biographies by Martin Stannard (1986, 1992), Selina Hastings (1994) and Douglas Lane Patey (1998). His reputation has also been sustained by television adaptations of *Scoop* (1986: ITV, scripted by William Boyd, directed by Gavin Millar), *Sword of Honour* (2001: BBC, scripted by William Boyd, directed by Bill Anderson) and Charles Sturridge's film of *A Handful of Dust* (1988), along with the film *Bright Young Things* (2003: scripted and directed by Stephen Fry), based on *Vile Bodies*.

Evelyn Waugh has always attracted passionate detractors. Both his writings and his caricature public persona of an irascible, tweed-suited 'old fogey' have been accused of snobbishness, elitism, boorishness, cruelty, misanthropy and racism. At the Hay-on-Wye Literary Festival in May 2003 Stephen Fry confirmed his intense admiration for his comic spirit but considered that in his later years Evelyn was 'more or less a howling shit'. Some elements of academia have also adopted a condescending tone. In the widely used student reference volume, *The New Pelican Guide to English Literature* (reprinted seventeen times between 1961 and 1983), Graham Martin dismisses him as an outmoded relic from another age, offering: 'mainly a period interest. He is essentially a pre-war novelist, and the post-war interest in him is a kind of hang-over, a nostalgic reaction, socially, but not critically, interesting'.[1] Also his various personae – decadent student, valiant soldier, devout Roman Catholic, country squire, iconoclastic commentator and aged misanthrope – have been damaging to his posthumous appeal, tending to deflect attention from the writings: 'the life has become more compelling than the fiction'.[2]

Considerable disagreement remains over which of his novels possess lasting literary qualities. Debate is usually polarized between the outrageous comedies (*Decline and Fall, Black Mischief, Vile Bodies, A Handful of Dust, Scoop* and *The Loved One*), or the more sombre wartime works (*Brideshead, Put Out More Flags* and *Sword of Honour*) which are circumscribed by his traditionalist, stoically unyielding Catholic morality. Evelyn's absurdist world of pre-1940 comedies is overtly godless, with the wicked thriving and the innocent exploited. It seems inconceivable that any benign or omniscient God could have created this arbitrarily callous universe in which the pursuit of instant gratification and pleasure invariably dominate over virtuous hopes and relationships. Fragmentary elements of Evelyn's early life, especially his school-mastering, travels and high-society socializing, shimmer through his early comedies. But these works are not autobiographical in any meaningful sense since they merely reflect his mischievous recognition of the superficial pointlessness of modern life. Essentially, they provide a zestful, escapist indulgence within a range of amoral fantasy worlds.

The latter half of his literary career was more substantially 'auto-biographical'. His later novels grew seriously self-reflective – not just because of his conversion to Catholicism but also through the vicissitudes of his wartime engagements, family life and the processes of ageing – and were more imaginatively rooted in his own feelings and experiences. Inevitably, the anarchic delight in disorder of his earlier writings substantially diminished from *Brideshead* onwards as he sought to define essential truths about the human condition and to promulgate his belief in the need for a Divine moral authority over one's personal life. Although his darkly comic view of an irredeemably self-interested world occasionally resurfaced, notably in *The Loved One* (1948) and *Basil Seal Rides Again* (1963), the last two decades of Evelyn's literary life were dominated by more serious philosophical and religious concerns.

Of particular importance to his later writings is an idealized, if elusive, concept of the family as the sustaining core of a healthily productive society – both on a personal level and as part of a global Catholic community. His own family life, of course, did not always match such elevated concepts. He preferred when his children were young to minimize his daily contacts with them; and his long-suffering wife, Laura, had to cope with his unpredictable mood-swings and growing disillusionment with English society. But such real-life vicissitudes seem only to have strengthened his conceptual veneration in his later fictions for man's insistent psychological need to belong to some kind of identifiable family or social grouping. The traumatic breakdown of his first marriage to She-Evelyn impacted directly on the manuscript of *Vile Bodies*, converting its latter half into a much darker picture of the vacuous pointlessness of 1920s high society. Afterwards, and until his marriage to Laura, Evelyn's fictional protagonists were often cast as intrinsically decent but rootless wanderers, lost in a cruel world which shows them little compassion or companionable solace. But in *Brideshead*, Charles Ryder, 'homeless, childless, middle-aged, loveless' (330) – the product of an absentee mother and an emotionally disengaged father – is ultimately drawn into the spiritually reinvigorating family of Catholicism. Similarly, Guy Crouchback generously adopts Trimmer's child and, thereby, finally achieves contentment with his second wife, Domenica, and their own two children in the nurturing environment of his family's ancestral house at Broome.

If the *Sword of Honour* trilogy is viewed as the culmination of Evelyn's novels and a spiritual rewriting of *Brideshead*, then Guy becomes his ultimate figure of redemption. The term, 'unconditional surrender', refers not only to the defeat of the Axis powers but also to Guy's final acceptance of Divine providence and his renewed membership of the Catholic family. He now realizes that personal fulfilment lies in his closest familial relationships, even if they have been artificially constructed through his charitable adoption of Trimmer's child. He has also been taught through his father's inspiring example that sons must be answerable to the moral example set by respected ancestors. Both Ryder and Guy finally accept the essentially fallen state of the world and, as a counterbalance, the operation of Divine grace. They realize that they are no longer alone in a hostile and unforgiving world but, instead, may rely upon the protective and nurturing support of their spiritual family. But, unlike the still solitary Ryder, for Guy the idyll is completed by his loving family life with Domenica and their children.[3]

Family literary heritage: Arthur and Alec

Aside from critical debate over the respective merits of his writings, Evelyn Waugh's continuing artistic heritage is uniquely connected with the remarkable creativity of his own family. Since the late nineteenth century the Waughs have been perhaps the most productive English literary dynasty. As publisher and author, Arthur Waugh's personal associations within late-Victorian and Edwardian literary society were impressively diverse and his treasured collection of signed first editions was probably unrivalled, at least until 1935 when Evelyn accidentally set his father's library on fire. Beginning with the publication of Arthur's Newdigate Prize Poem in 1888, the immense literary output of his two sons, Alec and Evelyn, was followed by that of Evelyn's son, Auberon and his daughters Margaret and Harriet. Auberon's wife, Lady Teresa Waugh, is also a translator and novelist and three of their children, Sophia, Alexander and Daisy, are writers. The Waughs have published approaching 200 books and numerous articles, reviews, newspaper and magazine columns. Alexander Waugh remarks that 'all of us Waughs only became writers to impress our fathers'; and his *Fathers and Sons* (2004) concludes with cautionary paternal advice to his own son, Auberon (b.1998):

> Bear the name of Waugh with pride . . . Do not let it browbeat you into thinking you have to become a writer, that it is your destiny or your duty to do so. It isn't. There is no point in writing unless you have something to say and are determined to say it well.[4]

Evelyn's elder brother Alec remained an industrious writer from the late-1950s to the late-1970s. As an enthusiastic connoisseur of wine (like his nephew Auberon) he reputedly invented the cocktail-party and hosted rum swizzle (rather than tea) parties during the 1920s. He published the *Merchants of Wine: House of Gilbey* (1957); *In Praise of Wine* (1959), a discursive guide to the major wine types; and *Wines and Spirits* (1968) for the Time-Life series, 'Foods of the World'. More significantly, his volumes of autobiographical reminiscences provide a wealth of anecdotal detail about the Waugh family, beginning with *The Early Years of Alec Waugh* (1962) up to 1930. Evelyn wrote to Alec on 12 July 1961, suggesting they should compare notes on autobiographies and was keen to know whether Alec was drafting personal memoirs or a family history. Alec duly sent him an advance copy of *The Early Years* which Evelyn utilized when drafting his own *A Little Learning*. Alec's *My Brother Evelyn and Other Portraits* (1967) provides an intimate impression of Evelyn's life up to his conversion to Catholicism. It also includes personal recollections of prominent literary figures, such as Edmund Gosse, Robert Graves, Siegfried Sassoon and W. W. Jacobs, and other long-forgotten ones, such as Temple Thurston whose first novel, The *Apple of Eden*, was about a fallen priest; and Desmond Coke whose schoolboy stories, especially *The Bending of the Twig* (1906), inspired Alec's *The Loom of Youth*. His two final volumes of recollections, *A Year to Remember* [1931] (1975a) and *The Best Wine Last* [1932–69] (1978), were among the most interesting of his numerous publications.

In *My Brother Evelyn*, Alec describes himself as 'restless, rootless, eager for change, avid of the sun, finding his plots between capricorn and cancer' (1). His longstanding interests in the West Indies produced *The Sugar Islands* (1949) and *A Family of Islands: A History of the West Indies 1492 to 1898* (1964). He also wrote *Bangkok: The Story of a City* (1970b), offering a personalized history of the city documenting his fascination with Thai society and cultures which dated back to his first visit there in 1926 (as described in *Hot Countries*). Exotic locations were also used in his collection of short stories, *My Place in the Bazaar* (1961), and in his later novels, including *Fuel for the Flame* (1960), set on an imaginary island in the South China Sea and a forgettable 'erotic comedy', *A Spy in the Family* (1970a). Following Evelyn's lead in utilizing his own war-time service in *Sword of Honour*, Alec's *The Mule on the Minaret* (1965), was based on his British counter-intelligence activities in the Middle East and included a 'Postscript' explaining how it echoed his experiences in Beirut, Cairo and Baghdad with the Spears Mission.

The Fatal Gift (1973) is set in England and Dominica and has Alec as its narrator but it now remains of interest through its casting of Evelyn as a semi-fictional character. His Oxford set is vividly depicted, including Harold Acton and Brian Howard, into which is inserted Alec's imaginary hero, Raymond Peronne, the younger son of an English peer. It also recalls the Cave of Harmony, Evelyn's jape of bringing one of their friends into college disguised as a man and his problematic relationship with Dean Cruttwell.[5] Although its plot is slowed by Alec's cloying descriptions of society love affairs, the vicissitudes of the privileged but distrait Raymond (who ends up living alone on Dominica) owe a clear debt to Sebastian's personal degeneration towards a paradoxical later contentment in *Brideshead*.

Alec's next novel, *Brief Encounter* (1975b), was based on Carlo Ponti's film of Noel Coward's famous play, *Still Life* (1938) and the 1945 film with Trevor Howard and Celia Johnson. His final novel, *Married to a Spy* (1976), was another limp attempt at 'erotic' fiction set in Tangier about the Basque Liberation Movement. Alec died on 3 September 1981 at Tampa, Florida, aged eighty-three and his ashes were brought back to St-John-at-Hampstead churchyard for interment with his parents. His nephew, Auberon, concluded that Alec will 'be remembered as a great survivor, rather than as the author of any particular work of talent'.[6]

Auberon Waugh

The diverse literary talents of Auberon Waugh, Evelyn's eldest son, were of a significantly higher order than those of his uncle Alec, although he shared his intense work ethic and deep-rooted need to write. As a sixteen-year-old schoolboy at the Benedictine monastery school of Downside, the sceptical and satiric vision of his later writings was already flourishing as the impact of his father's intense Catholicism waned. His housemaster, Dom Aelred Watkin, wrote to Evelyn on 22 December 1955: 'I don't think he is irreligious, though I don't think religion means a great deal to him . . . to a boy of Bron's cast of mind religious pageantry seems something bourgeois'.[7] Nevertheless, during spring 1955 he drafted a series of short stories on broadly religious themes and secretly sent them off to various magazines. 'The Twelve Caesars' and 'The Cheerful Rivalry' had no takers but 'The Mills of God' was accepted by *Lilliput* when the editor spotted that the contributor was Evelyn's son. Auberon's desire for anonymity was overridden by the editor's payment of twenty-five guineas (of which only ten guineas were guilefully disclosed to the author's proud parents).[8]

In December 1956 Auberon was awarded an exhibition in English at Christ Church, Oxford, but elected first to take an extended break in Italy and then to complete his National Service. He stayed in Florence with Harold Acton and afterwards drafted an unpublished novel about two seventeen-year-old friends travelling around Italy, based on his own experiences with a school-friend, Rob Stuart.[9] Returning home, he was commissioned in September 1957 into the Royal Horse Guards (the Blues) and after his passing out ceremony in March 1958 was sent to Nicosia, Cyprus. On 9 June he was checking a faulty machine gun when it fired six rounds through him and, although he was fortunate to survive, it was without a lung, spleen, several ribs and a finger. Following a lengthy recuperation, he went up to Oxford in autumn 1959 to read not English but (unwisely) Politics, Philosophy and Economics. After failing his first year examinations, he left university with new hopes of a career in journalism.

While still recovering from his wounds during summer 1959 Auberon made another trip to Italy. By August he was in a lodging house at Bologna and half way through drafting a novel satirizing life at Downside and recalling his time in hospital. It was completed over Christmas but his father was far from encouraging over its publication, reminding him that he was still a minor and could not sign a book contact without parental permission. Evelyn seemed wary of his precocious son publishing a potentially scandalous school novel (recalling the family anxieties engendered by Alec's *The Loom of Youth*), just as his own biography of *Ronald Knox* was due to appear in print. But Auberon secretly sent it to Chapman and Hall and secured an immediate offer of a contract. In early March 1960 Evelyn read *The Foxglove Saga* in proof and expressed delight in its originality and vitality, especially commending its army scenes. Like his father, Auberon was at his best when his fictions were directly inspired by personal experience. The English edition claimed on its dust-jacket that it was the 'first novel by the youngest member of a distinguished family' and the American edition made the startling claim that it was 'this decade's *Vile Bodies*'. More realistically, Graham Greene advised Auberon that comparisons with his father's work were unavoidable but considered that *The Foxglove Saga* has 'only one parent and stands magnificently alone'.[10]

After leaving Oxford Auberon worked as a copy editor at *Queen* magazine but when his boss, Quentin Crewe, contributed a venomous review of *The Foxglove Saga* to the *Sunday Express*, he swiftly moved to a sub-editor's post at the *Daily Telegraph*. This first novel brought Auberon financial success but his father warned him of the difficulties of following up on such instantaneous fame, citing the example of Alec who had endured almost four decades of undistinguished literary industry between *The Loom of Youth* (1917) and *Island in the Sun* (1955). Interspersed with unsuccessful interviews with the British Secret Service, Auberon doggedly continued to seek a literary career. His second novel, *Path of Dalliance*, was published in November 1963 and focused on his brief Oxford experiences. Advertised as a 'comedy with tragic overtones', it focuses on the Sligger family, especially young Jamey whose brief Oxford career is followed by a period in a Fleet Street sub-editor's office. Its Cleeve Abbey School recalls Downside and the inanities of the aristocratically biased Godolphin Hall echo Auberon's experiences at Christ Church. A few nods to his father are also incorporated, including references to Hertford College and the fictional Halberdiers. While the eccentricities of Jamey's parents and the religious brothers at Cleeve are effectively delineated, the preoccupations of its gauche adolescent characters now seem rather limited. The novel's blurb eloquently promises everything and nothing, claiming that 'Auberon Waugh is a born writer and writes like himself', and *Books and Bookmen* named it 'novel of the year' for 1963. Alec and John Betjeman (who grandly compared it to Dickens) were loyally supportive but Evelyn constructively deduced from this evidence that Auberon would not be able to sustain a living as a novelist.[11]

Inspired by a period as a feature's writer for *Woman's Own*, Auberon's next novel, *Who Are the Violets Now?* (1965), borrowed its title from Shakespeare's *Richard II* (V.2, 'who are the violets now that strew the green lap of the new come spring?'). It follows the experiences of a young hack journalist, Arthur Friendship, who ekes out a living writing book reviews and ghosting other columns for the relentlessly upbeat *Women's Dream*. As awkward as Paul Pennyfeather, Arthur's is besotted with the kindly Liz Pedal but she is unresponsive and instead falls for Thomas Gray, a mercurial black civil rights speaker. Arthur becomes embroiled in a global black conspiracy through his involvements with the International Peace Studies organization, directed by the cosmopolitan Mr Besant who turns out to be a wanted Nazi war criminal. Although laced with flashes of comic brilliance (especially in its use of a repetitive pet animal motif), the novel unexpectedly ends in tragic bathos as Arthur, now horribly scarred from a fire, is killed when his motorcycle crashes into a car on his way to see Liz. The novel was dedicated to Evelyn and Laura who received this filial gesture with gratitude, prompting Evelyn's assurance that it was so far his most skilfully constructed and controlled writing as a novelist.[12]

Consider the Lilies (1968) traces the activities of a cynical clergyman, Nicolas Trumpeter, and his atheist wife in a huge rectory in Berkshire; and

A Bed of Flowers (1971) focuses on a hippy commune in Somerset, controlled by the immensely wealthy John Robinson. The other characters in this latter novel, including Celia, Rosalind, Orlando, Oliver, Adam, Touchstone and Jaques (a former Roman Catholic priest), carry obvious references to *As You Like It*. As a disintegrating English society struggles through a cannabis haze of indifference, the melancholy Jaques repeatedly echoes Evelyn in pointing to the decline of religious belief as a key factor in the diminution of the modern world. Opening to a Labour General Election win and the beginning of Harold Wilson's first premiership (1964–70), the novel also echoes themes from Auberon's involvements in the Biafran conflict, with Rosalind's baby christened Biafra Sunshine Ojukwu. This fifth and last novel was far more contrived and whimsical than its predecessors and received only hardback publication in the UK, failing entirely to find an American publisher.[13]

With a growing family to support, Auberon now concentrated on satirical, polemical and literary journalism since his prior experience in these challenging fields was already diverse. He began in 1960 by working as a cub reporter on the *Daily Telegraph*'s Peterborough gossip column. During 1963–4 he was a columnist for the *Catholic Herald*, and (as his father's son) was an unsparing critic of the post-Second Vatican Council English Church, led by Archbishops Basil Cardinal Hume and Derek Warlock. During 1970–1 he also began a weekly Saturday column for *The Times* on current affairs. His long-standing association with *The Spectator* began in the mid-1960s, with a powerful review (May 1966) of his father's obituaries, leading to his appointment first as the magazine's political correspondent (1967–70), then book reviewer (1970–3) and finally columnist (1976–95).

His most prominent humanitarian work was produced from 1968 as an acerbic commentator on the disastrous conflict in Biafra, a mainly Catholic province that had attempted in May 1967 to secede from Nigeria. He visited the country in July 1968 and became a fearless opponent of the Wilson government's tacit condoning of mass starvation via blockades by the federal government against the Biafran Ibos. His fourth child was christened Nathaniel Thomas Biafra; he lectured widely the UK and the US on the crisis; co-authored with Suzanne Cronjé a disturbing exposé, *Biafra, Britain's Shame*; and stood as a 'Save Biafra' candidate in his local Bridgewater by-election.[14] Other journalism on national newspapers and journals from the 1970s onwards included work for the *Evening Standard* (1973–80), *Books and Bookmen* (1972–80), *New Statesman* (1973–6), *The Daily Mail* (1981–6), *Sunday Telegraph* (1981–90, 1996–2001), *The Literary Review* (editor from 1986), *The Independent* (1986–9), and the *Daily Telegraph* (1990–2000) as the writer of the *Way of the World* column three times per week.

Some of his most pungent literary journalism – blending absurdist fantasies and virulent personal abuse with a humanitarian distaste for veniality and rapaciousness – appeared in 'Auberon Waugh's Diary' (1972–86) for the satirical magazine, *Private Eye*, edited by Richard Ingrams. He was immensely proud of these satires which parodied a column then popular in *The Sunday Times*. They allowed imaginative flights of comic fantasy as he inserted himself into whatever real political, social or religious contexts took his fancy.[15] These columns were later collected together in two anthologies: *Four Crowded Years: The Diaries of Auberon Waugh, 1972–76* (1976) and *A Turbulent Decade: The Diaries of Auberon Waugh, 1976–85* (1985). Reviving the spirit of his father's early satiric novels, Auberon's 'Diary' castigated a fallen and riotously amoral world, in which temporal gratification and self-aggrandizement reigned comically supreme.

The range of material covered in these *Private Eye* diaries was diverse, encompassing high society, business, media stars, international affairs and the church. Politics was an especially important area of attack and his tone was often characterized by a deep-rooted suspicion of American imperialism, balanced by a cautiously positive view of European integration. Some individuals regularly attracted attention, especially Shirley Williams because of her support for comprehensive education and the Liberal Party leader, Jeremy Thorpe, who stood trial for conspiracy to murder. Following the suspicious shooting of a dog, Rinka, owned by Norman Scott, with whom Thorpe was alleged to have had a homosexual liaison, Auberon stood in the 1979 General Election in his local constituency for the 'Dog-Lover's Party' – a gesture also recalling his father's long-standing vendetta against his Oxford tutor, Cruttwell. He wrote a separate account of Thorpe's trial, *The Last Word: an Eyewitness Account of the Thorpe Trial* (1980); and his *Another Voice – an Alternative Anatomy of Britain* (1986) gave vent to his disillusionment with Margaret Thatcher's economic policies as he grew to regard them as socially and culturally destructive.[16]

Will This Do? (1991), offers illuminating insights into Auberon's early family life, his often fraught relationship with his father and the waning of his orthodox Catholic religious beliefs. Its introductory 'Apologia' begins with Evelyn's diary for 23 December 1946 noting that the seven-year-old 'Bron is clumsy and dishevelled, sly, without intellectual, aesthetic or spiritual interest' (7); and he frankly views himself as a 'monstrous child and even worse adolescent' (8). He discusses the idea of sin and the small child, the traditional Catholic piety of his Herbert relatives, his Anglican clergymen ancestry, and the more disreputable aspects of Catholic school-life at Downside. After his wounding in Cyprus, he recalls being ferried to hospital while the Catholic army chaplain read the *De Profundis* and receiving the last rites from an Irish priest. The efficacy of prayer tends to be more obvious after machine-gunning oneself and his letters home during recuperation sometimes conclude with the heartfelt request for his family to 'KEEP PRAYING'. As a young journalist, Auberon adopted the attitudes of a staunchly conservative Catholic but he gradually ceased to practise his father's adopted faith, especially when its post-Second Vatican Council ceremonials no longer bore any resemblance to those espoused by his father.[17] Although Evelyn's children were all sent to Catholic schools and given religious gifts by their parents, as Alexander Waugh notes, 'the zeal of the convert is seldom passed down on the hereditary principle'. Nevertheless, he also confirms his father's firm belief that 'Man's relationship to God is an intensely private affair, the most intimate and personal of all his relationships'.[18]

Auberon Waugh died on 16 January 2001 at Combe Florey and was vituperatively attacked by Polly Toynbee in an article illustrated with a sketch of his corpse being swilled down a lavatory. She condemned his world as a 'coterie of reactionary fogeys', centred on the *Spectator* and the *Telegraph*, who still held Evelyn as an 'icon' in their veneration for the 'aristocracy and old Catholicism'. Keith Waterhouse later remarked: 'never in a lifetime spent in this black trade have I read a nastier valedictory for a fellow scribe'.[19] Despite Toynbee's denunciations, Auberon Waugh remains one of England's most inventive and pungent comic satirists – a journalist who dynamically revived for his own times the spirit of both William Hogarth's eighteenth-century social commentaries and his father's early novels.

His younger sister, Margaret or 'Meg' (1942–86), was also a writer and in December 1955 she won, aged thirteen, a short-story competition in the *Observer*. While assisting Father Caraman at Farm Street in 1961 she drafted hagiographical pamphlets on the Catholic martyrs, Nicholas Owen and Ralph Sherwin. Her informative biography, *The Man Who was Greenmantle* (1983), traced the life of her maternal grandfather, Aubrey Herbert, whom John Buchan had used as a model for Richard Hannay. It boded well for her still-developing literary career but she was fatally injured by a car in 1986.[20] Her youngest sister, Harriet (b.1944), became a novelist, publisher's reader and reviewer of crime fiction. Her first novel, *Mirror, Mirror* (1973) bears comparison with the grotesque world of her father's *Love Among the Ruins*. It is a grisly black comedy of middle-class domestic intrigue, laced with an insistent fear of incipient madness and mortality. Its anti-hero, Godfrey Pettlement is so repellently ugly that he is only gains admission to Oxford while wearing bandages over his face but then drives his horrified college room-mate to madness. After university he undergoes extensive plastic surgery and emerges as a handsome force for destruction. He exacts revenge on the cruel world by initiating a death-cult and eventually he suffers a biblically traumatic end. This disturbing fantasy fiction, laced with the language of horror and religious allegory, echoes Harriet's father's concerns with a moribund English society pervaded by spiritual and emotional bankruptcy.

Harriet's other fiction offers worlds in which Basil Seal, Dennis Barlow (*The Loved One*) and Miles Plastic (*Love Among the Ruins*) would undoubtedly thrive. *Mother's Footsteps* (1978), is an ironic study of the fraught relationships between a feckless mother-in-law, her neurotic daughter and devious son-in-law; and *Kate's House* (1983), portrays a manipulatively malevolent four-year-old child. Her *The Chaplet of Pearls* (1997) seems at first a more staid social comedy, focusing on a literary appreciation society of wealthy elderly ladies. They venerate the Victorian novelist, Charlotte M. Yonge, a champion of virtuous self-control and temperance. Her 1868 novel of the same name had traced the bloody sectarian struggles in late-sixteenth-century France between the Catholics and Protestant Huguenots. Instead of sectarian hostilities, lethal enmities break out in Harriet's novel when a strident feminist critic, Hilary Greep, plans to write a revisionist biography of Yonge, laced with lesbianism and incest. Plans for her murder ensue among the polite ladies of the Chaplet since like the young (but for different reasons) the old feel they have little to lose. It is easy to imagine Evelyn and Nancy Mitford gleefully following this mischievous 'lady-killers' plot-line.

On 1 July 1961 Auberon married Lady Teresa Onslow (b.1940), a daughter of the sixth Earl of Onslow. She has published an impressive range of translations, including *The Travels of Marco Polo* (1984b), Jean Tulard's *Napoleon: The Myth of the Saviour* (1984c), Jean Gimpel's *The Cathedral Builders* (1993), Benedetta Craveri's *Madame Du Deffand and Her World* (1994a) and Anka Muhlstein's *A Taste for Freedom: The Life of Astolphe de Custine* (2000). She is also a prolific novelist, including *Painting Water* (1984a), tracing the life of an estate agent's wife in Surrey; *An Intolerable Burden* (1988), focusing on a social worker in London; and *Song at Twilight* (1989), about a retired schoolteacher in Somerset. During the 1990s her literary productivity continued with more novels: *Sylvia's Lot* (1994b), *The Gossips* (1995), *A Perfect Day* (1999b) and, most disturbing, *A Friend Like Harvey* (1999a), about a Basil Seal like fantasist who damages the lives of everyone who comes into contact with him and ultimately ends up in prison.

Teresa Waugh's second novel, *Waterloo, Waterloo* (1986), is a melancholy comedy of manners about a retired major, Jack Bennett, who lives in the village of Chadcombe, Devon. His harmless life in retirement is defined by his fascination with military history and a particular admiration for Napoleon, recalling Guy Crouchback's once innocently idealistic view of army life. His first wife, Bobby, was the sister of a fellow officer and, although childless, their marriage had been a happy one until her death from cancer. His second wife, Peggy, is a selfish divorcee sixteen years younger than himself whose unappetizing son, Nigel (a secret flasher), works in the linen department of a West End store. They have a daughter, Josephine, whom Jack genuinely loves. After leaving the army at fifty-five and then working for ten uninspiring years as a bursar of a minor girls' school, he retires with Peggy to Chadcombe where she runs the chaotic village shop. The novel traces Jack's gradual ageing process and increasing isolation, including Peggy's affair with the local driving instructor and their death together in a car crash. Nigel takes over managing the shop and marries his dim girlfriend, Suzanne, who becomes pregnant. With Peggy dead and a baby on the way, the novel concludes with Jack in despair, being shipped off to an old people's home. Tautly written and with sharply defined characters,

Waterloo, Waterloo moves steadily from comedy to pathos, confirming the mundane ordinariness of sad, pointless lives – a callous world without redemption which the likes of Tony Last (*A Handful of Dust*) would have readily recognized.

In contrast, *The House* (2002) is a murder-mystery, recounting the vicissitudes of a debt-laden, dilapidated Palladian country house, Cranfield, from 1945 until 1950 and prior to it becoming a National Trust property. It is the time of rationing, post-war austerity and the great freeze of 1947 and the novel traces the declining fortunes of the English aristocracy. The narrative deftly unfolds via the letters and diaries of four main characters: the owner, Sydney, Lord Otterton, a shell-shocked war veteran who collects exotic birds; his five-year-old daughter Georgina (who matches the author's age in 1945); Annie Jerrold, a reliable but inscrutable maid; and Zbigniew Rakowski, a Polish historian of Whig aristocracy who is officially compiling the Otterton's family history but is also in love with Lady Otterton and secretly writing a murder-mystery about the house. There are also two dominant female characters, Lord Otterton's ruthless mother, Lady Lilian, and his wife, Priscilla. The House has been read as a *roman-à-clef*, with Lord Ollerton as the author's father, Lord Onslow; Cranfield as Teresa Waugh's childhood home Clandon Park. But, like Brideshead, it is the fictional great house which ultimately becomes the presiding presence in the novel as a dominating, timeless framework for the joys and vicissitudes of its family.

Sophia (b.1962) and Daisy (b.1967), the daughters of Auberon and Teresa Waugh, are both writers. Sophia has published book reviews for *The Observer* and contributed to the 'Bookends' column in the *Spectator*. With her husband Julian Watson, she has also published *A Lazy Contentment: A History of the Carnarvon Arms Hotel* (1999), a classic sporting hotel on Exmoor. Her younger sister, Daisy, is a prolific journalist, travel writer, novelist and television presenter, restaurant critic and agony aunt (*The Independent*). She has written a weekly newspaper columns from Los Angeles and the West Country ('Country City Mole', 2005–07) and the 'Waugh Zone' column for the *Sunday Times* magazine. Her travel and lifestyle books include, *A Small Town in Africa* (1994); *The New You Survival Kit* (2002); *Ten Steps to Happiness* (2003); *Bordeaux Housewives* (2006); and *The Desperate Diary of a Country Housewife* (2008). She is also an established novelist with six titles to her name, beginning with *What is the Matter with Mary Jane? A Cautionary Tale* (1988) and concluding (so far) with a semi-fictional romance, *Last Dance with Valentino* (2011).

Their brother, Alexander (b.1963), is a writer, musician, record producer, cartoonist, journalist, television presenter, historian and archivist of the Waugh family. In his *Fathers and Sons*, he explores the problems of finding oneself a scion of a literary dynasty and how it renders it impossible to write 'interesting or amusing things about the world' if everything has first to be 'passed through the Evelyn-Auberon masher'. Consequently, his career as a writer has been pragmatically focused on 'non-fiction books and classical-music criticism'.[21] As a youth he also supplied cartoon strips to the *Literary Review* and for the *Daily Telegraph*. He was chief opera critic of the *Mail on Sunday* (1990–1) and the London *Evening Standard* (1991–6) and published *Classical Music: A New Way of Listening* (1995) and *Opera: A New Way of Listening* (1996). His 'Bon Voyage' (2000), co-written with his brother Nathaniel, won the 12th Vivian Ellis Award for Best New Musical. His television credits include documentary films based upon his *Fathers and Sons* (2005) and 'The Piano – A Love Affair' (2006). His account of a tragically malfunctioning family, *The House of Wittgenstein: A Family at War* (2008), was commended by Terry Eagleton as an 'eminently readable, meticulously researched account of the Wittgenstein madhouse' (*The Guardian*, 8 November 2008).

His *Time: From Microseconds to Millennia, a Search for the Right Time* (1999) is one of the most intriguing books produced by Evelyn Waugh's descendants. Ranging through religious, classical and renaissance scholarship, it blends past beliefs and theories, often in gently subversive ways, with more recent scientific thought. It is presented in the form of a series of witty and ironic monologues and its chapters steadily expand from 'Initium – Beginning', through historically diverse concepts of seconds, minutes, hours, days, weeks, months years, decades, centuries, millennia, eras and eternity, concluding with 'Primitive Time', 'Complex Time' and, as the culminating challenge of human understanding, 'Finis – End'. Alexander's grandfather would surely have been intrigued by this Erasmian questioning of humanity's innate need to make conceptual sense, often within religious frameworks, of time, mortality and eternity. He would also have been gratified by this book as an artistic object. Its inner-board is illustrated by Thomas Kelly's engraving (1822/23) of 'Adam Naming the Creation' (*Genesis*, II.XIX) and its end-board by a detail from William Hogarth's last engraving before his death, 'The Bathos' (1764), depicting the expiry of Time represented by a dying winged male figure, collapsed against a shattered column with his scythe, hour-glass and pipe broken. At the centre of the picture stands a grim wooden signpost for 'The World's End'.

If Evelyn had lived to be ninety-six, he could have received a presentation copy of this book from his grandson. But what would he have made of its sceptical and often wisely childlike modes of interrogating religious belief? Its first page opens with the resounding biblical truth: 'In the beginning, God created Heaven and Earth', but then immediately juxtaposes this statement with the seven-year-old schoolboy Bertrand Russell asking: 'If God made everything, who made God?' (1). While never dismissing the staunch religious faith espoused by his grandfather, Alexander seems in *Time* to temper it with the secular scepticism of his father, Auberon. It is as though his grandfather presides over the book's opening biblical illustration, 'Adam Naming the Creation', while the *Private Eye* persona of his father stands alongside its concluding image of Hogarth's 'The Bathos'.

As he reads on, grandfather Evelyn might ponder the archaeologically supported theory that the biblical Genesis was borrowed by the Jews from earlier Assyrian myths, which themselves may have derived from Sumerian legends. He could then consider the Septuagint's calculation that that universe was created 5500 years before Christ, in contrast to the Venerable Bede's estimation of the true date as 3951 years before Christ, or Archbishop James Ussher's confident reassessment in 1656 that the world was created on 23 October (precisely) 404BC. Elsewhere, lavishly illuminated and jewel-encrusted late-medieval Books of Hours are discussed. Surviving examples are now acclaimed as magnificent works of art but also seem to convey a more elitist message: 'He who possessed the handsomest copy of the *Book of Hours* might consider himself the most worthy, the most pious, the most learned and the most powerful of all' (56). Evelyn, who took great pleasure in his own huge and ostentatiously bound Missal, might pause over the implicit tension hinted at here between the requisite humility of private devotions and the aesthetic pleasures of beautiful but expensive religious objects. He may even nod knowingly at Alexander's ultimately unanswerable question as to why God took six days to create the world, followed by a day of rest, when an omnipotent God could surely have created 'the world in one day, or even in one second' (78).

As a careful compiler of historical sources for his biographies of Campion and Knox, the nonagenarian Evelyn would certainly approve of his grandson's thorough analysis in *Time* of proposed datings for the Crucifixion, the Julian and Gregorian Calendars and the Church of Rome's determined attempts to suppress Galileo's reputedly heretical confirmation of Copernicus's heliocentric theories. In contrast, he would probably be peeved, given his long-standing friendships with Fathers D'Arcy, Knox and Martindale, with his grandson's depiction of the Jesuits as the secret 'crack troops of the Catholic Church' whose mission was to 'infiltrate the highest echelons of society in the hope that their message would percolate downwards to the ordinary people'. Alexander suggests that 'so much power allied to so much secrecy was a recipe for disaster which led inevitably to a festering contempt for the order right across Europe' (123). He traces their expulsion from France (1594), Venice (1607), England (1759), Spain (1767) and Naples (1768). Similarly, would Evelyn appreciate his grandson's sympathy with Oscar Wilde's summation of the human condition: 'The terror of society, which is the basis of morals, the terror of God, which is the secret of religion – these are the two things that govern us' (214)? *Time*'s final chapter, 'Finis – End', concludes with Bertrand Russell's tracing of parallels between Marxist Communism and the Christian schema, comparing the:

> materialistic dialectic of the Marxist scheme to the biblical God, the proletariat to the elect, the Communist Party to the Church, the revolution to the Second Coming, and the Communist commonwealth to the millennium. (276)

Such heretical thoughts would surely have shocked Evelyn. But if he had still been haunting the library at Combe Florey three years later aged ninety-nine, he could have examined an even more challenging work from his grandson. Alexander's biography of *God* (2002) was based upon his eclectic readings of the Bible, the Apocrypha, the Qur'an, the texts of Nag Hammadi, Quman and other Jewish mystical literature. Its completion had proved extremely stressful since it coincided with Auberon's death in January 2001 and was almost prevented by a major loss of computer files:

> If God seriously thought He could prevent publication of His biography by killing my father and scrambling my work, He was in error. All He succeeded in doing was to set my heart against His ways so that I produced a portrait which, in the end, was far less flattering to Him that it might otherwise have been.[22]

In the 'Forward' to *God* Alexander explains how shortly before he died his father, presumably fearful of the controversial nature of this study, offered to match the advance for the book, provided he withdrew it from publication.

Yet, despite its potential to arouse theological and sectarian ire, *God* seeks not to stir up controversy but rather to explore the infinitely complex and often paradoxical nature of religious belief in a Divine being. As Alexander reasonably argues, since 'human brains are *finite*, they should not be expected to understand the *infinitude* of God, for the whole (that is to say God, the universe and everything in it) cannot be explained with the use of a single part (a finite human brain)' (3–4). Evelyn would certainly agree with his grandson's premise that 'God is the most perplexing and yet most compelling figure in human history' (7). Given his anthropological interest in non-Christian theism in his African travel writings, he would also understand the shrewd narrative strategy of presenting a 'book of shifting premises, preached from several pulpits at once' (6).

The seven Shakespearean sections of *God* – 'Mewling and Puking', 'Shining Face', 'Furnace', 'Strange Oaths', 'Justice', 'Pipes and Whistles', 'Sans Everything' – offer intriguing textual claims and openly address questions which most devout Christians should at least occasionally ask themselves. For example, why do the traditions of Islam seem to have 'preserved more details about how God made Adam than are found in the Book of Genesis' (49)? Similarly, key questions are posed over the problematic nature of the Garden of Eden: Why did God create a tree that specifically allowed knowledge of evil? Why did he then put Adam and Eve in close proximity to it? Shouldn't an omnipotent God have already known exactly what would happen to his creations? If God is all-powerful, why does he seem less able to persuade Adam and Eve than Satan? Of course, the answers to such logical questions, a pious but indulgent grandfather might reply, lie in the primacy not of God's awesome Old Testament powers but rather in the Divine gift of free will to humanity and the self-sacrifice of the New Testament Jesus Christ.

God also offers a detailed checklist of God's body-parts as mentioned in scripture and other ancient texts, including face, feet, hands, bowels, breasts, phallus and womb and it gives due consideration to whether God is black or androgynous. In a wry literary nod to Evelyn, a section on '*Vile bodies*' discusses attitudes towards physicality and the 'Christian mistrust of sex' (127). Alexander then offers a compendium of biblically supported thoughts on such issues as whether God has a sense of humour; how to pray; the comparative size of Heaven or Hell; the concept of the Trinity; kinds of angels; and, returning to the thesis of *Time*, God and temporality. Evelyn would surely be impressed by the complex range of biblical and textual scholarship displayed in these sections. In contrast, Alexander's citing of Jean-Paul Sartre's famous assertion from *The Devil and the Good Lord* seems a deliberately subversive gesture towards his grandfather, not least because the quotation is headed: '*French joke*' – exactly how Evelyn had viewed the philosophic self-aggrandizement of French existentialism during the 1950s:

> I supplicated, I demanded a sign, I sent messages to Heaven – no reply. Heaven ignored my very name. Each minute I wondered what could be in the eyes of God. Now I know the answer: nothing, God does not see me, God does not hear me . . . I am going to tell you a colossal joke: God does not exist. (268)

Ultimately, however, Alexander Waugh's *God* displays no profound scepticism over the personal value of religious belief but rather offers a humane demonstration that all knowledge is necessarily finite and often contradictory. His ninety-nine-year old grandfather would readily endorse this view as confirmation that sometimes only a humble acceptance of religious faith can make total emotional sense in the face of endlessly conflicting rational arguments and empirical evidence.

NOTES

Preface

1 Stannard, *Critical Heritage*, 506; Stannard, I.xiv.
2 Sherry, I.121.
3 *Tablet*, 5 June 1948; Stannard, *Critical Heritage*, 164–6; Sherry, II.296.
4 Stannard, I.1.
5 Patey, xvii, 3.
6 Hastings, 229–30.
7 Ibid, 205; Woodman, 28–30.
8 Alexander Waugh, *Fathers and Sons* (FS), 41.
9 Ibid, 34.
10 Hastings, 5.
11 Ibid, 26.
12 *Complete Stories* (CS), 549–50.

Chapter 1

1 *FS*, 32.
2 Sykes, 9–12.
3 Stannard, I.36; *FS*, 83–5.
4 *Diaries*, 9.
5 *My Brother Evelyn* (MBE), 167.
6 CS, 537–9; *Diaries*, 5.
7 Hastings, 30–3; CS, 545–8.
8 *FS*, 125–6; see also 103, 119–24.
9 Stannard, I.177; *FS*, 162.
10 *Diaries*, 112.
11 Hastings, 29.
12 *Essays*, 6–8.
13 Patey, 4–5.
14 Stannard, I.57; Hastings, 58–70.
15 *FS,* 155.
16 *Diaries*, 127; Hastings, 76–9.

17 *Essays*, 9–12; Stannard, I.64–5.

18 *MBE*, 172; Wykes, 29–30.

19 *CS*, 583–91; Stannard, I.78.

20 *FS*, 175–8.

21 Patey, 12.

22 *CS*, 578–82; Wykes, 34–5.

23 Stannard, I.84–9.

24 *CS*, 583–91; Hastings, 92–5, 100–4.

25 Ibid, 96–8, 106; Byrne, 53–9.

26 Hastings, 106–15.

27 Stannard, I.91.

28 Sykes, 55–6; Byrne, 68–70.

29 Hastings, 122–6, 131, 140–2, 150.

30 Ibid, 122, 127–8.

31 *Letters*, 23.

32 Hastings, 134–6.

33 *Diaries*, 233.

34 Ibid, 240.

35 *CS*, 3–42; Wykes, 46–8; Byrne, 82–3.

36 *Diaries*, 281.

37 *CS*, 43–54.

38 *Diaries*, 284.

39 *Essays*, 22–5.

40 Stannard, I.140, 144; Wykes, 55–8.

41 *Letters*, 25–6, n.3.

42 *Diaries*, 289.

43 Stannard, I.148–9; Hastings, 167–71; Ker, 155–62.

44 Patey, 66.

45 *Night and Day*, 52.

Chapter 2

1 Hastings, 180–3.

2 Stannard, I.175–7; Hastings, 178–87.

3 *MBE*, 191–2; McDonnell, 8–16.

4 *Essays*, 94–6; Sykes, 96; Stannard, I.184–5, 189; Hastings, 220.

5 Ibid, 211–12; Patey, 86.

6 Hastings, 224.

7 Ibid, 225.

8 *Daily Express*, 20 October 1930; *Essays*, 103–5.

9 *Diaries*, 792–3; Stannard, I.228–32.

10 Stannard, I.234–5; Wykes, 84–92; Patey, 88–9.

11 *Harper's Bazaar*, 9 December 1933; CS, 146–56; Stannard, I.347; Patey, 96.

12 Byrne, 131–60.

13 Hastings, 264–5.

14 Ker, 170–1.

15 Hastings, 282–4.

16 Stannard, *Critical Heritage*, 132–40; Stannard, I.336–40.

17 *Letters*, 80; Hastings, 284–94.

18 *Letters*, 84; Sykes, 137–43; Hastings, 296–301.

19 Ibid, 301–6.

20 Bergonzi, 24–7; Patey, 118–9.

21 CS, 157–65; DeVitis, 31–3; Ker, 171–5.

Chapter 3

1 *Letters*, 87.

2 Patey, 129.

3 *Evening Standard*, 13 February 1935; *Essays*, 162–4.

4 CS, 93–120, 157–216, 238–42; FS, 230–1; Byrne, 238–40.

5 *Essays*, 190; FS, 229–30.

6 Stannard, I.422–3, 439–41.

7 Hastings, 357–67.

8 *The Telegraph*, 5 October 2003.

9 Patey, 162–3.

10 Stannard, I.471.

11 Ibid, I.477–8.

12 Hastings, 374–9; Brennan, *Graham Greene*, 56–64.

13 Hastings, 376–7.

14 Stannard, I.483–5.

15 *Essays*, 238–59; Stannard, I.488; CS, 217–37.

16 Ibid, 243–86; Sykes, 223–7.

17 CS, 243–340.

18 Stannard, I.495–500, II.xvii; Hastings, 387–90; Patey, 171–4.

19 Stannard, II.13–14, 22; FS, 247–8.

20 *Diaries*, 438; Hastings, 383–7.

21 *Letters*, 146; Stannard, II.18–24.

22 Ibid, II.28–31; Hastings, 417–31.

23 Stannard, II.59; Wykes, 133–5.

24 Stannard, II.42–4, 112.

25 *Diaries*, 548; Stannard, II.87; Hastings, 446–54; Patey, 190–1.

26 Stannard, II.100, 104; Hastings, 456–62.

27 *Diaries*, 785; Hastings, 463–72.

28 *Essays*, 282–5; Stannard, II.115, 138–43; Hastings, 474–81; Patey, 214–19.

Chapter 4

1 *Letters*, 146.

2 *Diaries*, 240.

3 Bergonzi, 27–30.

4 Hastings, 482.

5 Stannard, II.100; Ker, 181–90.

6 Stannard, II.100.

7 Byrne, 324–6.

8 Ibid, 189–97.

9 Stannard, II.222.

10 Ibid, II.92–4.

11 Patey, 226, 229.

12 *Diaries*, 664; Stannard, II.148.

13 Ibid, II.xx.

14 *Essays*, 312–16; Stannard, II.165–6.

15 CS, 430–44.

16 Stannard, II.163.

17 CS, 374–429; Stannard, II. 168–70.

18 Patey, 267.

19 Hastings, 502.

20 Stannard, II.150; Hastings, 509; Patey, 250.

21 *Essays*, 300–4.

22 Patey, 257.

23 *Essays*, 339–43.

24 Hastings, 516–18.

25 Stannard, II.205–10; Patey, 278.

26 *Essays*, 368–9.

27 *Life*, 19 September, 1949; *Essays*, 377–88; Stannard, II.248–9.

28 Ibid, II.238–42; Hastings, 536–8.

29 Stannard, II.215–16.

30   Hastings, 507.

31   *Tablet*, 5 June 1948; *Essays*, 360–5; *Letters*, 280; Brennan,
     Graham Greene, 84.

32   *CS*, 445–68; Stannard, II.220.

Chapter 5

1   Stannard, II.275–9; Wykes, 158–64.

2   *Letters*, 339; DeVitis, 60–7; Sykes, 318–22; Stannard, II.156–7, 173, 300;
     Patey, 245–6.

3   Patey, 290.

4   *Letters*, 315.Stannard, II.253.

5   Ibid, II.256, 289–90.

6   Stannard, II.263–4.

7   Patey, 300–1.

8   Hastings, 543–6.

9   Stannard, II.293–300.

10   *Will This Do? (WTD?)*, 22.

11   Stannard, II.43, 227, 269.

12   *Letters*, 353.

13   *Sunday Times*, 29 October 1961.

14   Stannard, II.281.

15   *Letters*, 386; Stannard, II.308–9.

16   Patey, 309.

17   *Sunday Express*, 30 November 1952; *Essays*, 426–8; Stannard, II.312–14,
     323–5.

18   *CS*, 469–501.

19   *Essays*, 448–56; Stannard, II.315–16, 371.

20   Ibid, II, 338, 343; Hastings, 159.

21   Sykes, 359–72; Hastings, 560–8.

22   Stannard, II.347–9, 392–3; Patey, 309, 338–9.

23   Stannard, II.349–50; Hastings, 571–4; Patey, 327–30.

Chapter 6

1   *Essays*, 468–70; Stannard, II.351, 362–4, 373, 382–5.

2   Ibid, II.362.

3   Ibid, II.425.

4   *Sunday Times*, 25 September 1961.

5 Stannard, II.415.

6 Ibid, II.415–18.

7 Stannard, *Critical Heritage*, 271–2; McDonnell, 208–11.

8 *Essays*, 538–40; Stannard, II.425–7.

9 Ibid, I, 2; II.430.

10 Bergonzi, 32–6; Stannard, II.437.

11 Patey, 349–51.

12 Bergonzi, 29; Sykes, 427–8; Hastings, 597–8; Wykes, 204–6; Patey, 243.

13 *CS*, 445–68; Stannard, II.235, 441–2; Patey, 349–50.

14 *Guardian*, 27 October 1961.

15 *Letters*, 564; *Essays*, 561–8; Stannard, II.444–6.

16 *Essays*, 583–6, 592–6; Hastings, 604–7; Patey, 358–9.

17 *Essays*, 572–7; Hastings, 601.

18 *CS*, 502–34; Stannard, II. 323, 424, 448–50.

19 Ibid, II.456–61, 473.

20 Hastings, 612–15.

21 *Essays*, 602–9, 614–18, 628–30; Stannard, I.479–80; Hastings, 616–19, 623.

22 Ibid, II.485.

23 Stannard, *Critical Heritage*, 476–80.

24 *MBE*, 184; *Spectator*, 10 July 1964; Stannard, I.99; *Essays*, 625–8.

25 Stannard, II.476–91; Hastings, 620–6.

Chapter 7

1 *The Guardian*, 27 May 2003; Ford (ed.), *Pelican Guide*, 479.

2 *The Telegraph*, 5 October 2003.

3 Patey, 350.

4 *FS*, 450, 453.

5 Hastings, 99.

6 *Oxford Dictionary of National Biography*, 'Alec Waugh'.

7 Stannard, II.369.

8 *FS*, 318–19.

9 *Ibid,* 347–51, 382.

10 Stannard, II.419, 429; *FS*, 13, 376, 387.

11 Ibid, 387–90.

12 Ibid, 411.

13 *WTD?*, 210–11.

14 Ibid, 192–8.

15 Ibid, 216, 221.

16 *Kiss Me, Chudleigh* provides a diverse sampling of Auberon Waugh's satirical writings.

17 *FS*, 366; *WTD?*, 187.

18 *God*, 1; *FS*, 308, 435.

19 *The Guardian*, 19 January 2001; *FS*, 5.

20 Stannard, II.369, 447–9; 494.

21 *FS*, 11, 448.

22 Ibid, 10.

SELECTED BIBLIOGRAPHY

Bergonzi, Bernard (1963), 'Evelyn Waugh's gentleman', *Critical Quarterly*, 5, 23–36.

Boyd, William (5 October 2003), 'Behind the pose', *The Telegraph*, 5 October 2003.

Brennan, Michael G. (2010), *Graham Greene Fictions, Faith and Authorship*, London and New York: Continuum.

Byrne, Paula (2009), *Mad World: Evelyn Waugh and the Secrets of Brideshead*, London: Harper Press.

DeVitis, A. A. (1956), *Roman Holiday: The Catholic Novels of Evelyn Waugh*, New York: Bookman Associates.

Ford, Boris (ed.) (1961; revised edition, 1983), *The New Pelican Guide to English Literature: From James to Eliot*, Vol. 7, Harmondsworth: Penguin.

Greene, Graham (1939; rpt. 2002), *The Lawless Roads*, London: Vintage.

— (1940; rpt. 2004), *The Power and the Glory*, London: Vintage.

— (1948: rpt. 2004), *The Heart of the Matter*, London: Vintage.

— (1951; rpt. 2004), *The End of the Affair*, London: Vintage.

— (1980; rpt. 1999), *Ways of Escape*, London: Vintage.

— (1982; rpt. 2006), *Monsignor Quixote*, London: Vintage.

— (ed.) (1985), *Night and Day*, ed. Christopher Hawtree, London: Chatto & Windus.

Hastings, Selina (1994), *Evelyn Waugh: A Biography*, London: Sinclair-Stevenson.

Ker, Ian (2003), *The Catholic Revival in English Literature, 1845–1961*, Notre Dame, IN: University of Notre Dame Press.

McDonnell, Jacqueline (1985), *Waugh on Women*, London: Duckworth.

Oxford Dictionary of National Biography (2004), ed. H. C. G. Matthew and B. Harrison, Oxford: Oxford University Press (on-line edition).

Patey, Douglas Lane (1998; rpt. 1999), *The Life of Evelyn Waugh: A Critical Biography*, Oxford: Blackwell.

Sherry, Norman (1989), *The Life of Graham Greene, Vol. 1: 1904–1939*, London and Toronto: Jonathan Cape and Lester & Orpen Dennys.

Stannard, Martin (ed.) (1984), *Evelyn Waugh: The Critical Heritage*, London: Routledge & Kegan Paul.

—(1986), *Evelyn Waugh: The Early Years, 1903–1939*, London and Melbourne: J. M. Dent & Sons.

—(1992), *Evelyn Waugh: No Abiding City, 1939–1966*, London: J. M. Dent & Sons.

Stopp, Frederick John (1958), *Evelyn Waugh: Portrait of an Artist*, London: Chapman and Hall.

Sykes, Christopher (1975), *Evelyn Waugh: A Biography*, London: Collins.

Waugh, Alec (Alexander) Raban (1917), *The Loom of Youth*, London: Chapman and Hall.

—(1918), *Resentment: Poems*, London: G. Richards.

—(1919), *The Prisoner of Mainz*, London: Chapman and Hall.
—(1921), *Pleasure*, London: G. Richards.
—(1922a), *Public School Life*, London: Collins.
—(1922b), *The Lonely Unicorn*, London: G. Richards.
—(1923), *Myself When Young: Confessions*, London: G. Richards.
—(1924), *Card Castle*, London: G. Richards.
—(1925), *Kept: A Story of Post-War London*, New York: A. and C. Boni.
—(1926a), *Love in These Days*, London: Chapman and Hall.
—(1926b), *On Doing What One Likes*, Kensington: The Cayme Press.
—(1928a), *Nor Many Waters*, London: Chapman and Hall.
—(1928b), *The Last Chukka: Stories of East and West*, London: Chapman and Hall.
—(1929), *Three Score and Ten*, London: Chapman and Hall.
—(1930a), *"Sir!" She Said*, New York: Farrar and Rinehart.
—(1930b), *The Coloured Countries (Hot Countries)*, London: Chapman and Hall.
—(1931a), *Most Women*, New York: Farrar and Rinehart.
—(1931b), *So Lover's Dream*, London: Cassell.
—(1932a), *Leap Before You Look*, London: E. Benn.
—(1932b), *No Quarter*, London: Cassell.
—(1932c), *Thirteen Such Years*, New York: Farrar and Rinehart.
—(1933), *Wheels Within Wheels*, London: Cassell.
—(1934), *The Balliols*, London: Cassell.
—(1936), *Jill Somerset*, London: Cassell.
—(1937), *Eight Short Stories*, London: Cassell.
—(1938), *Going Their Own Ways*, London: Cassell.
—(1941), *No Truce with Time*, New York: Farrar and Rinehart.
—(1944), *His Second War*, London: Cassell.
—(1948a), *The Sunlit Caribbean*, London: Evans.
—(1948b), *These Would I Choose*, London: Sampson Low.
—(1948c), *Unclouded Summer*, London: Cassell.
—(1949), *The Sugar Islands*, New York: Farrar and Straus.
—(1950), *The Lipton Story*, New York: Doubleday.
—(1951), *Where the Clocks Chime Twice*, London: Cassell.
—(1952), *Guy Renton*, London: Bloomsbury.
—(1955), *Island in the Sun*, New York: Farrar, Straus and Cudahy.
—(1957), *Merchants of Wine: House of Gilbey*, London: Cassell.
—(1959), *In Praise of Wine*, London: Cassell.
—(1960), *Fuel for the Flame*, London: Cassell.
—(1961), *My Place in the Bazaar*, London: Cassell.
—(1962), *The Early Years of Alec Waugh*, London: Cassell.
—(1964), *A Family of Islands: A History of the West Indies 1492 to 1898*, London: Doubleday.
—(1965), *The Mule on the Minaret*, London: Cassell.
—(1967), *My Brother Evelyn and Other Profiles*, London: Cassell.
—(1968), *Wines and Spirits*, New York: Time-Life.
—(1970a), *A Spy in the Family*, New York: Mayflower.
—(1970b), *Bangkok: The Story of a City*, London and New York: W. H. Allen.
—(1973), *The Fatal Gift*, London: W. H. Allen.
—(1975a), *A Year to Remember* [1931], London: W. H. Allen.
—(1975b), *Brief Encounter*, London: W. H. Allen.

—(1976), *Married to a Spy*, London: W. H. Allen.

—(1978), *The Best Wine Last: An Autobiography* [1932–69], London: W. H. Allen.

Waugh, Alexander (1995), *Classical Music: A New Way of Listening*, London: Macmillan.

—(1996), *Opera: A New Way of Listening*, New York: Stewart, Tabori and Chang.

—(1999), *Time: From Micro-Seconds to Millenia, a Search for the Right Time*, London: Headline.

—(2002), *God*, London: Review.

—(2004), *Fathers and Sons: The Autobiography of a Family*, London: Headline.

—(2008; rpt. 2009), *The House of Wittgenstein: A Family at War*, London: Bloomsbury.

Waugh, Arthur (1888), 'Gordon of Africa', *Newdigate Prize Poem*, Oxford: A. T. Shrimpton.

—(1890), *Schoolroom and Home Theatricals*, London: Cassell.

—(1892), *Tennyson*, London: Heinemann.

—(1896), *Johnson's Lives of the Poets*, London: Kegan Paul.

—(1898), *Legends of the Wheel*, London: Privately Printed.

—(1899), *The Square Book of Animals*, London: Heinemann.

—(1900), *Robert Browning*, Small, London: Maynard & Co.

—(1915), *Reticence in Literature*, London: J. G. Wilson.

—(1919), *Tradition and Change*, New York: Dutton.

—(1930), *Chapman and Hall, A Hundred Years in Publishing*, London: Chapman and Hall.

—(1931), *One Man's Road: Being a Picture of Life in a Passing Generation*, London: Chapman and Hall.

Waugh, Auberon (1960), *The Foxglove Saga*, London: Chapman and Hall.

—(1963), *Path of Dalliance*, London: Chapman and Hall.

—(1965), *Who are the Violets Now?*, London: Chapman and Hall.

—(1968), *Consider the Lilies*, London: Michael Joseph.

—(1969), *Biafra: Britain's Shame*, London: Michael Joseph.

—(1971), *A Bed of Flowers*, London: Michael Joseph.

—(1976), *Four Crowded Years: The Diaries of Auberon Waugh, 1972–76*, London: Harper Collins.

—(1980), *The Last Word: An Eyewitness Account of the Thorpe Trial*, London: Michael Joseph.

—(1985), *A Turbulent Decade: The Diaries of Auberon Waugh, 1976–85*, London: Private Eye.

—(1991), *Will This Do? The First Fifty Years of Auberon Waugh: An Autobiography*, London: QPD.

—(2001), *Closing the Circle: The Best of Way of the World from The Daily Telegraph*, London: Macmillan.

—(2010), *Kiss Me, Chudleigh: The World According to Auberon Waugh*, ed. William Cook, London: Coronet.

Waugh, Daisy (1988), *What is the Matter with Mary Jane? A Cautionary Tale*, London: Sceptre.

—(1994), *A Small Town in Africa*, London: Heinemann.

—(2002), *The New You Survival Kit*, London: Harper Collins.

—(2003), *Ten Steps to Happiness*, London: Harper Collins.

—(2006), *Bordeaux Housewives*, London: Harper.

—(2008), *The Desperate Diary of a Country Housewife*, London: Harper.

—(2011), *Last Dance with Valentino*, London: Harper.

Waugh, Evelyn (1916), *The World to Come: A Poem in Three Cantos*, London: Privately Printed.

—(1926), *P.R.B.: An Essay on the Pre-Raphaelite Brotherhood, 1847–54*, London: Alastair Graham.

—(1928a; rpt. 1986), *Decline and Fall*, Harmondsworth: Penguin.

—(1928b; rpt. 1931), *Rossetti: His Life and Works*, London: Duckworth.

—(1930; rpt. 1955), *Vile Bodies*, Harmondsworth: Penguin.

—(1932; rpt. 1983), *Black Mischief*, Harmondsworth: Penguin.

— (1934a; rpt. 1986), *Ninety-Two Days*, Harmondsworth: Penguin.

—(1934b; rpt. 1984), *A Handful of Dust*, Harmondsworth: Penguin.

—(1938; rpt. 2003), *Scoop*, London: Penguin.

— (1939; rpt. 1940), *Robbery Under Law: The Mexican Object-Lesson*, London: The Catholic Book Club.

—(1942a; rpt. 1975), *Put Out More Flags*, Harmondsworth: Penguin.

— (1942b; rpt. 1951), *Work Suspended and Other Stories*, Harmondsworth, Penguin.

— (1945; rpt. 1978), *Brideshead Revisited*, Harmondworth, Penguin.

— (1946; rpt. 1951), *When the Going was Good*, Harmondsworth, Penguin.

—(1948; rpt. 1951), *The Loved One*, London: Penguin.

— (1950; rpt. 1953) *Helena*, Harmondsworth: Penguin.

—(1952a; rpt. 1984), *Men at Arms*, Harmondsworth: Penguin.

— (1952b), *The Holy Places*, New York: Queen Anne Press.

—(1955; rpt. 1984), *Officers and Gentlemen*, Harmondsworth: Penguin.

—(1957; rpt. 1962), *The Ordeal of Gilbert Pinfold*, Harmondsworth: Penguin.

—(1961; rpt. 1964), *Unconditional Surrender*, London: Penguin.

—(1964; rpt. 2010), *A Little Learning*, London: Penguin.

—(1976), *The Diaries of Evelyn Waugh*, ed. Michael Davie, London: Weidenfeld and Nicolson.

—(1980), *The Letters of Evelyn Waugh*, ed. Mark Amory, London: Weidenfeld and Nicolson.

—(1983), *The Essays, Articles and Reviews of Evelyn Waugh*, ed. Donat Gallagher, London: Methuen.

—(2000), *The Complete Stories of Evelyn Waugh*, [including 'The Balance', 'The Man Who Liked Dickens', 'Out of Depth', *Mr Loveday's Little Outing*, 'My Father's House', 'Charles Ryder's Schooldays', *Scott-King's Modern Europe*, 'Compassion', *Love Among the Ruins*, and *Basil Seal Rides Again*], New York, Boston and London: Little, Brown.

—(2001; rpt. 2005), *Two Lives: Edmund Campion – Ronald Knox* [1935, 1959], London and New York: Continuum.

—(2003), *Waugh Abroad: Collected Travel Writings* [including *Labels, Remote People, Ninety-Two Days, Waugh in Abyssinia, Robbery Under Law, The Holy Places, A Tourist in Africa*], ed. Nicholas Shakespeare, London: Everyman.

Waugh, Harriet (1973), *Mirror, Mirror*, London: Littlehampton Book Services.

—(1978), *Mother's Footsteps*, London: Weidenfeld and Nicolson.

—(1983), *Kate's House*, New York: St. Martin's Press.

—(1997), *The Chaplet of Pearls*, London: Bloomsbury.

Waugh, Lady Teresa (1984a), *Painting Water*, London: Hamish Hamilton.

—(tr.) (1984b), *The Travels of Marco Polo*, London: Sidgwick & Jackson.

—(tr.) (1984c), Tulard, Jean, *Napoleon: The Myth of the Saviour*, London: Wiedenfeld and Nicolson.

—(1986), *Waterloo, Waterloo*, London: Hamish Hamilton.

—(1988), *An Intolerable Burden*, London: Hamish Hamilton.

—(1989), *Song at Twilight*, London: Hamish Hamilton.

—(tr.) (1993), Gimpel, Jean, *The Cathedral Builders*, New York, Harper Colophone.

—(tr.) (1994a), Craveri, Benedetta, *Madame Du Deffand and Her World*, Boston, MA: David R. Godine.

—(1994b), *Sylvia's Lot*, London: Sinclair-Stevenson.

—(1995), *The Gossips*, London: Sinclair-Stevenson.

—(1999a), *A Friend Like Harvey*, London: Victor Gollancz.

—(1999b), *A Perfect Day*, London: Travelman Publishing.

—(tr.) (2000), Muhlstein, Anka, *A Taste for Freedom: The Life of Astolphe de Custine*, New York: Helen Marx Books.

—(2002), *The House*, London: Weidenfeld and Nicolson.

Waugh, Margaret ('Meg') (1961), *Blessed Nicholas Owen: Jesuit Brother and Maker of Hiding Holes*, London: Office of the Vice-Postulation.

—(1962), *Blessed Ralph Sherwin*, London: Office of the Vice-Postulation.

—(1983), *The Man Who was Greenmantle*, London: Murray.

Waugh, Sophia (1999), *A Lazy Contentment: A History of the Carnarvon Arms Hotel*, Exebridge: Lonsdale Press.

Weston, William (1955), *The Autobiography of an Elizabethan*, tr. Philip Caraman with a foreword by Evelyn Waugh, London: Longmans.

Woodman, Thomas (1991), *Faithful Fictions: The Catholic Novel in British Literature*, Milton Keynes and Philadelphia: Open University Press.

Wykes, David (1999), *Evelyn Waugh: A Literary Life*, Basingstoke and New York: Macmillan and St. Martin's Press.

INDEX